Transgender and the Literary Imagination

Transgender and the Literary Imagination

Changing Gender in Twentieth-Century Writing

Rachel Carroll

EDINBURGH
University Press

Edinburgh University Press is one of the leading university presses in the UK. We publish academic books and journals in our selected subject areas across the humanities and social sciences, combining cutting-edge scholarship with high editorial and production values to produce academic works of lasting importance. For more information visit our website: edinburghuniversitypress.com

© Rachel Carroll, 2018

Edinburgh University Press Ltd
The Tun – Holyrood Road,
12(2f) Jackson's Entry,
Edinburgh EH8 8PJ

Typeset in 11/13 Adobe Sabon by
IDSUK (DataConnection) Ltd, and
printed and bound by CPI Group (UK) Ltd, Croydon, CR0 4YY

A CIP record for this book is available from the British Library

ISBN 978 1 4744 1466 1 (hardback)
ISBN 978 1 4744 1467 8 (webready PDF)
ISBN 978 1 4744 1468 5 (epub)

The right of Rachel Carroll to be identified as the author of this work has been asserted in accordance with the Copyright, Designs and Patents Act 1988, and the Copyright and Related Rights Regulations 2003 (SI No. 2498).

Contents

Introduction: Transgender and the Literary Imagination: Changing Gender in Twentieth-Century Writing — 1

1. 'Two men, so dissimilar': Class, Marriage and Masculinity in George Moore's *Albert Nobbs* (1918) and Simone Benmussa's *The Singular Life of Albert Nobbs* (1977) — 37

2. 'She had never been a woman': Second Wave Feminism, Femininity and Transgender in Angela Carter's *The Passion of New Eve* (1977) — 64

3. Playing the Breeches Part: Feminist Appropriations, Biographical Fictions and Colonial Contexts in Patricia Duncker's *James Miranda Barry* (1999) — 87

4. Two Beings/One Body: Intersex Lives and Transsexual Narratives in *Man into Woman* (1931) and David Ebershoff's *The Danish Girl* (2000) — 125

5. Blue Births and Last Words: Rewriting Race, Nation and Family in Jackie Kay's *Trumpet* (1998) — 158

6. Never an Unhappy Hour: Revisiting Marriage in Film Adaptations of *Albert Nobbs* (2011) and *The Danish Girl* (2016) — 191

Bibliography — 233
Index — 243

Introduction

Transgender and the Literary Imagination: Changing Gender in Twentieth-Century Writing

A figure in the throes of a furious struggle is illuminated against the darkness by the intermittent flash of a photographer's bulb, the sounds of extreme human exertion and the slap of fists and feet against hard, damp surfaces testifying to an otherwise invisible contest between the human body and inanimate matter. In *Becoming an Image* (2012–) the performance artist Cassils applies the prowess and agility of a body disciplined by intensive training to the task of transforming a monumental block of clay. Capturing the artist in postures which are both frozen and fleeting, photographic documentation does more than simply record: it frames the audience's experience of the performance, imprinting images which are both arbitrary and forceful. One still image in particular uncannily evokes the traditions of classical statuary, depicting a human figure seemingly seated atop a battered pedestal in a posture of Promethean ambiguity: is this a body emerging out of the clay, moulded by a hidden hand? Or is this the figure of the artist, fixed to the rock in eternal punishment for the crime of creative presumption?[1] Originating as a commission by the ONE Archives in Los Angeles, home to a longstanding LGBTQ archive, *Becoming an Image* draws attention to what is neither seen nor recorded: it is a testament to the struggle to make an impression in the field of representation, to gain visibility in conditions of unseeing and to find a foothold in the institutions of cultural memory. Cassils's work speaks powerfully to the themes of this book, which examines questions of visibility, recognition and representation in relation to literary narrative. A key concern for this study is the way in which transgender lives – whether historical or fictional – have been 'authored by others': named, defined and appropriated in ways which obscure, displace or erase transgender experiences, identities and histories. By revisiting twentieth-century narratives and their afterlives this book aims to examine the legacies of this representational history, exploring the extent to which transgender potential can be recovered and realised.

Transgender and the Literary Imagination examines a selection of literary fiction by British, Irish and American authors first published between 1918 and 2000, each text featuring a protagonist (and in some cases two) whose gender identity differs from that assigned to them at birth: George Moore's naturalistic novella set in an 1860s Dublin hotel, *Albert Nobbs* (1918); Angela Carter's dystopian feminist fantasy *The Passion of New Eve* (1977); Jackie Kay's contemporary fiction inspired by the life of a post-war jazz musician, *Trumpet* (1998); Patricia Duncker's historical novel based on the life of a nineteenth-century colonial military surgeon, *James Miranda Barry* (1999); David Ebershoff's historical fiction *The Danish Girl* (2000), based on the life of Lili Elbe, reputed to be the first person to undergo gender reassignment treatment. An interest in the intertextual relationship between these narratives and a range of source and adapted texts is central to this study, which explores memoir, biography, drama and film, including historical biographies of James Miranda Barry, Niels Hoyer's 1931 'memoir' of the life of Lili Elbe, *Man into Woman*, and Simone Benmussa's 1977 stage adaptation *The Singular Life of Albert Nobbs*; the afterlives of these narratives are explored with a special focus on contemporary film adaptation, specifically *Albert Nobbs* (directed by Rodrigo García, 2011) and *The Danish Girl* (directed by Tom Hooper, 2016). 'Transgender' is a term whose current meanings can be traced to its origins in the 1990s in a combination of contexts, including community formation, political activism and scholarly enquiry. The first decades of the twenty-first century have witnessed the entry of debates about transgender rights and representation into mainstream public discourse and popular culture.[2] In this context, this study returns to the narrative representations of an earlier era, examining how they reflect, shape or transform changing understandings of gender in the twentieth century and beyond. By identifying and analysing the narrative strategies and motifs which have characterised the representation of transgender lives in literary fiction prior to the twenty-first century, this book investigates the relationship between these narratives and dominant ideas about the origins, meaning and significance of conventional categories of sex and gender.

The American campaigner Virginia Prince (1912–2009) is widely credited as being the first to coin the term 'transgender'.[3] However, the publication in 1992 of Leslie Feinberg's pioneering *Transgender*

Liberation: A Movement Whose Time Has Come is seen by many as playing a pivotal role in establishing transgender as a concept referring to 'an imagined political alliance of all possible forms of gender antinormativity'.[4] As T. Benjamin Singer writes:

> Feinberg's manifesto resonated with an early 1990s social imaginary that infused the category transgender with the collective energy of a social movement – enabling a range of different bodies to congregate underneath a single umbrella. Without this sense of political collectivity, it would not have been possible to visually render transgender as an umbrella instead of a continuum of gender-nonconforming identities and behaviours or as a particular mode of being.[5]

Singer notes that the 'original purpose' of the term, as conceived by Feinberg, was for 'political advocacy',[6] and from the late twentieth century onwards transgender activists and organisations have variously challenged conventional assumptions about sex and gender and campaigned for social and legal change.[7] While the term and its meanings have continued to evolve over the decades, it is worth reflecting on the distinctive characteristics of this formative formulation. Firstly, the adoption of the term 'transgender' represents a rejection of existing clinical terms and definitions, with their origins in medical and psychiatric discourse, and an assertion of the right to self-determination: in this way, it constitutes a refusal to be named by others and an expression of a developing sense of collective identity and agency. Secondly, the term embraces an identity grounded in the experience of transition, defying the pressures to conceal or deny a differently gendered past. In an essay which has proved a founding text for the field of transgender studies, 'The Empire Strikes Back: A Posttranssexual Manifesto', Sandy Stone wryly observed that the 'highest purpose of the transsexual is to erase him/herself, to fade into the "normal" population as soon as possible'.[8] To identify as transgender is to refuse the invisibility – whether social, political or cultural – which Stone describes. In *Second Skins: The Body Narratives of Transsexuality*, Jay Prosser conveys this conceptual shift in the following way:

> If transsexual has been conceived conventionally as a transitional phase to pass through once the transsexual can pass and assimilate as nontranssexual – one begins as female, one becomes a transsexual, one is a man – under the aegis of transgender, transsexuals, now refusing to pass through transsexuality, are speaking en masse as transsexuals, forming activist groups, academic networks, transgender 'nations'.[9]

Indeed, the emergence of 'transition' as 'the vernacular term of choice' for 'describing the process or experience of changing gender'[10] is important here; where the phrase 'sex change' has acted to imply an irrevocable rupture effected by medical intervention, 'transition' foregrounds a durational experience without a single, fixed or finite destination. Finally, transgender is an inclusive category which provides space for a diverse range of gender identities. It is not simply equivalent to, nor a substitute for, 'transsexual' (a term referring to someone who seeks or has undergone gender reassignment treatment) but rather provides an organising 'umbrella' for a range of people who, in Talia Mae Bettcher's words, 'do not appear to conform to traditional gender norms by presenting and living genders that were not assigned to them at birth or by presenting and living genders in ways that may not be readily intelligible in terms of more traditional conceptions'.[11] This book does not seek to define, explain or delimit who counts as transgender in literary fiction but rather to examine the narrative strategies at work in the representation of characters whose lived gender identity or expression differs to that assigned to them at birth. In doing so it aims to examine how narrative conventions have shaped the ways in which characters with transgender potential are read, interpreted or understood in literary fiction in particular, and cultural representation more broadly.

The challenges of cultural intelligibility and the struggle for self-determination are especially evident in twentieth-century texts in the form of two recurring and closely related motifs: the prominence of modes of life writing and the persistence of tropes of forcible revelation. Life writing – both biography and autobiography – has proved an important genre in relation to transgender representation and has been the focus of key works on cultural representation in the field of transgender studies.[12] Jack Halberstam's critique of transgender biography in his pivotal essay 'Telling Tales: Brandon Teena, Billy Tipton, and Transgender Biography' demonstrates the ways in which transgender lives have been forcibly 'dismantled and reassembled',[13] imposing normative assumptions about sex and gender and overwriting the reality of lived experience. By contrast, autobiography could be seen as a form of self-expression through which such misrepresentations might be redressed. The genre is given close consideration in Prosser's *Second Skins*, where he proposes that 'every transsexual, as a transsexual, is originally an autobiographer'.[14] Indeed, the publication of a number of widely read transgender memoirs over the course of the twentieth century has shaped popular perceptions about the forms such life stories take. However, consideration of the contexts in which these narratives have been produced draws attention to the specific discursive conditions of some transgender life writing. As Prosser argues: 'The autobiographical act for the transsexual begins even before the published autobiography – namely, in the clinician's office where, in order to be diagnosed as transsexual, s/he must recount a transsexual autobiography.'[15] The complex relationship between auto/biographical and fictional accounts of transgender lives will be examined in this book with reference to the narrative afterlives of James Miranda Barry (c. 1799–1865), Lili Elbe (1882–1931) and Billy Tipton (1914–89), with an emphasis on the extent to which these narratives perpetuate or resist the dynamic outlined in Halberstam's essay. The narrative of forcible, and often posthumous, exposure is not only a recurring trope in historical biographies of transgender subjects but also extends across a range of cultural narratives. It is exploited in particular ways in visual culture, including film and television drama, where the spectacle of revelation has been used to achieve effects ranging from comedy to horror. This trope raises central questions to do with self-determination and representation, especially as it typically mobilises demeaning, pathologising or sensationalist meanings which negate the transgender subject's self-definition. In an essay on what she terms the 'reveal' as a narrative device, Danielle M. Seid argues:

> Structuring an audience's knowledge of a character's transgender status as a reveal can contribute to the perception that living a transgender life involves concealing 'the truth' of sexed bodies. The moment of the reveal provokes a struggle over the meaning of the trans body, a struggle in which the trans person often 'loses' to dominant discourses about trans lives, the conclusion being: that's *really* a man. [emphasis in original][16]

The protagonists who feature in the texts examined in this study are repeatedly subject to unwanted acts of revelation which rewrite their identity, typically reversing their lived gender identity: for George Moore's Albert Nobbs, Patricia Duncker's James Miranda Barry and Jackie Kay's Joss Moody this takes the form of a posthumous exposure, whereas for Tristessa in Angela Carter's *The Passion of New Eve* it instigates a series of events which conclude with her murder. The varying treatment of this theme will be examined in close detail, culminating with an extended exploration of Kay's unravelling of the narrative dynamics of forcible exposure in her novel *Trumpet*. Drawing on the insights of leading scholars in the field of transgender studies, this book aims to provide new frameworks for the analysis of literary fiction as a significant form of cultural representation. More specifically, by situating a selection of key texts in a range of historical, cultural and intertextual contexts, it will examine the following topics: questions of historical representation in relation to historical fiction; the influence of genres of transgender life writing, including memoir and biography; the legacies of Second Wave feminist critiques of transsexuals; the impact of narratives of gender crossing on the interpretation of transgender lives; the relationship between transsexual narratives and intersex bodies; the role of colonial contexts and discourses of 'race' in the construction of gender normativity. The sections which follow provide a more extended consideration of critical frameworks essential for the project of rereading representations of transgender in twentieth-century literary fiction: the first section addresses debates to do with transgender historiography; the second and third sections consider the relationship between transgender studies and feminism and queer theory respectively; the fourth and final section reflects on contemporary debates about the limits of identity politics. This introduction will conclude with an overview of the book structure, providing summaries of each chapter.

Paradoxical Projects: Transgender Historiography

In a founding intervention in the field of transgender studies, 'The Empire Strikes Back: A Posttranssexual Manifesto', Sandy Stone observes that 'it is difficult to generate a counterdiscourse if one is programmed to disappear'.[17] Historically, assimilation – whether coercive, strategic or desired – has served an important function as a means by which people perceived to be non-normative in terms of their sexed or gendered identity could seek to evade the social penalties of stigma, discrimination and prejudice. In this context, questions of visibility have proved a recurring preoccupation within the field of transgender historiography. Indeed, Halberstam has described transgender history as a 'paradoxical project' in that it 'represents the desire to narrate lives that may wilfully defy narrative'.[18] By contrast, a 'refusal to disappear'[19] is identified by Prosser as a defining characteristic of transgender identification in contemporary contexts, expressing as it does a collective affirmation of identity in defiance of a culturally coerced invisibility. The recovery of a hidden history has been an imperative for many identity politics movements seeking to redress a legacy of cultural misrepresentation. However, the relationship between the needs of contemporary rights movements and the evidence of historical record is a complex one, characterised by the challenge of recovering minority histories from historical sources which may obscure or deny their existence. Moreover, the potential subjects of a transgender history can be subject to competing claims given that the historical practice of 'gender crossing' has acquired significant meanings in women's, lesbian and gay, and queer historiography. Finally, the tensions between historically specific constructions of identity and the historical records of lived experience which predate them pose further questions of interpretation across time.

In a 2008 essay exploring narratives of female cross-dressing in late Victorian London, Katie Hindmarch-Watson articulates some of the concerns that have been expressed about transgender historiography: 'The ahistorical transgender subject is the latest manifestation of a politically useful but historically problematic attempt to locate nonnormative gendered individuals within a grand narrative culminating in present-day transgendered lived experience.'[20] Firstly, there is a concern about the anachronistic imposition of contemporary categories of identity on past historical subjects; such a methodology is understood as ahistorical because it universalises current understandings without due regard for historical difference. Moreover, integral to this critique is a sense that retrospection is being put to improper use, with the historical past conjured as a mirror image of the present. Finally, the imposition of a linear, teleological narrative whose only destination is the present moment is at odds with the insights of postmodern historiography, with its emphasis on the textuality, contingency and multiplicity of historical narrative and its implication in uneven dynamics of power. It is interesting to note that this observation is situated in the context of a historical analysis of 'female cross-dressing'. Indeed, the author acknowledges that this figure has been the object of interpretative struggles: 'Usually, passing women are divided into those who, through their intimate and sexual relations with women, are considered the rightful subjects of lesbian history and those whose heterosexual relations remove them from the scholarship about sexual deviance.'[21] The question of who constitutes the 'rightful subject' of any historical enquiry – especially those concerned with gender or sexual minorities – is a potent one. The broader context of Hindmarch-Watson's compelling historical analysis is worth further reflection. The allusion to feminist and lesbian feminist historiography reminds us that questions of identity, visibility and methodology are not unique to transgender history. To take lesbian historiography as one example, in their introduction to *Sapphic Modernities* (2007), Laura Doan and Jane Garrity suggest that 'scholars in lesbian studies have been inordinately preoccupied with the question of "who counts" or "what is it that we count" in assigning modern categories of sexuality (lesbian, bisexual, straight, etc.)', concluding that 'such questions are, in fact, at the crux of lesbian historiography'.[22] In their survey of lesbian historiography they note that leading scholars (such as Judith Bennett and Martha Vicinus) have emphasised the 'importance of avoiding ahistoricism by differentiating between questions that concern us now (the urge and desire to know for sure) and what the historical record allows us to conclude (what might never be known)'.[23] Foucault's hypothesis, outlined in his *History of Sexuality*, that homosexuality as a category of sexual identity – indeed the very idea of sexual identity as a category – is the effect of a unique confluence of legal, medical and psychological discourses in the late nineteenth century has been central to debates about lesbian and gay historiography. Some scholars, including in the field of lesbian history, have questioned the usefulness of Foucault's theories on the grounds that they appear to render invisible the historical existence of lesbians and gay men prior to the late nineteenth century. However, in other contexts, and especially within queer historiography, Foucault's insights into the discursive and historically specific production of sexed, gendered and sexual identities have significantly extended the field of historical enquiry. In her 2004 essay 'Queer Physiognomies: Or, How Many Ways Can We Do the History of Sexuality?', Dana Seitler describes how this historicising of categories of identity has informed queer perspectives on the past:

> Ostensibly moving away from the assumptions of identity politics, queer theory has had as its promise a project that was less interested in 'discovering' stable sexual subjects from the past than in developing an understanding of the process of deviant subject formation that helped constitute the prescriptions for compulsory heterosexuality.[24]

Similarly, leading theorists in the field of transgender studies have offered strategies for reconstructing potential transgender histories without projecting contemporary categories on to the past. Indeed, in 'Telling Tales', Halberstam does not aim to name, identify or categorise the historical subjects of her essay, but rather to recognise their narratives as 'unresolved tales of gender variance that will follow us from the twentieth century to the twenty-first century: not resolved, not near, not understood'.[25] Similarly, for Susan Stryker 'transgender phenomena'[26] are not limited to questions of individual identification but rather extend to 'anything that calls our attention to the contingency and unnaturalness of gender normativity'.[27] In the following account Stryker gives some indication of the kind of locations in historical archives where the 'transgender phenomena' of the past might be discerned: 'appear[ing] at the margins of the biopolitically operated-upon body, at those fleeting and variable points at which particular bodies exceed or elude capture within the gender apparatus when they defy the logic of the biopolitical calculus or present a case that confounds an administrative rule or bureaucratic practice.'[28] Indeed, K. J. Rawson has argued that a history of transgender people may be dispersed across a range of sources, rather than residing in any single archive:

> Prior to the development of 'transgender' as a discrete identity, a variety of state-sponsored materials – dress code laws, police documents, immigration reports, homicide records – provide a glimpse of the troubled meetings between gender-nonconforming people and the social and legal mechanisms that have attempted to define, control, and dictate gender norms.[29]

These 'glimpse[s]' of 'troubled meetings' are what the historian of transgender phenomena might be alert to, whether working in the medium of historical record or fictional reconstruction. David Getsy's concept of 'transgender capacity'[30] is immensely helpful in conceptualising a methodology conducive to transgender historiography and is defined as follows: 'Transgender capacity is the ability or the potential for making visible, bringing into experience, or knowing genders as mutable, successive, and multiple.'[31] Getsy explains how recognition of 'transgender capacity' might be applied to historical methodology:

> With regard to historical analysis, transgender capacity poses particularly urgent questions, since it is clear that there is a wealth of gender variance and nonconformity that has simply not been registered in the historical record. Without projecting present-day understandings of transgender identities into the past, one must recognize and make space for all of the ways in which self-determined and successive genders, identities, and bodily morphologies have always been present throughout history as possibilities and actualities.[32]

Hence, it is with these 'unresolved tales' (Halberstam), historical 'glimpses' (Rawson), and 'possibilities and actualities' (Getsy) in mind that this study approaches the question of historical existence within cultural representation and narrative, whether memoir, biography, fiction, drama or film. Within the field of literary criticism, characters whose gendered identity is at odds with prevailing assumptions about the relationship between sex and gender have historically tended to be the provenance of feminist, lesbian and gay and queer readings.[33]

For the purposes of this study, a focus on the 'transgender capacity'[34] of the protagonists of each text will be the starting point for analysis. This is not to suggest that the protagonist – whether fictional or historical – should only be read as transgender, nor is it to preclude other readings of his or her gendered identity. Rather, these readings are offered as a counter discourse to dominant narratives (historical, literary and critical) which have either overlooked the transgender potential of the figure concerned or defined it in negative or disparaging terms. It is not the intention of this study to anachronistically impose contemporary categories of identity – themselves dynamic and subject to change – on to historical subjects which predate their emergence. Nor does it seek to judge historically contingent texts – and their authors – against protocols of address which they could not have anticipated. However, it does aim to examine a specific set of narrative strategies employed in the telling of lives which we might now wish to call transgender and to examine how these strategies both produce and deny different narrative possibilities. In her 2008 book *Transgender History*, Susan Stryker notes: 'What counts as transgender varies as much as gender itself, and it always depends on historical and cultural context.'[35] This study will pay attention to the variety of contexts at work in the production and reception of the texts examined, including the period in which the narrative is situated (ranging from the British Empire in the early nineteenth century, to 1860s Dublin and early-twentieth-century Europe), the era in which the text was written and published (from 1918 to 2000), the cultural conditions in which adaptations for the stage and screen were produced, and the present moment from which the cultural productions of the last century – and their afterlives – are revisited. A historicising approach is also essential when considering the relationship between transgender representation and a critical framework which has played a formative role in the reception of transgender motifs in twentieth-century writing: feminism.

The Empire Writes Back: Transgender and Feminism

The relationship between transgender and feminism is a complex one, especially in relation to feminist perspectives on literary and cultural representations of transgender bodies or identities. Composed of competing, and even contradictory, histories, politics and discourses, this relationship has taken different forms at different times. Four contexts are important to consider when attempting to unravel the close but sometimes contentious relationship between feminism and transgender: firstly, a tradition of women's writing and feminist literary criticism which champions female-to-male gender crossing as an important metaphor for feminist subversion; secondly, a history of Second Wave feminist polemic which denounces male-to-female transsexuals as victims of sex role ideology and agents of patriarchal infiltration; thirdly, the impact of queer theory, and specifically Butler's theories of gender performativity, on feminist perspectives on transgender; finally, new efforts on the part of feminist and transgender theorists to confront past and current tensions and to renew and theorise a 'transfeminist' alliance. The influence of all contexts can be seen in the diversity of contemporary feminist positions both on the existence and rights of transgender people and on their representation in literature and culture.

Gender crossing – whether historical or figurative – has occupied a significant place in traditions of women's writing and feminist literary criticism. The existence of historical records and reports testifying to a long history of female-to-male gender crossing has proved an important source of inspiration for generations for women writers and feminist critics who have embraced the gender-crossing figure as symbol of feminist defiance. In her 1989 book *Amazons and Military Maids: Women Who Dressed as Men in Pursuit of Life, Liberty and Happiness*, Julie Wheelwright cautions against the 'temptation to claim these women as our feminist forebears',[36] given that their success was in many ways conditional on their compliance with gender convention, but does interpret their actions as indicative of a deep and systemic dissatisfaction with conventional gender roles: 'The thread that pulls these stories together is women's desire for male privilege and a longing to escape from domestic confines and powerlessness. Many vividly describe a lifelong yearning for liberation from the constraints they chafed against as women.'[37] Wheelwright's narrative rescues the female-to-male gender-crossing subject from the margins of history; no longer an exceptional, anomalous or aberrant figure, she is placed within a larger history of women's struggle for freedom and independence, providing an inspiring antecedent for future generations. For lesbian feminist historians, the female-to-male gender-crossing figure can further be placed within cultural histories of 'female masculinity'[38] as one of the ways in which women expressed their gendered and sexual identity; in this way a 'hidden history' is made visible and the gender-crossing subject claimed for a larger history of female same-sex desire and lesbian identity. In this kind of narrative, historical reality and historical metaphor combine to produce a concept of gender crossing whose figurative uses have been extensively employed in traditions of women's writing and feminist literary criticism. Virginia Woolf's historical fantasy *Orlando*, first published in 1928, has played an important role in the tradition of women's writing and feminist literary criticism in which gender crossing as a symbolic trope is embraced as an expression of feminist defiance or subversion. Moreover, the novel's dedication to Vita Sackville West and its widespread interpretation as a tribute to Woolf's lover have meant that the novel has been situated in traditions of lesbian feminist writing. In this irreverent pastiche of historical fiction and biography, Woolf depicts sex as inessential and gender as culturally contingent; as a literary conceit, the character of Orlando combines the historical and the figurative in a way which was to have a lasting effect on traditions of women's historical fiction – including those embracing postmodern strategies – and on feminist literary criticism. In this way, Orlando's change of sex – as presented in a novel which lays claim to both historical reference and the licence of fantasy – has served as a kind of feminist literary prototype for the depiction of gender crossing as a metaphor for women's position in a patriarchal world and for female same-sex desire and lesbian identity. In these contexts, motifs of 'sex change' or 'gender crossing' are understood primarily as metaphors for women's experience, with the unintended consequence that the transgender potential of these narratives has often been overlooked or obscured.

In the tradition of women's writing and feminist literary criticism considered above, motifs of gender crossing or changing sex – whether historical or fantastical – are considered subversive in ways which are both playful and empowering. By contrast, the actual lived existence of some male-to-female transsexuals has been less celebrated in some feminist contexts. A series of public expulsions of transgender people from 'women only' cultural spaces in the US in the early 1970s, combined with the publication of Janice Raymond's *The Transsexual Empire: The Making of the She-Male* in 1979, had the effect of constructing transgender identity, especially in relation to male-to-female transsexuals, as a focal point for heated debates about what constitutes women's identity in feminist contexts. Male-to-female transsexuals form the principal focus of attention in Raymond's book, which offers a critique based on two major assumptions: that male-to-female transsexuals are intent on both colonising women's spaces (understood in terms of identities, bodies and communities) and appropriating women's power (aligned with women's creativity and attributed to reproductive capacity). In this context, male-to-female transsexuals are repeatedly figured as intruders in disguise, seeking to penetrate and colonise 'women's mind, women's space, women's sexuality'[39] and to capture and usurp 'female creative energy and power'.[40] Insistent throughout is the assertion that 'Transsexuals are *not* women. They are *deviant* males . . .' [emphasis in original][41] and their actions are compared to rape and pornography, the principal objects of Second Wave critiques of male sexual violence and objectification. Raymond defines the 'transsexual empire' as 'the medical conglomerate that has created the treatment and technology that makes anatomical sex conversion possible'.[42] Her argument that transsexual identity is the product of medical technology – an effect of modern science rather than the expression of individual agency – is one which challenges its authenticity and legitimacy: 'Historically, individuals may have wished to change sex, but until medical science developed the specialties, which in turn created the demand for surgery, sex conversion did not exist.'[43] The implication is that medical science, long recognised in feminist, gay and lesbian critiques for its role as an agent of coercive normativity, conspires with the transsexual patient to enable them to fulfil an illusion of gender which only perpetuates patriarchal power. Where figurative gender crossing had been embraced in longstanding feminist contexts as subversive, the actual existence of male-to-female transsexuals was now denounced in ideological terms.

The third context is one which serves to explain the recuperation of the transgender subject within the field of feminist enquiry in the 1990s and beyond. Seemingly bypassing the problematic legacy of Second Wave feminist hostility to transsexuals, this 'return' is made possible by the impact of queer theory, and more specifically the influence of Judith Butler's theories of performativity, on feminism. This definition reflects a period of theorising in the 1990s which equated the transgender subject with the subversion of binary categories of identity; aligned with radical politics, transgressive practice and deconstructive theory, 'transgender' is figured as a trope which exemplifies cutting-edge thinking about identity.[44] However, as we will see in the next section, this emphasis on transgender as a conceptual category exemplifying queer theories of subjectivity has been problematised; the transgender subject is arguably reduced to a metaphor in service to frameworks of identity which are not principally concerned with the experience and interests of transgender people.

Finally, recent decades have seen the emergence of new feminist scholarship on transgender which seeks to acknowledge and address the divisive legacy of some aspects of Second Wave feminism, to examine the affinities between transgender studies and feminism and to forge new alliances. Central to this movement is an understanding of the importance of a relationship which is both self-reflexive and reciprocal, acknowledging a complex and controversial history (and present) at the same time as working to identify political affinities and potential alliances. In the face of what Talia Bettcher and Ann Garry describe as 'unfriendly theorizing',[45] these critics seek to emphasise the common cause which transgender studies and feminism share. In their introduction to a special issue of the feminist philosophy journal *Hypatia*, dedicated to transgender studies and feminism, Bettcher and Garry challenge the basis of some feminists' hostility to male-to-female transsexuals by placing particular emphasis on shared experience: 'Many trans women are well acquainted with the mechanisms of sexism and sexual violence to which they may fall prey, precisely because trans women are recognized as *women*' [emphasis in original].[46] Similarly, in her 2003 essay 'Feminist Solidarity after Queer Theory: The Case of Transgender', published in the longstanding feminist journal *Signs: Journal of Women in Culture and Society*, Cressida Heyes argues that 'many transgendered people are daily the victims of the most intense and public attempts to discipline gender in ways feminists have long criticized'.[47] However, beyond assertions of affinity and pledges of allegiance, this work is often characterised by a quality of critical self-reflexivity and an ethics of responsibility which is principally concerned with the impact of debates about the 'proper subject' of feminist activism and theory, past, present and future. Indeed, the use – and abuse – of transgender issues in feminist theory has become the object of significant theoretical reflection. Heyes acknowledges the ways in which debates about transgender have been employed as a kind of limit case in feminist theory: 'Whether appropriated to bolster queer theoretical claims, represented as the acid test of constructionism, or attacked for suspect political commitments, transgender has been colonised as a feminist theoretical testing ground.'[48] Reversing the colonising metaphor which was used to such provocative effect by Janice Raymond, Heyes suggests that it is feminist theory which should be held accountable for acts of appropriation. The theoretical uses to which the transgender figure has been put in feminist theory are explored in detail in Vivian Namaste's essay 'Undoing Theory: The "Transgender Question" and the Epistemic Violence of Anglo-American Feminist Theory', where she argues that

> For nearly twenty years, then, Anglo-American feminist theory has been preoccupied with the 'Transgender Question.' This phrase – the 'Transgender Question' – refers to the ways in which feminist theory depends on looking at transsexual and transgendered bodies in order

to ask its own epistemological questions. Current discussions within Anglo-American feminist theory – notably the central question of considering how gender is constituted – take place primarily through citing transsexual and transvestite bodies. Anglo-American feminist theory asks the Transgender Question in order to go about its business.[49]

Namaste demonstrates the way in which feminist theory has relied on the concept of transgender to undertake its own enquiries. The 'transgender question' takes on a hypothetical status in this context, existing as a philosophical conundrum rather than a lived reality. In other words, transgender is constructed as the 'other' against which feminism defines and tests its own identity and boundaries: variously expelled and appropriated, the concept of transgender does considerable labour on behalf of feminist theorising and is hence the source of a significant but often unacknowledged intellectual debt. This work foregrounds the way in which feminist theory has been reliant on the construction of 'others', a tendency which has also been interrogated in relation to questions of race, class and sexuality amongst others. For many of the contributors to this debate, feminism's capacity to engage with the questions posed by transgender studies is understood as crucial for its future. Gayle Salamon contends that feminism, 'particularly but not exclusively in its institutionalized form, has not been able to keep pace with non-normative genders as they are thought, embodied, and lived'.[50] In this context she argues that such a project is vital:

> Genders beyond the binary of male and female are neither fictive not futural, but are presently embodied and live, and the discipline of women's studies has not yet taken account of this. Until women's studies demonstrates a more serious engagement with trans studies, it cannot hope to fully assess the present state of gender as it is lived, nor will it be able to imagine many of its possible futures.[51]

As we have seen, the relationship between feminism and transgender studies is a long and complex one, whose contrasting histories and competing positions encompass a range of motifs and debates, including: the role of 'sex change' or 'gender crossing' as figurative tropes in cultural representation; the competing claims of feminist, lesbian feminist and transgender historiography on the figure of the female-to-male gender-crossing subject; the continuing legacy of Second Wave critiques of transsexuals as complicit in patriarchal ideologies of gender; the relationship between Butler's theories of performativity and pre-existing feminist perspectives on gender crossing. These debates are central to this study, which examines the impact of a variety of feminist perspectives on the production, reception and adaptation of narratives about transgender lives, including Simone Benmussa's 1977 stage adaptation of George Moore's *Albert Nobbs* (1918) and Patricia Duncker's *James Miranda Barry* (1999), but with a special focus on Angela Carter's *The Passion of New Eve* (1977), which will be considered in the context of Second Wave feminist critiques of male-to-female transsexuals.

Troubling Transgender: Queer Theory and Performativity

The methodologies and practices of queer theory are generally understood to have served as a formative origin for many aspects of transgender studies. Indeed, Heather Love identifies important affinities between queer theory and transgender studies when she writes that 'queer and transgender are linked in their activist investments, their dissident methodologies, and their critical interrogation of and resistance to gender and sexual norms'.[52] Similarly, Prosser notes parallels consisting in 'Coming out; pride in marginality; a politics that deconstructs identity' and concedes that 'many of transgender's tenets *are* queer' [emphasis in original].[53] However, while transgender theorists have acknowledged the importance of queer theory as an enabling condition, they have also identified significant differences and critical tensions between the two fields. Susan Stryker's playfully and provocatively titled essay 'Transgender Studies: Queer Theory's Evil Twin' revives the imagery of Gothic doubling which she employed to such powerful effect in her landmark essay 'My Words to Victor Frankenstein above the Village of Chamounix: Performing Transgender Rage'. For Stryker, transgender studies exists in a productively critical relationship with its theoretical forebear:

> If queer theory was born of the union of sexuality studies and feminism, transgender studies can be considered queer theory's evil twin: it has the same parentage but wilfully disrupts the privileged family narratives that favour sexual identity labels (like *gay*, *lesbian*, *bisexual* and *heterosexual*) over the gender categories (like *man* and *woman*) that enable desire to take shape and find its aim. [emphasis in original][54]

Moreover, Stryker identifies two tendencies which problematise the conflation of queer and transgender: the first concerns the politics of assimilation and the second concerns the processes of displacement.

She suggests: 'While queer studies remains the most hospitable place to undertake transgender work, all too often queer remains a code word for "gay" or "lesbian," and all too often transgender phenomena are misapprehended through a lens that privileges sexual orientation and sexual identity as the primary means of differing from heteronormativity.'[55] In other words, the nominally 'subjectless'[56] critique of queer theory often takes – or is assumed to take – gay and lesbian identity as its proper subject. Where assimilation entails implicit subordination, the second tendency makes use of processes of displacement, in a process by which gay and lesbian identity secures inclusion within normative structures through the expedient projection of non-normativity on to transgender 'others'.[57] As Stryker puts it: 'Most disturbingly, "transgender" increasingly functions as the site in which to contain all gender trouble, thereby helping secure both homosexuality and heterosexuality as stable and normative categories of personhood.'[58]

When considering the relationship between transgender and queer theory it is important to acknowledge the role played by readings of Judith Butler's work on performativity, as outlined in her 1990 book *Gender Trouble: Feminism and the Subversion of Identity*, in establishing transgender as a 'key queer trope'.[59] This phrase belongs to Jay Prosser, and his delineation of misinterpretations of Butler's work, and its implications for transgender studies, is essential reading when considering how and why transgender has come to be conflated with queer theory through popular digests of Butler's work. The tendency to read transgender lives – whether fictional or not – as illustrative embodiments of key queer concepts is both persistent and problematic. Indeed, it might be argued that this habitual interpretative reduction of transgender identities and bodies to exemplary ciphers for queer theoretical paradigms is currently one of the principal obstacles encountered when analysing representations of transgender in literary fiction. Prosser suggests that 'in the cultural imagination [the] figure of the body as costume is surely welded most firmly to the transsexual'.[60] This trope is a popular one in literary and cultural studies indebted to theories of social construction. Metaphors of performance are often deployed to communicate a shift from thinking about the self as innate and fixed to thinking about identity as provisional and contingent; if the self is an unmediated expression of an inner essence, the subject is just one iteration of identity in specific historical, cultural and discursive conditions. The idea that we may be unknowingly performing a 'role' scripted by the dominant culture draws on the distinction between the actor and the performance to suggest that the roles we play may not be of our own making.[61] According to this analogy, we are all actors; some may experience significant personal investment in their roles giving rise to a vivid sense of authenticity, where others may experience alienation resulting from constraint or coercion. Nevertheless, a recurring motif in the depiction of transgender people reveals that the insights of social construction theory are often unevenly applied. As Talia Mae Bettcher puts it, in her 2014 essay 'Trapped in the Wrong Theory: Rethinking Trans Oppression and Resistance': 'Consider: If all the world's a stage on which we all play a part, trans individuals play actors.'[62] While theories of social construction implicitly question the unexamined authenticity of all identity roles, transgender people are often assumed to exemplify this insight more fully than non-transgender people; to put it in other words (with apologies to George Orwell), if all genders are constructed, some are more constructed than others. Indeed, motifs of inauthenticity, deception and imposture have been used not only to question the legitimacy of transgender lives but also to rationalise prejudice, discrimination and violence against transgender people. In this context, Bettcher has noted that 'if trans people are systematically subject to allegations of deception or pretense, the idea that sex and gender are constructs might seem especially threatening'.[63] This concern has prompted theorists such as Gayle Salamon to make significant efforts to clarify what theories of social construction can reasonably claim, with a view to contesting its misapplication and recovering its insights:

> To claim that the body is socially constructed is not to claim that it is not real, that it is not made of flesh, or that its materiality is insignificant. To claim that sex is a social construct is not to claim that it is irrelevant, or invariant, or incapable of being embodied or reworked. To claim that our experiences of our sexed and gendered bodies are socially constructed is not to claim that our experiences are fictive, or inessential, or less important than our theorizing about sexed and gendered bodies.[64]

In her phenomenological study, Salamon seeks to reconcile social construction with lived experience, in contrast to other contexts where the former has been deployed to discredit the latter in relation to transgender lives: 'What social construction offers is a way to understand how that felt sense arises, in all its historical and cultural variations, with all its urgency and immediacy, and to ask what it is, finally, that is delivered by that felt sense.'[65] It is notable that, in a 2014 interview with *The TransAdvocate*, Butler sought to clarify her position on social construction and the lived experience of transgender people, denouncing the use of the former to deny the reality of the latter:

> One problem with that view of social construction is that it suggests that what trans people feel about what their gender is, and should be, is itself 'constructed' and, therefore, not real . . . I oppose this use of social construction absolutely, and consider it to be a false, misleading, and oppressive use of the theory.[66]

Prosser cites Butler herself as commenting on the ways in which a relatively minor feature of her analysis in *Gender Trouble* has been deployed as the premise for persistent misreading: '"there were probably no more than five paragraphs in *Gender Trouble* devoted to drag [yet] readers have often cited the description of drag as if it were the 'example' which explains the meaning of [gender] performativity"' [brackets in original].[67] The logic by which 'drag' is equated not only with performativity but also with transgender is one which arguably has its origins outside of the rhetorical framework of Butler's text: while some drag performers may also be transgender people, the gender identity of transgender people is not a drag performance. Prosser's chapter 'Judith Butler: Queer Feminism, Transgender, and the Transubstantiation of Sex' can be situated in a larger body of work which has sought to remedy misreadings of Butler's work, but it has special significance for transgender studies because it foregrounds the implications of the conflation of 'queer' with 'transgender'. Prosser argues that the mistaken assumption that

> gender performativity means acting out one's gender as if gender were a theatrical role that could be chosen, led to the belief that Butler's theory of gender was both radically voluntarist and antimaterialist: that its argument was that gender, like a set of clothes in a drag act, could be donned and doffed at will, that gender *is* drag. [emphasis in original][68]

This assumption that gender can be subverted by individual acts of agency underestimates the very real and injurious constraints to which the expression of gender is often subject. For Prosser, the equation of transgender with performativity, and hence with subversive agency, is problematic for further reasons; in *Second Skins*, he argues for a return to the materiality of gender, observing that 'there are transgendered trajectories, in particular *transsexual* trajectories, that aspire to that which this scheme devalues [straight gender]. Namely there are transsexuals who seek very pointedly to be nonperformative, to be constative, quite simply, to *be*' [emphasis in original].[69] Prosser questions the 'assumption that transgender is queer is subversive'[70] and does so in a context in which he recognises the way in which 'transgender *gender* appears as the most crucial sign of queer *sexuality's* aptly skewed point of entry into the academy' [emphasis in original].[71] It is essential to take this important observation into account when considering the critical reception of literary representations of transgender bodies and identities; in contexts where this misreading of Butler's theories of performativity is employed under the sign of queer theory (including feminist contexts), the transgender figure is read (and indeed written) as a metaphor for gender subversion rather than an expression of gender identity. Reduced to a rhetorical vehicle for analogical thinking about the meaning of normative gender, the relationship between the transgender figure and the actual or potential lived experience of transgender people is obscured. This is not to argue that metaphorical representation is inevitably problematic, nor is it to make a case for mimetic representation only in relation to transgender representation. Rather it is to draw attention to the particular purposes to which transgender figures have been deployed in literary fiction and literary criticism and to recognise that these purposes, while nominally subversive, may in fact be mortgaged to normative assumptions. As will be demonstrated, motifs of performance are evident in the texts examined in this study but often in ways which are more likely to reinforce the perception of transgender characters as 'actors' than to subversively reveal the performativity of all gender roles.

Crossing the T: Identity Politics and the LGBT Umbrella

In the second decade of the twenty-first century transgender people, their rights and representation have acquired a new visibility in the public sphere as a consequence of the longstanding efforts of transgender activists. However, this visibility has taken a number of varying forms with different effects, ranging from the formal inclusion of transgender people in the equality and diversity policies and strategies of public and private bodies (including charities, NGOs and health care providers), to the prominence of some transgender people in popular culture and social media, especially in relation to celebrity, film and television drama, and fashion. In this context, the relationship between identity politics, discourses of rights and neoliberal agendas has been the subject of significant critical attention within the field of transgender studies. In particular, reflection on the inclusion of transgender within an expanded lesbian, gay, bisexual and transgender alliance, and on the relationship between LGBT politics and normative discourses, offers insights into the uses and limitations of identity politics in contemporary culture. The addition of transgender to the activist coalition of lesbian, gay and bisexual people – typified in the acronym LGBT – can be understood as an expression of solidarity and an extension of the benefits of collective action on the basis of common cause: the experience of prejudice, discrimination and violence shared on the grounds of sexual or gender non-normativity.[72] However, the inclusion of transgender as a category of identity within the LGBT umbrella has been the subject of critical debate in a number of contexts. Firstly, activists and theorists have expressed concern that the specific needs and interests of transgender people are confused, obscured and displaced through the apparent conflation of gender identity (transgender) with sexual identity (lesbian, gay and bisexual). Secondly, a broader critique of what has been termed (following Lisa Duggan) 'homonormative' trends in LGBT activism has raised questions about its investment in radical change. Finally, an emphasis on transgender people as the natural allies of lesbian, gay and bisexual people is thought to obscure alternative modes of alliance, including those to do with race, class and disability.

In an essay on the LGBT 'umbrella' in US contexts, Zein Murib observes that

> The ubiquitous use of LGBT initialism across the various social, academic, and political discursive contexts ... suggests that the constitutive categories of lesbian, gay, bisexual, and transgender are equivalent, informed by similar experiences, and, as such, appropriate to collapse into a single category: LGBT.[73]

'Equivalent' and 'collapse' are key terms here. The logic of analogy – by which parallels are drawn between experiences of oppression by different groups of people – has the potential to identify collective experience and to mobilise an empowering sense of solidarity. However, the inclusion of transgender within the LGBT umbrella potentially serves to exacerbate public misunderstanding about what the term 'transgender' means: the alliance of gay, lesbian and bisexual people is founded on the organising category of sexual identity, but transgender is not a sexual identity.[74] The experiences of transgender people are not identical to the experiences of lesbian, gay and bisexual people and there is a concern that those experiences which do not serve to bolster the strategic analogy may be overlooked or marginalised. As Susan Stryker puts it in her essay 'Transgender History, Homonormativity, and Disciplinarity': '"T" becomes a separate category to be appended, through a liberal politics of minority assimilation, to gay, lesbian, and bisexual community formations.'[75] Stryker's critique of the 'liberal politics of minority assimilation' can be placed in a broader context of critical debates about the political direction of mainstream LGBT activism, or what Stryker terms

> the same developmental logic that transformed an antiassimilationist 'queer' politics into a more palatable LGBT civil rights movement, with T reduced to merely another (easily detached) genre of sexual identity rather than perceived, like race or class, as something that cuts across existing sexualities . . .[76]

Questions of assimilation, inclusion and appropriation are central to debates which focus on the impact of neoliberal contexts and the advent of homonormativity.

The term 'homonormativity' was first coined by Lisa Duggan in her 2003 book *The Twilight of Democracy? Neoliberalism, Cultural Politics, and the Attack on Democracy*. It describes a perceived trend in lesbian and gay activism, especially that pursued by mainstream advocacy organisations, which, in Stryker's words, 'does not challenge heterosexist institutions and values, but rather upholds, sustains, and seeks inclusion within them'.[77] While the term did not originate in transgender contexts, Stryker suggests that it serves a need 'to name the ways that homosexuality, as a sexual orientation category based on constructions of gender it shared with the dominant culture, sometimes had more in common with the straight world than it did with us'.[78] Moreover, these norms are seen by critics of homonormativity as symptomatic of a historically specific neoliberal politics. This critique is central to David Valentine's *Imagining Transgender: An Ethnography of a Category* (2007) and Dean Spade's *Normal Life: Administrative Violence, Critical Trans Politics and the Limits of Law* (2015). As Spade puts it, 'the quest for inclusion in and recognition by dominant US institutions' began to supplant 'questioning and challenging the fundamental inequalities promoted by those institutions'.[79] Valentine provides the following overview of the new neoliberal consensus as it emerged in the United States in the late twentieth century:

> In a time frame that maps onto the ascendency of identity-based politics in the United States, since the early 1970s a broad (and sometimes contradictory) range of neoliberal policies have asserted

business rights over public life, increasingly privatized public services and public space, undercut labor and class-based progressive alliances, and reframed 'rights' in terms of a framework of consumption in the United States and beyond.[80]

This mapping of 'identity politics' against market-driven social change alerts us to the complex relationship – what Spade calls the 'paradox of rights'[81] – between nominally radical social movements and the social and economic structures which frame them. Spade refers to 'co-optation and incorporation' as the 'hallmarks of neoliberalism' whereby 'the words and ideas of resistance movements are frequently recast to produce results that disserve the initial purposes for which they were deployed, and instead become legitimizing tools for white supremacist, capitalist, patriarchal, ableist political agendas'.[82] For Spade, Valentine and others, an emphasis on individual and privatised experience and an embrace of normative institutions (such as marriage, the reproductive family and the military) are defining characteristics of homonormative politics. As Spade argues: 'Trans resistance is emerging in a context of neoliberal politics where the choice to struggle for nothing more than incorporation into the neoliberal order is the most obvious option.'[83] One consequence of this insistence on integration is the assimilation of LGBT organisations within the political status quo; another is the consolidation of existing racial, class and other privileges. Firstly, there is an emphasis on similarity rather than difference. As Valentine suggests: 'One of the primary sites of such institutionalization has resulted from the mainstream gay and lesbian activist claims that homosexual people are essentially the same as heterosexual Americans but for one fact of privately experienced and conducted sexual desire and practice.'[84] Such a strategy makes a case for the extension of privileges to an excluded group on the grounds that their inclusion will not compromise the status of existing social structures but rather consolidate and fortify them. Secondly, such a strategy assumes that sexuality is the only disqualifying characteristic suffered by LGBT citizens; as such it arguably serves to principally benefit those already privileged by gender, race, class or ability. Indeed, Spade argues that the LGBT rights agenda has 'shifted toward preserving and promoting the class and race privilege of a small number of elite gay and lesbian professionals while marginalizing or overtly excluding the needs and experiences of people of color, immigrants, people with disabilities, indigenous people, trans people, and poor people'.[85] In this way the goal of homonormative strategies is implicitly to 'restore privileges of the dominant systems of meaning and control to those gender-conforming, white, wealthy gay and lesbian US citizens who are enraged at how homophobic laws and policies limit access to benefits to which they feel entitled'.[86] For Valentine, this strategy is 'effectively a claim to invisibility – a dense condensation of gendered, sexual, racial, and class normality'.[87] In other words, it takes for granted an 'invisibility' which only normative subjects can assume and which is unavailable to those who are 'marked' by gender, race, class or ability. By situating their critique of homonormativity in the broader context of neoliberal politics, these critics enable us to think beyond prevailing paradigms of identity politics and to place transgender rights in the context of global patterns of political and economic marginalisation and exploitation; as Stryker has argued: 'The current attention to homonormativity has tended to focus on gay and lesbian social, political, and cultural formations and their relationship to a neoliberal politics of multicultural diversity that meshes with the assimilative strategies of transnational capital.'[88] Indeed, the inclusion of transgender within the LGBT umbrella and the prevalence of homonormative strategies in leading LGBT organisations is considered problematic by Spade, Stryker, Valentine and others because of the ways in which it obscures commonalities of experience and potential political alliances with groups not principally defined by sexuality or gender. As Stryker observes:

> Central issues for transgender activism – such as gender-appropriate state-issued identification documents that allow trans people to work, cross borders, and access social services without exposing themselves to potential discrimination – suggest useful forms of alliance politics, in this instance with migrant workers and diasporic communities...[89]

In her 2008 book *Transgender History*, Stryker similarly argues that: 'The restrictions on movement in the post-9/11 United States give transgender people more in common with immigrants, refugees, and undocumented workers than they might have with the gay and lesbian community.'[90] This issue is also pivotal for both Valentine and Spade. Valentine states: 'My central question here is: by identifying transgender people as experiencing discrimination or violence along the axis of gender identity, or describing gender-variant people through the framework of transgender, how are other kinds of social experience elided?'[91] Spade places particular emphasis on 'specific sites of intersection'[92] when he argues: 'Finding overlap and inspiration in the analysis and resistance articulated through women of color feminism, disability justice politics, prison abolition, and other struggles against colonialism, criminalization, immigration enforcement, and capitalism has far more to offer trans people.'[93]

Debates about the limits of identity politics are especially pertinent when considering two important but often overlooked motifs which have emerged in this analysis of twentieth-century narratives of transgender lives. The first is to do with the relationship between narratives of transsexual identity and intersex experience; the second is to do with the role played by normative categories of gender in constructions of 'race', including whiteness. To date, little critical attention has been given to the complex relationship between narratives of transgender identity and narratives of intersex experience. The potential affinity and common cause between intersex and transgender people has been acknowledged by critics including Iain Morland, who writes that 'both intersex and transsexuality raise the question of what kind of body one needs to have in order to claim membership in a gender and whether a person's sense of belonging to a gender is colored by the experience of living in a body that has been touched by medical technology'.[94] However, in the context of contemporary identity politics and activism, vigilance with regard to the problems arising from misleading conflations, both within activist contexts and within the public sphere, has been paramount. The possible inclusion of intersex people within the transgender umbrella has provoked concern that the needs and priorities of intersex people will be subsumed under those of transgender people, and that the equivalence suggested by the 'umbrella' will act to exacerbate public misunderstanding about intersex people. Historically, understandings of intersex, transsexual and homosexual people, including in the discourses of sexology, have been mobile and overlapping. Records indicate that James Miranda Barry and Lili Elbe may have been people with intersex variations; the treatment of this possibility in biographical and fictional accounts of Barry's life is considered in a postscript to Chapter 3, which serves as a prelude to a fuller treatment of this topic in Chapter 4, which examines how retellings of a life story central to the canon of transsexual life writing might serve to obscure narratives of intersex existence and experience.

The motif of border crossing is a longstanding one in transgender studies, with Halberstam noting that 'myths of travel and border crossings are inevitable within a discourse of transsexuality'[95] and Prosser examining 'transition as a geographic trope' which enables an understanding of 'transsexuality as a passage through space, a journey from one location to another'.[96] However, significant shifts can be observed in the treatment of this trope in the twenty-first century. Where earlier studies emphasise the metaphorical parallels between the crossing of national borders and the 'borders' between sexed and gendered identities, more recent work has situated motifs of mobility within the global politics of the movement of peoples, whether forced or elective. Aren Aizura contrasts the economic and racial privilege which can often serve as a prerequisite for the geographical journeys sometimes required to access gender reassignment treatment with the forced displacement of disempowered subjects. From this perspective new light is cast on the use of metaphors of travel, border crossing and migration in transgender narratives:

> trans theory has examined those figural 'borders' regulating traffic between genders rather than watching what happens to gender-variant people at real borders, appropriating the metaphor of the immigrant 'without land or nation' to understand transgender experience without considering that many trans people are, in fact, immigrants.[97]

This study seeks to make visible the processes of racial 'othering' and privileges of whiteness in narratives where mobility and migration are significant themes. In doing so it aims to redress the displacement or erasure of issues to do with race, nationality and migration in narratives about transgender subjects. The role of racial 'othering' in the construction of white femininity is evident in both Angela Carter's *The Passion of New Eve* and David Ebershoff's *The Danish Girl* but the colonial contexts in which James Miranda Barry's white masculinity is situated in biographical and fictional accounts of his life are considered in more detail in Chapter 3. Joss Moody's identity as a Scottish man of African heritage is central to the discussion of Kay's *Trumpet* in Chapter 5; in this novel narratives of origin – whether national, racial, gendered or familial – are placed in question, defying any attempt to fix or reduce identity to a singular category.

Chapter Overview

Chapter 1, '"Two men, so dissimilar": Class, Marriage and Masculinity in George Moore's *Albert Nobbs* (1918) and Simone Benmussa's *The Singular Life of Albert Nobbs* (1977)', examines a critically overlooked literary fiction by an Irish writer whose legacy has tended to be overshadowed by the modernist generation which succeeded him. Moore's *Albert Nobbs* depicts the lives of not one but two female-bodied men working in a Dublin hotel in the 1860s. In striking contrast to the more sensationalist accounts of transgender lives which came to dominate popular cultural representations in the decades following the Second World War, these characters are presented in a naturalistic fashion and neither pathologised nor demonised. Moore's novella provides an alternative origin for a literary history of transgender representation, one which focuses on lived experience and social reality rather than the motifs of historical travesty and speculative fantasy established by Virginia Woolf's *Orlando*, published ten years later. This chapter aims to articulate the 'transgender capacity'[98] of Moore's novella, and explore the insights it offers into the social and economic functions of gender through a focus on class, marriage and masculinity. Moreover, the afterlives of Moore's novella – specifically its adaptation for the stage and screen – provide an opportunity to track the changing ways in which transgender motifs have been treated across the course of the twentieth century and beyond. Simone Benmussa's 1977 stage adaptation, *The Singular Life of Albert Nobbs*, has been canonised as a classic of feminist theatre and reflection on its critical reception offers insights into the ways in which transgender motifs have been interpreted in Second Wave feminist contexts. More specifically, this chapter will investigate how narratives of women's gender crossing have come to displace the narrative's transgender potential, establishing a pattern of feminist appropriation which is replicated in very different ways in Angela Carter's *The Passion of New Eve* (1977) and Patricia Duncker's *James Miranda Barry* (1999).

Second Wave feminist perspectives on transgender motifs are the central concern of the second chapter, '"She had never been a woman": Second Wave Feminism, Femininity and Transgender in Angela Carter's *The Passion of New Eve* (1977)', which focuses on a novel by a writer whose reputation as one of the most innovative and influential authors of the late twentieth century is firmly established. The centrality of Carter's work to feminist literary culture is widely recognised and celebrated, as is her passionately combative engagement with the feminist orthodoxies of her time. Through a focus on the contrasting depictions of an involuntary transsexual, the eponymous Eve (who is subject to sex reassignment surgery without her consent), and an elective transgender person, Tristessa (who is refused medical treatment despite living as woman), this chapter aims to address the critical legacies of specific strands of Second Wave feminist critique. It will do so by placing the novel within the context of debates and controversies about the place of male-to-female transsexuals in the women's movement contemporary to the era of its writing and reception. Where other critics have sought to incorporate Carter's work within later queer frameworks, most notably those informed by Judith Butler's theories of performativity,[99] this chapter aims to scrutinise the novel's relationship to competing feminist discourses of its time. Moreover, it will examine the impact of specific Second Wave feminist critiques – typified by Janice Raymond's *The Transsexual Empire* – on the critical reception of Carter's novel, focusing on the persistence of tropes which construct male-to-female transsexuals as agents of patriarchal constructions of femininity.

Where Carter's *The Passion of New Eve* provides opportunities to examine one of the more problematic legacies of Second Wave feminist perspectives on transgender motifs in literary fiction, Patricia Duncker's 1999 novel *James Miranda Barry* can be considered in a different tradition, one in which subversive narratives of women's gender crossing are prominent. Chapter 3, 'Playing the Breeches Part: Feminist Appropriations, Biographical Fictions and Colonial Contexts in Patricia Duncker's *James Miranda Barry* (1999)', examines a fictional reconstruction of the Irish-born and Scottish-educated colonial military surgeon James Miranda Barry (c. 1799–1865), whose life story has been irrevocably shaped by reports that he had been discovered after death to be female bodied. Barry has been the subject of a number of historical biographies but the narrative of strategic gender crossing which they have tended to adopt is notably absent in Duncker's depiction of Barry, which declines to disclose a definitive explanatory motivation or identification. However, a feminist narrative of gender crossing arguably emerges in displaced form in the novel through the expanded narratives of Barry's mother, Mary Ann, and imagined childhood sweetheart, Alice; in this novel Barry's gender identity serves as a vehicle through which women can express agency in a displaced manner and pursue ambition in a vicarious fashion. Barry's career took place in the theatre of empire but the racial politics of this era of British history are often overlooked in both biographical and fictional accounts of Barry's life; close attention to the treatment of colonial contexts will serve to demonstrate the role of white privilege and the construction of racial 'others' in these narratives.

Like Duncker's *James Miranda Barry*, David Ebershoff's 2000 novel *The Danish Girl* is a historical fiction based on the life of a real individual, Lili Elbe (1882–1931), reputed to be one of the first people to undergo gender reassignment treatment. The relationship between these fictions and their auto/biographical source texts merits special attention, especially given the prominent role played by genres of life writing in the representation of transgender lives. The relationship between historical record, autobiographical accounts and historical fiction is further complicated by the possibility that both James Miranda Barry and Lili Elbe may have been intersex people. The 'transgender capacity'[100] of the historical and fictional subjects of the texts examined in this study has provided the starting point for analysis in every chapter to date. By contrast, Chapter 4, 'Two Beings/One Body: Intersex Lives and Transsexual Narratives in *Man into Woman* (1931) and David Ebershoff's *The Danish Girl* (2000)', seeks to examine the ways in which the conventions of transsexual life writing may have the effect of obscuring or erasing narratives of intersex existence. This chapter will examine the novel's relationship to a formative source text, the generically hybrid auto/biography *Man into Woman: An Authentic Record of a Sex Change, the True Story of the Miraculous Transformation of the Danish Painter Einar Wegener (Andreas Sparre)* (1931), and its borrowing of the motif of 'two beings' in 'one body'.[101] The implications of the novel's reliance on the binary categories of identity prevalent in *Man into Woman* will be explored in relation not only to categories of sex but also to gender (especially femininity) and sexuality (specifically male homosexuality).

Posthumous exposure, often on the grounds of medical examination, has acted as the problematic vehicle through which a number of transgender lives have been bequeathed to history, with the perceived disparity between sex and gender serving as a pretext to forcibly rewrite the transgender person's identity in public memory. When Jason Cromwell refers to the '"Billy Tipton phenomenon"'[102] he evokes the memory of the American jazz musician who was subject to this fate on his death in 1989. Inspired by Tipton's life story, Jackie Kay's 1998 novel *Trumpet* explores the aftermath of a posthumous exposure but is notable for its purposeful thwarting of the narrative dynamics which conventionally accompany it. This novel will be examined in Chapter 5, 'Blue Births and Last Words: Rewriting Race, Nation and Family in Jackie Kay's *Trumpet* (1998)', which will examine how, in its focus on a Scottish musician of African heritage and his relationship with his adopted mixed-race son, *Trumpet* questions the privileging of essentialising narratives of 'birth', including those to do with gender, nation, race and family. Where Angela Carter's *The Passion of New Eve*, Patricia Duncker's *James Miranda Barry* and David Ebershoff's

The Danish Girl can be placed in the traditions of speculative fantasy and historical fiction respectively, *Trumpet* arguably returns to the realism of George Moore's early-twentieth-century novella and in doing so foregrounds lived experience over literary tropes. Its focus on gender normativity – Moody's masculinity is expressed in highly conventional ways in his role as husband and father within a heterosexual marriage – could be seen as anticipating twenty-first-century trends and this emphasis is also reflected in film adaptations of *Albert Nobbs* (2011) and *The Danish Girl* (2016).

Finally, Chapter 6, 'Never an Unhappy Hour: Revisiting Marriage in Film Adaptations of *Albert Nobbs* (2011) and *The Danish Girl* (2016)', returns to texts published at the opening and close of the twentieth century to examine their adaptation for the screen in twenty-first-century contexts. The retelling of transgender lives across different texts and contexts has been a recurring theme in this study; analysis of contemporary adaptations of twentieth-century texts will provide further opportunities to track the changing cultural meanings of these narratives. Released in a period in which the rights and representation of transgender people were attaining an unprecedented visibility in the mainstream media and popular culture, these films offer sympathetic portraits of their subjects but demonstrate an uneven engagement with contemporary understandings of transgender identity. The textual motif of 'two men, so dissimilar',[103] which draws attention to the differing personalities of Albert Nobbs and Hubert Page in Moore's novella, is all the more evident in the contrasting performances of Glenn Close and Janet McTeer in the 2011 adaptation *Albert Nobbs*. Benmussa's stage adaptation – in whose American premiere Glenn Close starred – is a crucial intertext for this adaptation, arguably shaping Close's interpretation of Albert as a tragically isolated cross-dressing woman. By contrast, the significant expansion of Hubert's character is achieved principally through the vehicle of his marriage to a milliner, with Hubert implicitly validated as the 'better man' in comparison with his abusive or absent male peers. Where Hubert's anticipated second marriage provides the resolution to the 2011 film, in the 2016 adaptation of *The Danish Girl* it is the protracted demise of the marriage between Einar Wegener (Eddie Redmayne) and Gerda Gottlieb (Alicia Vikander) which acts as the tragic heart of the drama, rather than Elbe's premature death. Moreover, *The Danish Girl* offers a largely normative depiction of femininity as the principal vehicle through which Elbe's gender identity as a woman is achieved, with the aesthetic conventions of period and costume drama mobilised to construct Elbe's transition in terms of the imperatives of passing. The prominence of marriage within these film adaptations of twentieth-century texts will be considered in the context of contemporary debates about LGBT activism and neoliberal politics.

In her 2004 book *Undoing Gender*, Judith Butler provides a powerful indication of what is at stake in the struggle for legal, social and cultural recognition for transgender people when she observes that gender 'figures as a precondition for the production and maintenance of legitimate humanity'.[104] In a chapter entitled 'Doing Justice to Someone: Sex Reassignment and Allegories of Transsexuality', Butler considers the 'conditions of intelligibility by which a human emerges'[105] and asks the following questions:

> What counts as a person? What counts as a coherent gender? What qualifies as a citizen? Whose world is legitimated as real? ... Who can I become in such a world where the meanings and limits of the subject are set out in advance for me? By what norms am I constrained as I begin to ask what I may become? And what happens when I begin to become that for which there is no place within the given regime of truth?[106]

The first decades of the twenty-first century have witnessed a transformation in the terms of public debate about transgender people, a change which can be attributed to the actions and interventions of generations of transgender activists, theorists, writers and artists. This context casts into new relief the ethical responsibility of scholarship in the arts and humanities to examine the role that culture can play in perpetuating or challenging assumptions which impact on people's lives and well-being. At a time when questions of self-determination are at the forefront of campaigns for transgender rights and debates about cultural representation, it is vital to examine the role played by historical, literary and film narrative in shaping 'conditions of intelligibility'. Grounded in feminist scholarship, informed by the insights of queer theory and indebted to the work of pioneering studies in the field of transgender studies, this book examines the uses to which transgender motifs have been put in twentieth-century narratives and their afterlives. By exploring the extent to which these texts give visibility or voice to transgender histories and identities, this study aims to contribute new insights to the complex, dynamic and ongoing history of transgender 'becoming' in the field of cultural representation.

Notes

1. *Becoming an Image Performance Still No. 2* (National Theatre Studio, SPILL Festival, London), 2013, photo: Cassils with Manuel Vason.
2. The 2006 Yogyakarta Principles on sexual orientation and gender identity have played a significant role in shaping global human rights discourses on transgender. The recommendations issued in the 2014 Amnesty International report, *The State Decides Who I Am: Lack of Legal Gender Recognition for Transgender People in Europe*, reflect the defining priorities of this movement, including: protection against discrimination and hate crime; the right to change legal names and gender markers on state-sanctioned identity documents; the abolition of prerequisites to legal recognition, such as the requirement to undergo medical diagnosis and treatment, to annul existing marriages or to meet minimum age requirements. See <https://www.amnesty.org/en/documents/EUR01/001/2014/en/> (last accessed 15 January 2018).
3. Susan Stryker argues that Prince originally intended the term to serve as a 'conceptual middle ground between transvestism (merely changing one's clothing) and transsexualism (changing one's sex)'. 'Transgender History, Homonormativity, and Disciplinarity', p. 146. By contrast, when the term was taken up by activists, communities and scholars in the 1990s, it expressed a very different position in relation to gender normativity.
4. Stryker, 'Transgender History, Homonormativity, and Disciplinarity', p. 146.
5. Singer, 'Umbrella', *TSQ: Transgender Studies Quarterly Special Issue – Postposttranssexual*, p. 260.
6. Singer, 'Umbrella', p. 259.
7. In the UK, for example, Press for Change was established in 1992 to campaign for legal equality for transgender people. In 2004 the Gender Recognition Bill allowed people to change their legal gender (providing they met predetermined criteria) and the 2010 Equality Act established gender reassignment as a protected characteristic under anti-discrimination legislation for the first time. In Ireland, Transgender Equality Network Ireland (TENI) was instrumental in securing the passage of the historic Gender Recognition Act in 2015.
8. Stone, 'The Empire Strikes Back: A Posttranssexual Manifesto', in Stryker and Whittle (eds), *The Transgender Studies Reader*, p. 230.
9. Prosser, *Second Skins*, p. 11.
10. Carter, 'Transition', *Postposttranssexual*, p. 235.
11. Bettcher, 'Evil Deceivers and Make-Believers: On Transphobic Violence and the Politics of Illusion', p. 46.
12. For a discussion of transsexual memoir, including Jan Morris's *Conundrum* (1974), Mark Rees's *Dear Sir or Madam: The Autobiography of a Female to Male Transsexual* (1996) and Renée Richards's *Second Serve* (1983), see Prosser, *Second Skins*.

13. Halberstam, 'Telling Tales: Brandon Teena, Billy Tipton, and Transgender Biography', in Sánchez and Schlossberg (eds), *Passing: Identity and Interpretation in Sexuality, Race, and Religion*, pp. 13–14.
14. Prosser, *Second Skins*, p. 101.
15. Prosser, *Second Skins*, p. 101.
16. Seid, 'Reveal', *Postposttranssexual*, p. 177.
17. Stone, 'The Empire Strikes Back', p. 230.
18. Halberstam, 'Telling Tales', p. 15.
19. Prosser, *Second Skins*, p. 11.
20. Hindmarch-Watson, 'Lois Schwich, Female Errand Boy: Narratives of Female Cross-Dressing in Late Victorian London', p. 72.
21. Hindmarch-Watson, 'Lois Schwich, Female Errand Boy', p. 73.
22. Doan and Garrity, 'Introduction', in Doan and Garrity (eds), *Sapphic Modernities: Sexuality, Women and National Cultures*, p. 5.
23. Doan and Garrity, 'Introduction', p. 5.
24. Seitler, 'Queer Physiognomies', p. 81.
25. Halberstam, 'Telling Tales', pp. 35–6.
26. Stryker, 'Biopolitics', *Postposttranssexual*, p. 40.
27. Stryker, 'Biopolitics', p. 40.
28. Stryker, 'Biopolitics', p. 40.
29. Rawson, 'Archive', *Postposttranssexual*, p. 24.
30. Getsy, 'Capacity', *Postposttranssexual*, p. 47.
31. Getsy, 'Capacity', p. 47.
32. Getsy, 'Capacity', p. 48.
33. Reflecting on his interpretation of a novel widely regarded as a classic in the canon of lesbian writing, Radclyffe Hall's *The Well of Loneliness* (1928), Jay Prosser observes that 'the writing of transsexual history will surely depend upon performing retroactive readings of figures and texts that have been central to the lesbian and gay canon'. Prosser, *Second Skins*, p. 167.
34. Getsy, 'Capacity', p. 47.
35. Stryker, *Transgender History*, p. 19.
36. Wheelwright, *Amazons and Military Maids*, p. 9.
37. Wheelwright, *Amazons and Military Maids*, p. 19.
38. See Halberstam, *Female Masculinity*.
39. Raymond, *The Transsexual Empire*, p. 104.
40. Raymond, *The Transsexual Empire*, p. xxiii.
41. Raymond, *The Transsexual Empire*, p. 183.
42. Raymond, *The Transsexual Empire*, p. xiv.
43. Raymond, *The Transsexual Empire*, p. xv. A similar critical position is adopted by Bernice Hausman in her 1995 book *Changing Sex: Transsexualism, Technology, and the Idea of Gender*, which has become the focus of critique in subsequent years.
44. See for example Roen, '"Either/Or" and "Both/Neither": Discursive Tensions in Transgender Politics'.

34 Transgender and the Literary Imagination

45. Bettcher and Garry, 'Introduction', *Hypatia Special Issue – Transgender Studies and Feminism*, p. 2.
46. Bettcher and Garry, 'Introduction', p. 4.
47. Heyes, 'Feminist Solidarity after Queer Theory', p. 1,094.
48. Heyes, 'Feminist Solidarity after Queer Theory', p. 1,098.
49. Namaste, 'Undoing Theory', p. 12.
50. Salamon, *Assuming a Body: Transgender and Rhetoric of Materiality*, p. 95.
51. Salamon, *Assuming a Body*, p. 96.
52. Love, 'Queer', *Postposttranssexual*, p. 172.
53. Prosser, *Second Skins*, p. 173.
54. Stryker, 'Transgender Studies: Queer Theory's Evil Twin', p. 212.
55. Stryker, 'Transgender Studies: Queer Theory's Evil Twin', p. 214.
56. See Eng, Halberstam and Muñoz: 'the "subjectless" critique of queer studies disallows any posting of a proper subject *of* or object *for* the field by insisting that queer has no fixed political referent' [emphasis in original]. 'Introduction: What's Queer about Queer Studies Now?', p. 3.
57. See Valentine, *Imagining Transgender*, and Puar, *Terrorist Assemblages*, for discussions of the relationship between the removal of homosexuality from, and the introduction of gender identity disorder to, the third edition of the *Diagnostic and Statistical Manual of Mental Disorders* in 1980.
58. Stryker, 'Transgender Studies: Queer Theory's Evil Twin', p. 214.
59. Prosser, *Second Skins*, p. 5.
60. Prosser, *Second Skins*, p. 62.
61. In a much quoted passage in *Gender Trouble*, Judith Butler describes gender as 'the repeated stylization of the body, a set of repeated acts within a highly rigid regulatory frame that congeal over time to produce the appearance of substance, of a natural sort of being' (pp. 43–4). Elsewhere, Butler describes gender 'as an act which has been rehearsed, much as a script survives the particular actors who make use of it, but which requires individual actors in order to be actualized and reproduced as reality once again'. 'Performative Acts and Gender Constitution: An Essay in Phenomenology and Feminist Theory', in Conboy, Medina and Stanbury (eds), *Writing on the Body: Female Embodiment and Feminist Theory*, p. 409.
62. Bettcher, 'Trapped in the Wrong Theory', p. 398.
63. Bettcher, 'Trapped in the Wrong Theory', p. 398.
64. Salamon, *Assuming a Body*, p. 76.
65. Salamon, *Assuming a Body*, p. 77.
66. 'Gender Performance: *The TransAdvocate* interviews Judith Butler', with Cristan Williams, *The TransAdvocate*, 1 May 2014, <http://www.transadvocate.com/gender-performance-the-transadvocate-interviews-judith-butler_n_13652.htm> (last accessed 15 January 2018).
67. Butler cited in Prosser, *Second Skins*, p. 25.
68. Prosser, *Second Skins*, p. 28.
69. Prosser, *Second Skins*, p. 32.

Introduction 35

70. Prosser, *Second Skins*, p. 29.
71. Prosser, *Second Skins*, p. 23.
72. In 2015 the leading UK lesbian, gay and bisexual rights organisation, Stonewall, published a report marking its formal commitment to trans inclusion. Reflecting on past practice and future strategy, *Trans People and Stonewall: Campaigning Together for Lesbian, Gay, Bisexual and Trans Equality* offers insights into the issues and opportunities presented by the LGBT alliance. See <http://www.stonewall.org.uk/sites/default/files/trans_people_and_stonewall.pdf> (last accessed 15 January 2018).
73. Murib, 'LGBT', *Postposttranssexual*, p. 118.
74. David Valentine questions this assumption, which is foundational for most other transgender theorists and activists, in *Imagining Transgender*.
75. Stryker, 'Transgender History, Homonormativity, and Disciplinarity', p. 148.
76. Stryker, 'Transgender Studies: Queer Theory's Evil Twin', p. 214.
77. Stryker, 'Transgender History, Homonormativity, and Disciplinarity', p. 145.
78. Stryker, 'Transgender History, Homonormativity, and Disciplinarity', p. 146.
79. Spade, *Normal Life*, p. 30.
80. Valentine, *Imagining Transgender*, p. 18.
81. Spade, *Normal Life*, p. 10.
82. Spade, *Normal Life*, p. 13.
83. Spade, *Normal Life*, p. 18.
84. Valentine, *Imagining Transgender*, p. 63.
85. Spade, *Normal Life*, p. 34.
86. Spade, *Normal Life*, p. 92.
87. Valentine, *Imagining Transgender*, p. 55.
88. Stryker, 'Transgender History, Homonormativity, and Disciplinarity', p. 145.
89. Stryker, 'Transgender History, Homonormativity, and Disciplinarity', p. 149.
90. Stryker, *Transgender History*, p. 150.
91. Valentine, *Imagining Transgender*, p. 17.
92. Spade, *Normal Life*, p. 1.
93. Spade, *Normal Life*, p. 12.
94. Morland, 'Intersex', *Postposttranssexual*, p. 114.
95. Halberstam, *Female Masculinity*, p. 165.
96. Prosser, *Second Skins*, p. 5.
97. Aizura, 'Transnational Transgender Rights and Immigration Law', in Enke (ed.), *Transfeminist Perspectives in and beyond Transgender and Gender Studies*, p. 135.
98. Getsy, 'Capacity', p. 47.
99. See Bristow and Broughton, 'Introduction', in Bristow and Broughton (eds), *The Infernal Desire Machines of Angela Carter: Fiction, Femininity, Feminism*.

100. Getsy, 'Capacity', p. 47.
101. *Man into Woman: The First Sex Change – A Portrait of Lili Elbe*, p. 24.
102. Cromwell, 'Passing Women and Female-bodied Men: (Re)claiming FTM History', in More and Whittle (eds), *Reclaiming Genders: Transsexual Grammars at the Fin de Siècle*, p. 53.
103. Moore, *Albert Nobbs*, p. 8.
104. Butler, *Undoing Gender*, p. 11.
105. Butler, *Undoing Gender*, p. 57.
106. Butler, *Undoing Gender*, p. 58.

Chapter 1

'Two men, so dissimilar': Class, Marriage and Masculinity in George Moore's *Albert Nobbs* (1918) and Simone Benmussa's *The Singular Life of Albert Nobbs* (1977)

Virginia Woolf's 1928 historical fantasy *Orlando* has assumed a central place within an Anglo-American literary tradition of representations of motifs of 'gender crossing' and 'changing sex'. The eponymous protagonist is famously transformed from a man into a woman midway through a narrative which opens in the Elizabethan era and closes in 1928; the narrator's bold and playful insistence that 'in every other respect, Orlando remained precisely as he had been'[1] exemplifies a challenge to conventional ideas about the relationship between sex and gender which has inspired subsequent generations of writers and critics. Indeed, some of the formative features of the treatment of transgender motifs in the literary imagination can be found in this novel. Firstly, it arguably helped to establish historical fiction and fantasy fiction as genres providing 'natural' homes for transgender characters or themes, which are often imagined as belonging to a bygone era or to a speculative future. Secondly, Woolf's narrative provides an important precedent for the figurative use of transgender as a conceptual conceit: that is, as a metaphorical vehicle for the exploration of abstract questions to do with identity. Finally, the legacy of *Orlando* has served to shape a particular relationship between transgender motifs, women's writing and feminist literary criticism, including in narratives which explore gender crossing as a form of feminist subversion (such as Patricia Duncker's *James Miranda Barry*) or which critique the cultural construction of femininity (such as Angela Carter's *The Passion of New Eve*). By contrast, George Moore's 1918 novella *Albert Nobbs* – published a decade before *Orlando* – has received much less critical attention than Woolf's extensively analysed fiction. Set in a Dublin hotel in the 1860s, it explores the repercussions of an encounter between two working men, hotel waiter Albert Nobbs and housepainter Hubert Page. The accidental revelation of Albert's sex to his temporary roommate prompts a disclosure by Hubert that he too is a female-bodied man; Hubert's accounts of his contented domestic life with his wife Polly inspire Albert to transform his own social and marital status, and his attempts to do so are central to the drama which subsequently unfolds. Moore's novella merits close and sustained critical attention for a number of reasons. Firstly, as a pioneer of European naturalism in the English language novel, Moore situates his protagonist in a specific social and economic environment in which the quest for paid employment, social mobility and property ownership on the part of an itinerant and vulnerable working population is a central concern. This emphasis on lived experience and social reality inhabits a different tradition of literary representation to that represented by *Orlando*. Secondly, in its depiction of not one but two female-bodied people living as men it departs from tendencies to depict transgender characters either as isolated, exceptional and aberrant figures or as universalising symbolic ciphers. Finally, Moore's novella has enjoyed an afterlife which offers insights into the different ways in which transgender characters have been appropriated, adapted and interpreted across the course of the twentieth century and beyond. Its adaptation for the stage by the French playwright Simone Benmussa, as *The Singular Life of Albert Nobbs*, in 1977 is widely identified as a key intervention in feminist theatre practice, and its reception exemplifies some of the ways in which transgender motifs have been appropriated in Second Wave feminist contexts.

Written during a long and prolific career which saw him act as both an advocate and a critic of a number of significant movements in the literary and visual arts, the literary output of George Moore (1852–1933) occupies a complex position in relation to periodisation. Indeed, his biographer Adrian Frazier has suggested that 'the non-categorical aspects of Moore's identity cause problems for those who would classify him'.[2] Moore's novella *Albert Nobbs* occupies a similarly elusive place not only in relation to histories of literary production and reception but also in relation to histories of gender and sexuality. The impact of social convention and class relations on the formation of character is at the heart of this fiction written by an author credited with introducing European naturalism to the Irish and English novel, especially in works such as *Esther Waters* (1894) with its sympathetic depiction of the struggles of an unmarried working-class mother. However, the narrative's formal and thematic interest in the interiority of its subjects also marks the modernity of the storytelling; moving fluently between interior monologue and free indirect discourse, it both inhabits the unique inner world of its protagonist and dramatises the collective life and communal voices of the servant quarters of Morrison's Hotel. Set in a period predating the emergence of discourses of sexology in the late nineteenth century, *Albert Nobbs* was first published at a time when these discourses were beginning to enter into wider circulation, including the literary and artistic circles responsible for an emerging modernist aesthetics. The pathologising discourses which were one of the legacies of sexology are notably absent from Moore's novella. Indeed, while the eponymous protagonist expresses feelings of loneliness and sadness when invited to tell his story, his narrative is not principally one of personal anguish and his plight is placed firmly in the context of social marginalisation and class exploitation. Nor are Albert's interior monologues used as a vehicle to explore psychologising speculations about non-normative gender identities but rather to investigate the challenges of navigating socially determined gender roles, especially in relation to marriage. Most significantly, Albert's disclosure of his apparent singularity is quickly undone by the doubling of his narrative in the form of Hubert Page, a female-bodied person living as a man and enjoying modest prosperity as a housepainter and personal satisfaction in his marriage to a milliner. The fact that Albert and Hubert are female-bodied men is disclosed to the reader in the early stages of the novella, but while the narrator (who is recounting their story retrospectively) refers to them by the female pronoun from this point onwards, he does not disclose their previous names as women. Moreover, their identity as men is never questioned within the close-knit community of the hotel household, where individuals of different age, class and gender live and work together in close proximity. With David Getsy's concept of 'transgender capacity'[3] in mind, this chapter will consider Albert and Hubert as they are understood in the social world of the narrative (as opposed to the perspective afforded by the framing narrative): that is, as men. The first part of the chapter aims to foreground the significance of class and marriage in Moore's novella, arguing that Albert's ill-fated attempt to stake a place for himself as a private individual in the capitalist economy serves to expose the sexual economy of marriage; it is the terms of that economy, rather than Albert's sexed identity, which prove the principal obstacle to his realisation of his dream of married life. The second part of the chapter will revisit Benmussa's play script and the critical reception of its production on stage in the late 1970s and early 1980s. It will explore the ways in which its canonisation as a classic of feminist theatre has served to construct the text as a narrative of female cross-dressing, arguably foreclosing its transgender potential as a narrative about a female-sexed person who lives his life as a man. By examining the afterlives of this text, this chapter – combined with the final chapter, which examines the 2011 film adaptation[4] – seeks to map the impact of contexts of reception and adaptation on the changing cultural significance of literary characters whose transgender potential extends beyond the provenance of the page from which they first emerged.

'Walking out' and 'strolling after a fare': Economies of Heterosexuality in George Moore's *Albert Nobbs* (1918)

'Two men, so dissimilar'[5] – such is the discerning judgement of Mrs Baker, the proprietor of a family hotel located in 1860s Dublin, on observing the very different temperaments of two of her employees. The first is Albert Nobbs, an exceptionally conscientious senior waiter, selflessly devoted to serving the Anglo-Irish gentry who frequent the establishment, and a long-term resident in the servant quarters of the household. In Mrs Baker's estimation he is the 'most dependable servant in the hotel', a status assured in her eyes by his apparent indifference to the more common pleasures and diversions likely to distract other working men from their responsibilities: 'no running round to public-houses and coming back with the smell of whisky and tobacco upon him; no rank pipe in his pocket; and of all, no playing the fool with the maid-servants.'[6] The second is Hubert Page, an itinerant housepainter whose youth, easy manner and charming demeanour make him a welcome presence in the hotel:

> everybody in the hotel, men and women alike, missed the pleasant sight of this young man going to and fro in his suit of hollands, the long coat buttoned loosely to his figure with large bone buttons, going to and fro about his work, up and down the passages, with a sort of lolling, idle gait that attracted and pleased the eye . . .[7]

If Albert's relentless industry attracts puzzled comments from his peers – 'I've heard the hall-porter say it was hard to understand a man living without taking pleasure in something outside of work'[8] – Hubert's leisurely professionalism seems to put the household in a kind of holiday mood, his status as a paid worker slipping into that of a favoured guest whose seasonal visits are anticipated with pleasure. Both men are defined by their occupation and both are engaged in modes of paid labour which place them in spaces whose relationship to the domestic sphere complicates the division between private and public realms. The hotel in which Albert works seeks to replicate the daily rhythms and social structures of the upper-class family home, with chambermaids and waiters substituting for the familiar presence of household staff. Hubert's employment as a housepainter requires temporary intrusion into private spaces, an intrusion which his leisurely demeanour seems designed to mitigate. However, the occasion which prompts Mrs Baker's observation – and its unspoken suggestion that one of the two men has been found wanting by comparison – is one which reflects badly on the 'dependable'[9] Albert rather than the 'lolling'[10] Hubert. Mrs Baker requests that Albert share his bed with Hubert to save the latter from a night of exposure to the elements as he awaits an early train to Belfast. Since Albert's bed and quarters are effectively the property of his employer this request is arguably a gesture of feigned courtesy rather than an appeal to his charity; his unexpected reluctance is an affront to the principle of hospitality which Mrs Baker is seeking to extend to the popular Hubert, who attempts to defuse an awkward encounter by offering to pass the night in walking the streets. In this encounter, Albert's virtues are transformed into vices in Mrs Baker's eyes when her efforts to sustain the appearance of gentility in her relationship with her workers is foiled by his resistance; the fastidious dedication to propriety which is prized in his paid labour presents itself as stubborn inflexibility when exercised in the name of his own private space. Economies of intimacy and their relationship to public and private spaces will prove a key concern in the analysis of this novella. Indeed, Mrs Baker's insistence on forcing the two men into a temporary intimacy in the space of a shared bed proves pivotal for the subsequent narrative. The reasons for Albert's apparent obstinacy are revealed in the course of the night. Tormented by another unwelcome intruder in the form of a flea, Albert unwittingly exposes his body to his apparently sleeping companion. He is interrupted in his attempts to dab soap on the insect as it rests on the tail of his night shirt by Hubert's exclamation: 'Lord amassy! what is the meaning of this? Why, you're a woman!'[11] Albert's fear and anxiety at this accidental disclosure are palpable as he tearfully begs on his knees: 'You won't tell on me, and ruin a poor man, will you Mr. Page?'[12]

Hubert expresses surprise and curiosity and listens with a seemingly disinterested sympathy as Albert tells his story, pondering aloud on the novelty of the situation and even coining a term for his seemingly unique plight:

> Seven years [at Morrison's Hotel], Page repeated, neither man nor woman, just a perhapser. He spoke these words more to himself than to Nobbs, but feeling he had expressed himself incautiously he raised his eyes and read on Albert's face that the word had gone home, and that this outcast from both sexes felt her loneliness perhaps more keenly than before.[13]

It is only after Albert has finished his tale and Hubert has suggested that he pursue the companionship of marriage as a solution to his loneliness that Hubert declares: 'I'm not a young man, I'm a woman.'[14] Hence Moore's novella unexpectedly offers not one but two narratives of transgender lives. Before Albert's situation can register in the reader's mind as an anomaly or aberration, the reader is presented with a double. Moreover, whereas the register of Albert's narrative is sombre, poignant and painful, Hubert's is pragmatic, action-driven and ultimately contented. Hubert – who has not 'known an unhappy hour since [he] married'[15] – is the narrative rejoinder to Albert's isolation; where Albert is an 'outcast' in a world of binary categories ('neither man nor woman'[16]), Hubert's gender, and its relationship to his sex, are seemingly no barrier to his integration in the heterosexual institution of marriage as a husband.

Hubert's presence within Albert's life is fleeting; his departure before Albert wakes in the morning leaves Albert preoccupied with a number of unanswered questions about Hubert's marriage which will continue to puzzle him for the remainder of his life. However, the impact of this encounter is pivotal as it sets in motion two narrative trajectories for Albert, one internal and one external. Albert's 'dream of a shop with two counters ... a shop with a door leading to her wife's parlour'[17] signifies the opening of a new interiority through the creation of an inner world independent of the needs and demands of others as mediated by the structures of paid labour. The language of economic servitude is mobilised in his apprehension of a new distinction between the life without and the life within: 'behind the show a new life was springing up – a life strangely personal and associated with the life without only in this much, that the life without was now a vassal state paying tribute to the life within.'[18] The coins which serve as tributes to his service are transformed into currency and capital, capable of generating a new life: the tips he receives are 'no longer mere white and yellow metal stamped with the effigy of a dead king or a living queen, but symbols of the future that await[s]' him.[19] Private property and domestic space, commercial enterprise and mutual companionship are combined in this fantasy, which Albert nurtures in his mind: 'the parlour behind the shop that she had furnished and refurnished . . . She had hung curtains about the windows in her imagination.'[20] This internal narrative of fantasy and longing – '[t]he furniture began to creep into her imagination little by little'[21] – is accompanied by an external narrative characterised by agency and action in which he undertakes to identify and court a suitable wife. In this way, property ownership becomes a metaphor for the emergence of an autonomous subjectivity and marriage the vehicle for individual agency in a capitalist economy. Albert's single-minded quest for a wife – which dominates the narrative of Moore's novella – has been read as a symptom of his 'innocence', with both readers and characters within the narrative expressing incomprehension at his apparent indifference to the role of sexual desire in the rituals of courtship.[22] Helen Dawes is exasperated and mystified at Albert's failure to make attempts to 'pull [her] about'[23] and declares to him that 'it doesn't seem natural to keep talking always, never wanting to put your arm about a girl's waist'.[24] She suspects an ulterior motive but her imagination fails to fathom what form such a motive could take in such a man: 'Was it a blind? Some other girl that he – Not being able to concoct a sufficiently reasonable story, Helen relinquished the attempt, without, however, regaining control of her temper . . .'[25] However, in the analysis which follows I wish to suggest that Albert's campaign to secure a wife reveals the economy of marriage as a heterosexual institution, played out through the transactions of courtship and paralleled (unfavourably) with prostitution. Albert's aspiration to act as a private individual in the economic structures and social institutions of Victorian society is powered by his belief in capital. However, his identification with his class position as a servant to the upper classes, and his single-minded pursuit of marriage as an institution which his capital entitles him to enter, generate tensions which expose the economic dynamics belied by myths of romantic love.

It is Albert's illegitimate birth, rather than his sex, which places him in an oblique relation to class, marriage and family from the outset of his narrative. On being invited by Hubert to 'begin at the beginning', Albert confesses: 'I don't know how to do that, for the story seems to me to be without a beginning; anyway I don't know the beginning. I was a bastard . . .'[26] However, his class identity is not of the kind most commonly associated with illegitimacy; he reports that his parents, although unknown to him, were thought to be 'grand folks' who paid a 'big allowance'[27] to the nurse who cared for him and the convent school where he received an education. Moreover, it is notable that he refers to 'parents' rather than just his mother; their combined action implicitly suggests that his mother was not the victim of coercion or abandonment. Unmarried but economically privileged, they are able to secretly provide for Albert, demonstrating that the stigma attached to the mothers of illegitimate children is a class as well as a gendered construction. Albert recalls the convent school as a refuge where 'all was good, quiet, refined and gentle';[28] in this way it is apparent that Albert's education has the effect of cultivating a certain class sensibility, one which makes it difficult to adjust to life without economic privilege. When Albert's parents die the allowance ceases. While Albert benefits from their class position while they are living, after his death he is deprived of one of the central pillars of the perpetuation of class position – inheritance. Indeed, he does not even inherit their name: Nobbs is the surname of his nurse, a woman who combines maternal functions in her role as his primary caregiver with the economic status of a paid employee. When Albert's allowance and Mrs Nobbs's wage come to an end they are both reduced to her class status as a working woman in service and compelled to find employment in chambers in the Temple district in London. Albert has not experienced the domestic sanctuary idealised in ideologies of the Victorian home and has received his education in an establishment where the boundary between private life and public service is dissolved; he and his nurse now enter into the workforce in conditions which further confuse and complicate the relationship between public and private. The chambers are both a professional and a private space, providing residential accommodation for bachelors, 'pleasant and considerate men'.[29] Here Albert becomes emotionally attached to a Mr Congreve, taking 'pleasure' in 'keep[ing] his pretty things clean, never breaking one of them'.[30] Albert is captivated by his refined masculinity which strongly signifies his class privilege: 'I can see him now as plainly as if he were before me – very thin and elegant, with long white hands, and beautifully dressed.'[31] By contrast, their new home among the working poor of Temple Lane becomes a place of dread and recoil: 'There was nothing wrong with them; they were honest enough; but they were poor, and when you are very poor you live like the animals, indecently, and life without decency is hardly bearable ...'[32] Here Albert lives in fear of encountering the 'rough men' and being 'caught hold of and held and pulled about',[33] his words echoing those of Helen and blurring the boundaries between consensual and abusive sexual encounters. Nor is he free from fear in this substitute family home. His nurse is 'obliged'[34] to keep her brother, an unemployed bandmaster, after he loses his berth; not only does this form of sibling exploitation further reduce the household income, but Albert is exposed to the advances of a man whose uninvited position in the home is effectively that of a maternal uncle: 'the bandsman wouldn't leave me alone, and many's the time I've waited until the staircase was clear, afraid that if I met him or another I'd be caught hold of and held and pulled about.'[35] Albert's heart sinks at the end of the working day which takes him from the gentility of Mr Congreve's quarters to their new home, where 'after four o'clock till we went to bed there was nothing for us to do but listen to the screams of drunken women'.[36] Here begins the habit of living vicariously through the lives of the upper classes whom he serves; this period is also the origin of his disinterest in life outside of work. Throughout Albert's youth we see a confusion of class, familial and marital roles: Albert is well-born but compelled to work in service; his birth parents provide enough to foster specific class expectations but deprive him of name and inheritance; the individual who mothers him as his 'nurse' is also his servant; he inherits the class position of the woman employed to care for him; his only experience of domestic refuge is of a bachelor residence combining work and leisure. Morrison's Hotel replicates the home life of the Irish gentry; in this context, Albert's employment offers him a compensatory proximity to upper-class family life.

If the vision of Hubert's marriage inspires Albert to pursue the dream of private property and domestic privacy, his entanglements with the rituals of heterosexual courtship reveal the economic dynamics underpinning the institution of heterosexual marriage. 'A certain shrewdness is not incompatible with innocence,'[37] observes the narrator as a prelude to Albert's proposal to Helen, whom Albert continues to court in full knowledge that his gifts of money have found their way into the pockets of Joe Mackins, the boyfriend with whom she is 'carr[ying] on'.[38] Albert is emboldened by the knowledge that Joe has 'nothing to offer Helen but himself',[39] in contrast to Albert's demonstrable purchasing power. Indeed, while a desire for companionship, affection and even parenthood are motivating factors in Albert's search for a wife, it quickly becomes clear from early engagements with the canny Helen that his campaign will be principally economic. Three working women in Moore's novella provide focal points for the exploration of different perspectives on heterosexual relationships: Helen Dawes, an unmarried kitchen maid at Morrison's, Kitty MacCan, whom Albert encounters at night 'strolling after a fare',[40] and Polly Page, a milliner and Hubert's wife. In each case the economic dimension of heterosexual relationships is revealed, from the giving and receiving of gifts in return for the promise of sexual favours in the context of courtship, to the payment of money in exchange for sexual access in the context of prostitution, to the sharing of economic resources by two marginalised subjects within the framework of a non-normative marriage. If Albert's shrewdness in his (ultimately unsuccessful) pursuit of a wife is sometimes less than romantic, it has the virtue of casting into relief the reality of marriage as a productive unit in the capitalist economy.

Albert's pursuit of a wife breaks with convention where romantic myths of heterosexual courtship are concerned, since his aspiration to marriage is not prompted by the love of a specific woman but by the desire to enter into a socially sanctioned institution. As the narrator observes, a 'changing figure was the wife in Albert's imagination'[41] and indeed a number of candidates – both particular and abstract – are subject to audition in the course of Albert's dreams. The unmarried women who work alongside Albert at Morrison's are appraised for their suitability. Personal compatibility is one of the criteria but more pressing, it seems, is an aptitude for shop work: Annie Watts is 'not chosen', despite her 'wistful eyes and gentle voice', on the grounds that her 'heart is not in her work';[42] Dorothy Keyes may be a 'glutton for work' but her appearance is 'unattractive' and her manner 'abrupt'; Alice has a 'small neat figure and quick intelligence' but is 'hot tempered'; Mary O'Brien's 'certain stateliness of figure' promises to make her an 'attractive shopwoman'[43] but she is dismissed because she is 'a Papist, and the experience of Irish Protestants shows that Papists and Protestants don't mix'.[44] Particular types of women are considered, in addition to specific personalities, and here Albert demonstrates an astute appreciation of the marginalisation of some women in terms of marriage, specifically widows and unmarried mothers. His calculations combine pragmatism and compassion; on the one hand he anticipates the need to manage his future wife's sexual expectations and maternal aspirations (perhaps assuming that those who have been married or borne children will have been sufficiently disabused of romantic dreams about sexual love), while on the other he is motivated by a desire to rescue the casualties of marriage as an institution, which renders women economically dependent on husbands and stigmatises those whose reproductive sexuality it constructs as illegitimate. The 'changing figure'[45] of Albert's dreams is sometimes

> accompanied by a child of three or four, a boy, the son of a dead man, for in one of her dreams Albert married a widow. In another and more frequent dream she married a woman who had transgressed the moral code and been deserted before the birth of her child.[46]

Indeed, Albert is proactive in his search for an unmarried mother, ever ready to deploy his legitimising power as a future husband to undo her social marginalisation: 'a girl in the family way appealed to her more than a widow . . . and Albert kept her eyes and ears open, hoping to rescue from her precarious situation one of those unhappy girls that were always cropping up in Morrison's Hotel.'[47] Albert is initially 'at once frightened and attracted' by Helen, whose 'flash[ing]' eyes, 'vindictive'[48] voice and sharp retorts would seem to exempt her from consideration, and indeed her temper continues to be a source of dread. However, he comes to admire this spirited young woman: 'Her way of standing on a doorstep, her legs a little apart, jawing a tradesman, and she'd stand up to Mrs Baker and the chef himself.'[49] He only regrets that she 'isn't in the family way, for it would be pleasant to have a little one running about the shop asking for lemon drops and to hear him calling us father and mother'.[50] By turn, Helen's assessment of Albert is candid and acute: 'Harmless in himself, she thought, and with a very good smell of money rising out of his pockets . . .'[51] If Albert has ulterior motives in pursuing Helen, driven as he is by the 'dream of a shop with two counters'[52] perhaps more than a desire for Helen herself, Helen is equally if not more calculating. Goaded by Joe Mackins, Helen takes full and conscious advantage of Albert's willingness to buy her gifts, pressing him beyond his means with a 'contemptuous look' and 'disdainful'[53] shake of the shoulders to purchase two costly boxes of chocolates when his judgement had baulked at one. Helen's 'expensive tastes' prompt Albert to rapidly calculate the costs of courtship – 'twenty eight shillings a month'[54] – and while the expense is painful, he seems to recognise the necessity of advance investment to secure his goal. Helen is puzzled that Albert does not insist on the usual terms of such transactions – 'It did seem odd that Albert should be willing to buy presents and not want to kiss her'[55] – but, pressed on by Joe, the currency of their courtship goes beyond gloves, parasols, shoes, stockings and kerchiefs to extend to pure capital in the form of gifts of money (a ruse to enable Joe to purchase a pipe and tobacco). In this way, the economic underpinnings of heterosexual courtship in the context of marriage are exposed and, by extension, the centrality of binary-categories sex is displaced. Helen understands that 'gifts' are offered in expectation of a return in the form of intimate access to her body, as a prelude to the exclusive access granted by marriage. The fact that Albert's motives are not principally sexual does not preclude him from participating in this ritual, with his demonstration of his surplus capital power serving as proof of his eligibility as a future husband regardless of his sexed identity.

This is not to underestimate Albert's disappointment and dismay when the courtship comes to an unhappy end; although he was once a figure of fun among his fellow workers for his naive pursuit of Helen, his sincere declaration of grief – 'I shall boil my pot and carry my can, but the spring is broken in me'[56] – turns the mood of the household in his favour, and before long (the narrator wryly observes) 'almost anyone of the women in the hotel would have married Albert out of pity'.[57] However, on the night of his break with Helen, as Albert wanders the street nursing his sorrow, he gains some sharp insights into the nature of marriage from Kitty MacCan, one of two women he encounters on the streets of Dublin 'strolling after a fare'.[58] Albert ponders the cost of the fare with simple curiosity rather than judgement – 'ten shillings or a sovereign, which? she asked herself'[59] – and expresses an unexpected envy of their situation: 'terrified by the shipwreck of all her hopes, she wished she were one of them. For at least they are women, whereas I am but a perhapser . . .'[60] The reality of their economic situation – selling sex on the streets – seems to guarantee the absolute clarity of their gender identity as women, revealing gender as economically determined rather than dictated by sex. There is fellow feeling between Albert and Kitty suggestive of a sense of common cause; Albert tries 'to lead the woman into a story of her life'[61] and Kitty intuits that Albert is 'in the middle of some great grief'.[62] Albert wishes that he could return home with Kitty so that they could 'both have a good cry together', observing without resentment: 'what matter would it be to the woman as long as she got the money she desired. She didn't want a man; it was money she was after, money that meant bread and board to her.'[63] Albert recognises that prostitution is not an expression of sexual desire but of economic necessity; unknown to him, Kitty's thoughts are indeed preoccupied with the need to pay the rent due the next day and the fear of 'return[ing] home without a gentleman',[64] her 'home' evidently being one in which her occupation is managed by those who have power over her. The question of Albert's sexed identity is likewise irrelevant; it is the economic exchange, not the sexual encounter, which is paramount. As Kitty makes her apologies and rushes off with a 'friend' and potential client, Albert wonders 'whether it were better to be casual, as they were, or to have a husband that you could not get rid of'.[65] In other words, for all the economic and social vulnerability of Kitty and her peers she is able to exercise an economic agency which would be denied in marriage, which institutionalises the right of male sexual access to women and their children in an arrangement where sexual (and reproductive) labour goes unpaid. Indeed, forced unpaid labour is the social punishment reserved for women who seek to exercise control of their bodies as sexual commodities; as Kitty remarks: 'you're not one of them . . . that think that we should wash clothes in a nunnery for nothing?'[66]

While Helen and Kitty occupy very different positions in relation to social respectability they inhabit the same heterosexual sexual economy, one in which sexual access to women is subject to economic exchange, whether through the state-sanctioned institution of marriage or its illicit mirror image, prostitution. Conscious of her currency on the marriage market as a respectable young woman working in service, Helen exploits Albert's interest in her without malice or remorse. Helen is not possessed of any special charm in Moore's narrative, where she is described as a 'thick-set, almost swarthy girl of three-and-twenty, rather under than above the medium height, with white, even teeth, but unfortunately protruding, giving her the appearance of a rabbit'.[67] In other words, her power over Albert is not attributed to her sexuality or her femininity. Nor is her character subject to any implied censure by the narrator; rather she is depicted with humour and some sympathy as an enterprising and pragmatic person, more than capable of advancing her own interests within the very limited field of action available to her as a young working-class woman in mid-nineteenth-century Ireland. Helen's unsentimental negotiations with Albert are an indirect expression of a form of sexual agency which is the unique and time-limited prerogative of a young woman within the established conventions of heterosexual courtship; given that marriage in this period marks the formal end of a woman's sexual and economic autonomy, it is perhaps no wonder that Helen presses her demands so relentlessly. In this context, the emotional labour which will be expected of her in her marital role is as firmly withheld by Helen as her entitlement to gifts is advanced. By contrast, it is Kitty who expresses feelings of sympathy and compassion for Albert; fiercely protective of her paid (sexual) labour, as an autonomous economic agent, Kitty is seemingly more at liberty to choose how to manage her interpersonal relationships with men. Moreover, it is with Kitty rather than any other woman that Albert imagines the possibility of emotional intimacy; paradoxically, the fact that Albert might be paying for Kitty's attention promises to liberate this imagined encounter from the subterfuges of heterosexual romance rather than compromise its authenticity. If Helen and Kitty occupy positions within the same economy – one negotiating the terms by which she will lose her sexual and economic autonomy in marriage, the other assuming a position of economic agency at the cost of sexual objectification – a third women represents an alternative position within the economy and marriage.

Polly Page is a character who plays a very significant role in Moore's novella without ever entering the action directly; indeed, she is only named by the narrator after her death,[68] and is given neither voice nor presence in the narrative. However, her position as Hubert's wife is central to the dreams which are triggered by the 'new life . . . springing up'[69] in Albert's mind. The question of when and how Hubert disclosed his story – and his sex – to his new wife is a recurring preoccupation in Albert's mind, with the wife taking on the role of gatekeeper to his anticipated new life; the terms of Polly's consent to the arrangement with Hubert are seen as crucial in enabling this alternative reality to acquire a life of its own. Hubert and Polly's courtship and marriage are presented very differently to the patterns of seduction, illegitimacy and abandonment evident elsewhere in the novella. Their relationship is characterised by candour, pragmatism and mutual affection. Indeed, the mutuality extends beyond the emotional to include the economic sphere; their partnership is explicitly described as a union of two working people with independent incomes, in which domestic harmony seems to follow from economic equality. As Hubert recalls:

> It was lonely going home to an empty room; I was as lonely as you, and one day, meeting a girl as lonely as myself, I said: Come along, and we arranged to live together, each paying our share. She had her work and I had mine, and between us we made a fair living; and this I can say with truth, that we haven't known an unhappy hour since we married.[70]

Entry into marriage is not the principal aim of the relationship; indeed, the terms of the partnership are established outside of the institution and the couple marry only to evade social scandal. Polly's profession is crucial to this relationship and the fact that she is identified as a milliner in Albert's mind seems especially symbolic; hats play a central role in the economy of Albert's courtship of Helen, with the demands of fashion rather than the requirements of utility escalating Helen's incursion into Albert's savings. On the breakdown of their relationship, Albert exclaims: 'Oh, the waste of money and the heart-breaking! What shall I do with the hat?'[71] By contrast, Polly is a producer rather than a consumer of this desirable commodity. As a skilled craftswoman in a trade which lends itself to cottage industry, Polly's profession can be imagined as unalienated labour. Elsewhere in Albert's story the conflation of private and public space in working environments is symptomatic of his deprivation of a home or family life; however, the 'dream of a shop with two counters ... with a door leading to her wife's parlour'[72] brings the public and private into a different kind of proximity. Entry into private enterprise marks Albert's imagined escape from a lifetime of service in a paternalist economy, but it also offers an alternative to the economy of heterosexual marriage. Polly and Hubert's marriage seems to offer an ideal of affectionate companionship and economic partnership and their home is a vision of a space unmediated by gendered hierarchies of class exploitation. Indeed, Albert attempts to conceptualise this new way of living as he travels towards his ill-fated rendezvous with Helen by the banks of the River Dodder: 'marriage should not be considered as a sexual adventure, but a community of interests.'[73] Travelling by tram through townships destined to swell into Dublin suburbs towards a location frequented by courting couples, Albert finds that 'his courage was again at an ebb';[74] in the face of the material and behavioural evidence of the perpetuation of social and sexual norms, the words are never spoken. Polly – and what she represents – remains an impossible figure for Albert and the dream of the 'community of interests' is never realised. Albert's unsuccessful struggle to improvise his way towards this dream gives rise to a narrative which some readers and critics have found tragic at best or pitiful at worst. However, it remains highly significant that for Hubert and his wife this life was not a dream but a reality. In this story of 'two men, so dissimilar'[75] the doubling structure of the narrative would seem to make it difficult to read Albert's narrative as somehow typical or representative; Hubert's life story stands as a retort to any attempt to deduce (from the evidence of Albert's narrative) that transgender lives are isolated, alienated and tragic. The significant expansion of Hubert's narrative in the 2011 film adaptation of *Albert Nobbs* will be examined in detail in the final chapter, but the role of an earlier adaptation is essential to consider first.

'The story was taken up by another voice': Simone Benmussa's *The Singular Life of Albert Nobbs* (1977)

Simone Benmussa's stage adaptation of George Moore's *Albert Nobbs*, which received its English language premiere (in a translation by Barbara Wright) in 1978 in London and in 1982 in New York, has played a pivotal role in the reception of Moore's novella in late-twentieth-century and twenty-first-century contexts. Its reception by feminist theatre and performance critics has played an important role in shaping how Moore's text and characters have been interpreted by subsequent generations of readers and audiences. Furthermore, it has served as an enabling bridge between the novella and the later film adaptation; Glenn Close, who played the part of Albert in the play's Off-Broadway premiere, was instrumental in bringing Moore's story to the screen, combining personal investment in the character with industry influence as an actor and producer. It could be argued that without the success of Benmussa's adaptation neither the novella nor its author, George Moore, would have been in a position to command the cultural recognition usually required for a viable adaptation. Moreover, the critical reception of Benmussa's adaptation has not only shaped how the play is perceived and placed in histories of twentieth-century theatre but also informed the contexts in which the later film adaptation was produced and consumed. This proliferation of framing narratives is entirely in keeping with the text itself, in which Albert's story is openly and self-consciously mediated by the contexts in which it is told. My concern here is not with recovering some original or more authentic 'Albert'. It is one of the great achievements of Moore's story that as an author and narrator he makes no claim to any absolute narrative truth; indeed, it is here that Albert's power as a character resides. It is inevitable – and certainly not regrettable – that Albert's character acquires new meanings and mobilises different possibilities in the different contexts in which he is read. However, my interest here is in tracking the specific meanings which have come to prevail in interpretations of Moore's *Albert Nobbs*, acquiring critical and cultural purchase in their capacity to shape future contexts of production and reception, foregrounding specific interpretative possibilities but arguably foreclosing others.

In recent years the somewhat neglected literary reputation of the Irish novelist, poet, art critic and autobiographer George Moore (1852–1933) has been subject to critical reappraisal thanks to the effort of a group of scholars and biographers who have been revisiting his work in all its diversity. Widely recognised as a 'pioneer of the French naturalist style in English',[76] Moore's advocates aim to extend his status within literary history beyond that of a footnote to the evolution of the novel in English. Adrian Frazier, the author of a major biography of the author published in 2000, has sought to establish Moore as deserving of a significant place in literary history: 'With George Bernard Shaw, Oscar Wilde, Bram Stoker and W. B. Yeats, Moore was one of the writers of Irish birth who remade English literature at the end of the nineteenth century.'[77] Ann Heilmann and Mark Llewellyn make similar claims for Moore's impact, in their introduction to a

2014 collection of essays which seeks to integrate and contextualise Moore's work through an emphasis on influence and collaboration: 'Innovative and provocative, his work and personality left a significant imprint on European art criticism, English realism and naturalism, the Irish Literary Revival, and life writing.'[78] In an editorial capacity in a further collection of essays, Mary Pierse refers to 'George Moore's substantial contribution to English and Irish literature' as 'ow[ing] much to French artistic influences, English models, and Irish heritage'.[79] The terms in which these claims are made already indicate some of the problems presented by Moore's work for conventional literary history, with its focus on period, national tradition, authorial identity and genre; Moore is at once a Victorian and a modernist, Irish, British and European, an artist, critic and life writer, and a naturalist, symbolist and realist. Indeed, Frazier reflects in some detail on the reasons for the decline in Moore's reputation, noting, firstly, that the author 'had no clear affiliation during his life with any single national tradition' and that 'no country wished to claim him after his death as part of its tradition'.[80] In addition, he identifies Moore's stylistic diversity and its impact on his authorial signature as complicating his literary status, combined with his interest in topics, such as sex and religion, which resulted in censorship in some contexts. Finally, Frazier proposes that Moore's 'greatest works are not novels'[81] but rather autobiographical narratives, many of which challenged the boundaries between literary fiction and biographical narrative. Indeed, the reputation of Moore's work as evading and troubling conventional literary taxonomies seems to extend to perceptions of his personality, no doubt compounded by his play with literary personae:

> Moore is sometimes represented as a peculiar, contradictory, or even incoherent man. The description of himself in his ironic *Confessions of a Young Man* as a 'man of wax' has been read as uninflected by irony, a mistake akin to taking *A Portrait of the Artist as a Young Man* as Joyce's straightforward autobiography. Yet the non-categorical aspects of Moore's identity cause problems for those who would classify him.[82]

The 'non-categorical' Moore defies the classifying imperatives of literary history because his work cannot easily be allotted to any single period, artistic movement or national tradition; his literary voice lacks the consistency and singularity required by the ideologies of authorship, by which literary property is wedded to literary provenance by way of its signature voice. Frazier suggests that the 'non-categorical' is not merely a quality of Moore's oeuvre but a recurring thematic preoccupation in his fiction, especially in relation to gender and sexuality; in a series of planned and published story cycles, including *Celibates* (1895), *In Single Strictness* (not published) and *Celibate Lives* (1927), Moore revisited the theme of '"men who do not care for women, and women who do not care for men"',[83] often returning to existing characters and rewriting published stories. Frazier refers to this motif as a 'theme that had drawn his attention again and again over the previous forty years: men and women without a match in the world, and in whom desire is not a desire for procreation'.[84] *Albert Nobbs* was one of three novellas published in the collection *Celibate Lives* but first entered print in the 1918 story sequence *A Storyteller's Holiday*, a publication which Frazier places in the category of autobiography despite it being 'not recollection at all, but an extravaganza of fabulation by the literary persona Moore had publicly evolved over decades of authorship'.[85] *Albert Nobbs* possesses a frame narrative which has its origins in *A Storyteller's Holiday*. Indeed, as Elizabeth Grubgeld puts it, this 'transposition creates some awkwardness'[86] given that the context of the storytelling and the identity of the interlocutor are neither explained nor justified to the reader who, as a consequence, may find it at best mystifying and at worst intrusive. In this context, it is striking that when adapting this self-reflexive fiction for performance on the stage, Simone Benmussa not only retains but foregrounds a narrative device whose 'awkwardness' on the page might seem difficult to reconcile with the imperatives of dramatic storytelling. Not only is the self-consciously literary frame narrative retained but the narration, including interjections by the interlocutor, interior monologues and dialogue are reproduced almost verbatim. However, this fidelity is employed to distinctly anti-naturalist ends as far as performance and character are concerned.

Frazier explains the 'frame-tale' for *A Storyteller's Holiday* in the following way:

> George Moore, famous novelist, visits Dublin after the Easter Rising and then takes a train to Mayo, where he meets Alec McDonnell, a fern-gatherer and *seanachie* [traditional Irish storyteller/historian]. The two men engage in a storytelling contest, the traditional versus the modern, with Alec telling the bawdy tales of holy Ireland and Moore retelling stories from the Bible and European novelists . . .[87]

When the story was republished in *Celibate Lives* in 1927 the frame was retained but without the context of the overarching narrative design. Grubgeld may be speaking for many readers when she spells out the consequences of this move: 'without the context of *A Story-Teller's Holiday*, the reader does not know why the storytelling is occurring, or the identity of "Alec" the listener, or the identity of the storyteller.'[88] To the uninitiated reader of *Albert Nobbs* (which has been published as a single volume since the release of the film adaptation), Alec's deference to the narrator, whom he addresses as 'your honour',[89] sits oddly with the liberty of his interjections; he interrupts the narrator, shattering the illusion of the embedded story for the reader, and is free with his opinions about how the story could have been improved when it comes to its rather inconclusive end. The ringing of the Angelus at the end of the frame narrative, and Alec's reference to the 'Ballinrobe cock',[90] seem to locate the frame narrative in rural Catholic Ireland, at some distance from the Anglo-Irish gentry at their leisure in Dublin. However, as Grubgeld points out, the 'Ballinrobe cock' and 'the Westport rooster'[91] are also the alter egos adopted by the two men in their storytelling battle, figures suggestive of a slightly comic competitive virility and hence reinforcing the homosocial context of the story's origins. In this context Albert's story could be seen as a narrative token strategically played in a battle of wits, the novel nature of the story's content a demonstration of its teller's narrative prowess and the topic of gender ambiguity a vehicle serving to confirm the masculine and class dominance of its metropolitan author over his rural rival. What is clear is that Moore the author enters the narrative as 'Moore' the narrator, a character in his own fiction; the generic ambiguity of the collection is only reinforced by an apprehension of the fictionality of the narrator, a figure who should not be simply conflated with the author.

In Benmussa's play script the frame narrative is retained but the scene of the telling is not dramatised on stage: 'Moore' and Alec exist only as disembodied voices. Moreover, Moore ventriloquises Albert's first lines, speaking for and through him; in later scenes, Albert 'speaks' through three voices, given in the play script as 'GEORGE MOORE'S VOICE', 'ALBERT NOBBS' and 'ALBERT NOBBS'S VOICE', the last representing Albert's inner voice. The voices conspire together to tell Albert's story, even engaging in a kind of internal dialogue in which the narratorial voice abets Albert's fantasies:

> GEORGE MOORE'S VOICE: Two rooms and a kitchen were what she foresaw. The furniture began to creep into her imagination little by little. A large sofa by the fireplace covered with a chintz!
> ALBERT NOBBS: But chintz dirties quickly in the city.
> GEORGE MOORE'S VOICE: A dark velvet might be more suitable.
> ALBERT NOBBS: It will cost a great deal of money . . .[92]

In this way, the play script replicates the 'illusionary techniques of modern realism' employed to innovative effect by Moore in the novella: as Grubgeld observes, 'the narration proceeds almost entirely through indirect discourse and interior monologue, with a great deal of shifting between voices . . .'[93] The audience are left in no doubt that Albert's character is thoroughly mediated by the narrator and author; where the reader of the novella may become so immersed in the storytelling as to find the 'return' to the frame narrative disruptive and unwelcome, Benmussa's conversion of free indirect discourse into spoken dialogue, attributed to named characters and performed by different actors, ensures that the audience can never 'forget' the storytelling frame.[94] Through this strategy, the adaptation's fidelity to the source text (which might go unrecognised by audiences unfamiliar with Moore's novella) gives rise to effects at odds with theatrical naturalism. In Moore's novella none of the hotel's guests enter into the narrative as characters; they are identified only by the number of the room which they occupy, their presence signified by the ringing of service bells which punctuate the narrative, interrupting Albert's internal monologues: 'At that moment 35 rang his bell';[95] 'Albert received 54's order and executed it';[96] 'The people in 34 were leaving tomorrow'.[97] In Benmussa's adaptation, the hotel guests are similarly disembodied, their invisible passage across the stage and through the dramatic action signified by the closing and opening of doors. Indeed, it is in the stage design that Benmussa's play most ingeniously represents the thematic significance of the hotel as a spatial location for Albert's character. In Moore's novella, Morrison's Hotel is recalled by the narrator as a warren of stairways and corridors rather than as a collection of rooms: 'passages running hither and thither, and little flights of stairs in all kinds of odd corners by which the visitors climbed to their apartments . . .'[98] It is these functional but liminal public spaces which Albert occupies in the novella and stage play, his ever-ready presence within them representing his service to the lives of others, sometimes to uncanny effect. Reminiscing as a former guest of the hotel as a child, the narrator recalls that Albert was 'every hour . . . before them'[99] and recollects his dread at 'open[ing] the sitting-room door, for I'd be sure to find him waiting on the landing, his napkin thrown over his right shoulder'.[100]

Indeed, Benmussa's most significant departures from Moore's novella are non-verbal and serve to introduce another layer of self-reflexivity to the text, this time in relation to performance and costume. Two female servants, identified as chambermaids in the cast list, take on the non-speaking role of Albert's 'feminine doubles'.[101]

In a scene entitled 'The Dream' the stage directions indicate that a housemaid 'follows her, helps her and accompanies her in her reverie . . . Her feminine double hands her the duster and brush.'[102] In a scene titled 'The Break' two chambermaids take Albert's place during the confrontation with Helen which terminates their courtship: '*During the next scene the two chambermaids are always in the place where* ALBERT NOBBS *ought to be, facing* HELEN DAWES. HELEN DAWES *is thus encircled by two women Alberts and one man Albert.*'[103] In her introduction to the play script, Benmussa explains her rationale for this device: 'The woman in her transpires, emerges, is "represented" behind her, beside her, around her, as the maidservants, going about their work, make feminine gestures.'[104] The effect of this conceit is open to interpretation. The position of the two maids is defined by class as much as gender; the reference to 'feminine' gestures may suggest parody, in which case the doubles might seem to represent what Albert has escaped as much as what he has lost. Benmussa goes on to suggest that the 'woman in her cannot emerge in the professional milieu she is caught up in, in that Victorian paternalism which alienates her'.[105] On the one hand, the reference to historically specific ideology – Victorian paternalism – might be read as an allusion to the culturally constructed nature of femininity; on the other hand, the language of alienation and submersion suggests an identity already constituted but suppressed – that of 'woman'. The 'woman in her' might be Albert's 'true' or 'authentic' self but such a 'woman' can be no less mediated – and hence 'alienated' – by ideology than the maids.

Where the play script is highly conceptual and open to interpretation on the part of actors, directors and audiences, Benmussa's introduction is perhaps inevitably more polemical and introduces some interpretative themes which have proved recurring motifs in scholarship on the play. Indeed, the years following the English language premiere of Benmussa's play in 1978 saw the publication of a series of articles which situated it within specific feminist frameworks; all of the articles proceed from the assumption that Albert is a woman compelled to pass as a man and thus have established certain frameworks for the reception of questions of gender within the play. Sue-Ellen Case opens her 1984 essay, 'Gender as Play: Simone Benmussa's *The Singular Life of Albert Nobbs*', with the assertion that the play is based on a true story, a suggestion that (to my knowledge) has not been documented with evidence elsewhere: 'The story was based on an incident reported in a 19th century newspaper: Albert Nobbs, the presumed male head servant of a hotel in Dublin, was in fact a woman who had lived her life as a man. Her sex was discovered only after her death through the coroner's examination.'[106] This claim serves to place Albert's fictional story, told within a piece of anti-naturalist theatre, in the context of the documented history of female gender crossing, a history which has played a significant role in feminist and lesbian feminist historiography.[107] In feminist contexts women's gender crossing has often been interpreted as an act of defiance, transgression or subversion, empowering the passing subject to enjoy the liberties and privileges from which they would otherwise be excluded. By contrast, in feminist scholarship on Benmussa's play there are recurring motifs of imprisonment, alienation and loss, especially of sexual identity. Firstly, Albert's adoption of masculine modes of dress and occupation are depicted not as expressions of agency (albeit in highly constrained circumstances) but as a symptom of coercion depriving him of the freedom of self-determination: Case describes Albert as 'trapped', with her 'female self' 'forced to go into hiding';[108] Dolan depicts the play as 'chronicl[ing] a woman's imprisonment in her assumed male role';[109] Ammen refers to 'Albert's entrapment' and claims that he was 'forced by patriarchal society to pretend to be a man';[110] and finally Elam refers to 'Albert's imprisonment in drag'.[111] A second motif concerns internalisation, by which Albert's gender expression is assumed to be a form of 'false consciousness'; having established patriarchal culture as the cause of Albert's gender crossing, Albert himself becomes the object of critique. Case argues that it is 'her own male-identification, her internalization of the patriarchal modes of production that victimize[s] her personal, emotional life'[112] and this point is reiterated by Elam, who asserts that 'Albert is victimized by her own male-identification and internalization of the patriarchal economic system'.[113] Finally, Albert's gender identification is depicted as forfeiting his sexuality; in this reading, loss of access to an intimate life – variously imagined as personal, romantic or sexual – is represented as one of the most significant deprivations suffered by Albert as a consequence of his gender crossing. A number of elisions seem to be at work here: firstly, sexuality is equated with gender, with the loss of the latter inevitably forfeiting the former; secondly, access to romantic or sexual life seems to be assumed to be an essential component of womanhood; finally, this sexuality is assumed to be heterosexual, with the proper destination of Albert's thwarted desires being a man. Case proposes that Albert's 'male-identified professional life stops her from having a successful sexual and emotional life'[114] and Diamond suggests that Albert 'sells her sexuality'[115] in return for male privilege. Ammen proposes that the 'same patriarchy' that forced him to 'pretend to be a man' has 'supplied her with the romantic myths of a love that she can now never have'[116] and Elam argues that 'Albert's cross-gender disguise ... leads to isolation and repression, preventing her from finding any emotional satisfaction in her personal life'.[117] This understanding of femininity as a form of false consciousness and a symptom of ideological internalisation is one of the defining insights of Second Wave feminism and is also reflected in Benmussa's introduction:

> Albert Nobbs poses the problem of disguise, but breaks with the theatrical tradition of travesty. Plays on the theme of travesty are centred around revelation, unmasking ... There is always something temporary – a plot, a strategy triumphed over by the person who adopts the disguise, whereas in Albert Nobbs, it is her destiny. Starting as her refuge from society, this disguise becomes her prison, and then her grave.[118]

Indeed, the recurring motifs of disguise, alienation and internalisation which have characterised feminist interpretations of Albert Nobbs bear a striking, if inadvertent, resemblance to the terms employed by some Second Wave feminists to denounce transgender identity; this legacy will be explored in further detail in the next chapter, which examines the depiction of male-to-female transsexuals in Angela Carter's provocative 1977 dystopian fantasy, *The Passion of New Eve*.

In some ways, the critical reception of Benmussa's play as a feminist drama of women's gender crossing seems to owe more to the author's introduction to the published play script than to the text itself: the play's highly self-reflexive insistence on the inescapability of Moore's framing narrative arguably points to the impossibility of grasping a definitive or originating 'truth' about Albert Nobbs and his identity. However, Benmussa's introduction also includes the less quoted observation that '[e]ven Moore, a man who felt a certain tenderness towards this story, displayed a kind of violence towards Nobbs'.[119] Crucially, the playwright declines to 'do what Moore did and show Albert as a corpse – no, I just could not bring myself to do her that violence'.[120] In recognising the implicit violence of narratives of forcible exposure and refusing to be party to its effects, Benmussa's position seems to anticipate the critiques of cultural representation which were to prove central to founding works in the field of transgender studies. The afterlives of Moore's novella (including the 2011 film adaptation which will be discussed in the final chapter) in many ways typify the formative effect of contexts of critical reception on retrospective readings of transgender figures in twentieth-century writing. The project of revisiting transgender potential in twentieth-century literary fiction is then revealed as an exercise which is always at least double: it entails revisiting not only the texts in which these figures first appeared but also the multiple contexts in which their meaning and significance has been understood by subsequent generations of readers and scholars, contexts whose ongoing legacies are deserving of renewed critical attention.

Notes

1. Woolf, *Orlando*, p. 87.
2. Frazier, *George Moore 1852–1933*, p. xvii.
3. Getsy, 'Capacity', *TSQ: Transgender Studies Quarterly Special Issue – Postposttranssexual*, p. 47. Getsy defines 'transgender capacity' as 'the ability or the potential for making visible, bringing into experience, or knowing genders as mutable, successive, and multiple'.
4. *Albert Nobbs*, directed by Rodrigo García, screenplay by Glenn Close, John Banville and Gabriella Prekop, UK, Ireland, France, 2011.
5. Moore, *Albert Nobbs*, p. 8.
6. Moore, *Albert Nobbs*, p. 4.
7. Moore, *Albert Nobbs*, p. 7.
8. Moore, *Albert Nobbs*, p. 5.
9. Moore, *Albert Nobbs*, p. 4.
10. Moore, *Albert Nobbs*, p. 7.
11. Moore, *Albert Nobbs*, p. 12.
12. Moore, *Albert Nobbs*, p. 13.
13. Moore, *Albert Nobbs*, p. 29.
14. Moore, *Albert Nobbs*, p. 32.
15. Moore, *Albert Nobbs*, p. 33.
16. Moore, *Albert Nobbs*, p. 29.
17. Moore, *Albert Nobbs*, pp. 43–4.
18. Moore, *Albert Nobbs*, p. 44.
19. Moore, *Albert Nobbs*, p. 43.
20. Moore, *Albert Nobbs*, p. 84.
21. Moore, *Albert Nobbs*, p. 42.
22. On receipt of an unsatisfactory kiss from Albert, Helen Dawes declares: 'Well, you are an innocent!' Moore, *Albert Nobbs*, p. 69. Albert's 'innocence' is given by Glenn Close as one of the reasons for the character's appeal to her as a performer. Close, 'Foreword', in Moore, *Albert Nobbs*, p. ix.
23. Moore, *Albert Nobbs*, p. 56.
24. Moore, *Albert Nobbs*, p. 67.
25. Moore, *Albert Nobbs*, p. 57.

26. Moore, *Albert Nobbs*, p. 16.
27. Moore, *Albert Nobbs*, p. 16.
28. Moore, *Albert Nobbs*, p. 19.
29. Moore, *Albert Nobbs*, p. 18.
30. Moore, *Albert Nobbs*, pp. 18–19.
31. Moore, *Albert Nobbs*, p. 19.
32. Moore, *Albert Nobbs*, p. 17.
33. Moore, *Albert Nobbs*, p. 17.
34. Moore, *Albert Nobbs*, p. 17.
35. Moore, *Albert Nobbs*, p. 17.
36. Moore, *Albert Nobbs*, p. 18.
37. Moore, *Albert Nobbs*, p. 59.
38. Moore, *Albert Nobbs*, p. 59.
39. Moore, *Albert Nobbs*, p. 59.
40. Moore, *Albert Nobbs*, p. 75.
41. Moore, *Albert Nobbs*, p. 44.
42. Moore, *Albert Nobbs*, p. 46.
43. Moore, *Albert Nobbs*, p. 47.
44. Moore, *Albert Nobbs*, p. 47. This is one of the few references to religion in the novella, with the ringing of the Angelus at the close of the frame narrative (located in County Mayo) being another. That Mary should be presented as an exception confirms the Protestant Ascendancy milieu of the hotel setting.
45. Moore, *Albert Nobbs*, p. 44.
46. Moore, *Albert Nobbs*, p. 44.
47. Moore, *Albert Nobbs*, p. 45.
48. Moore, *Albert Nobbs*, p. 49.
49. Moore, *Albert Nobbs*, p. 63.
50. Moore, *Albert Nobbs*, p. 50.
51. Moore, *Albert Nobbs*, p. 51.
52. Moore, *Albert Nobbs*, p. 44.
53. Moore, *Albert Nobbs*, p. 52.
54. Moore, *Albert Nobbs*, p. 53.
55. Moore, *Albert Nobbs*, p. 57.
56. Moore, *Albert Nobbs*, p. 82.
57. Moore, *Albert Nobbs*, p. 83.
58. Moore, *Albert Nobbs*, p. 75.
59. Moore, *Albert Nobbs*, p. 75.
60. Moore, *Albert Nobbs*, p. 75.
61. Moore, *Albert Nobbs*, p. 76.
62. Moore, *Albert Nobbs*, p. 77.
63. Moore, *Albert Nobbs*, p. 78.
64. Moore, *Albert Nobbs*, p. 77.
65. Moore, *Albert Nobbs*, p. 79.
66. Moore, *Albert Nobbs*, p. 76.

67. Moore, *Albert Nobbs*, p. 49.
68. Moore, *Albert Nobbs*, p. 93.
69. Moore, *Albert Nobbs*, p. 44.
70. Moore, *Albert Nobbs*, p. 33.
71. Moore, *Albert Nobbs*, p. 72.
72. Moore, *Albert Nobbs*, p. 44.
73. Moore, *Albert Nobbs*, p. 64.
74. Moore, *Albert Nobbs*, p. 64.
75. Moore, *Albert Nobbs*, p. 8.
76. Heilmann and Llewellyn, 'Introduction', in Heilmann and Llewellyn (eds), *George Moore: Influence and Collaboration*, p. 3.
77. Frazier, *George Moore*, p. xiii.
78. Heilmann and Llewellyn, 'Introduction', p. 1.
79. Pierse, 'Introduction', in Pierse (ed.), *George Moore: Artistic Visions and Literary Worlds*, p. xi.
80. Frazier, *George Moore*, p. xiv.
81. Frazier, *George Moore*, p. xv.
82. Frazier, *George Moore*, p. xvii.
83. Frazier, *George Moore*, p. 420.
84. Frazier, *George Moore*, p. xiii.
85. Frazier, *George Moore*, p. xvi.
86. Grubgeld, *George Moore and the Autogenous Self: A Study of the Autobiography and the Fiction*, p. 96.
87. Frazier, *George Moore*, p. 405.
88. Grubgeld, *George Moore and the Autogenous Self*, p. 96.
89. Moore, *Albert Nobbs*, p. 97.
90. Moore, *Albert Nobbs*, p. 98.
91. Grubgeld, *George Moore and the Autogenous Self*, p. 97.
92. Moore, *Albert Nobbs*, p. 32.
93. Grubgeld, *George Moore and the Autogenous Self*, p. 97.
94. For a discussion of the influence of Bertolt Brecht's dramaturgy on Benmussa's stage adaptation see Grubgeld, '"The Little Red-Haired Boy, George Moore": Moore, Benmussa, García and the Masculine Voices of Albert Nobbs', in Brunet, Gaspari and Pierse (eds), *George Moore's Paris and his Ongoing French Connections*.
95. Moore, *Albert Nobbs*, p. 38.
96. Moore, *Albert Nobbs*, pp. 39–40.
97. Moore, *Albert Nobbs*, p. 43.
98. Moore, *Albert Nobbs*, p. 2.
99. Moore, *Albert Nobbs*, p. 5.
100. Moore, *Albert Nobbs*, pp. 3–4.
101. Benmussa, 'Introduction', in *The Singular Life of Albert Nobbs*, p. xi.
102. Benmussa, *Singular Life*, p. 29.
103. Benmussa, *Singular Life*, p. 51.
104. Benmussa, 'Introduction', p. xi.

105. Benmussa, 'Introduction', p. xi.
106. Case, 'Gender as Play', p. 22.
107. See Wheelwright, *Amazons and Military Maids: Women Who Dressed as Men in Pursuit of Life, Liberty and Happiness*.
108. Case, 'Gender as Play', p. 22.
109. Dolan, 'Gender Impersonation Onstage: Destroying or Maintaining the Mirror of Gender Roles?', p. 9.
110. Ammen, 'Transforming George Moore: Simone Benmussa's Adaptive Art in *The Singular Life of Albert Nobbs*', p. 308.
111. Elam, 'Visual Representation in *The Singular Life of Albert Nobbs*', p. 314. In her psychoanalytic reading Heilmann similarly describes Albert as 'remain[ing] trapped within her body' in '"Neither man nor woman"? Female Transvestism, Object Relations and Mourning in George Moore's "Albert Nobbs"', p. 257.
112. Case, 'Gender as Play', p. 23.
113. Elam, 'Visual Representation', p. 317.
114. Case, 'Gender as Play', p. 22.
115. Diamond, 'Refusing the Romanticism of Identity: Narrative Interventions in Churchill, Benmussa, Duras', p. 281.
116. Ammen, 'Transforming George Moore', p. 308.
117. Elam, 'Visual Representation', p. 315.
118. Benmussa, 'Introduction', p. vii.
119. Benmussa, 'Introduction', p. xi.
120. Benmussa, 'Introduction', p. xii.

Chapter 2

'She had never been a woman': Second Wave Feminism, Femininity and Transgender in Angela Carter's *The Passion of New Eve* (1977)

In her 2002 essay 'Gender as Performance: Questioning the "Butlerification" of Angela Carter's Fiction', Joanne Trevenna reflects on a significant trend in scholarship on the work of the celebrated British writer Angela Carter (1940–92), a trend which was first identified by Joseph Bristow and Trev Broughton in their 1997 edited collection *The Infernal Desire Machines of Angela Carter: Fiction, Femininity, Feminism*. Bristow and Broughton observed that it had become 'almost impossible to read Carter's novels and short stories in the 1990s without noticing how uncannily they anticipate certain strands of current feminist theory' and, more specifically, how they seem to 'invite comparison'[1] with the work of Judith Butler, among others.[2] Revisiting what Bristow and Broughton term the 'after-the-fact "Butlerification" of Carter',[3] Trevenna notes that the queer frameworks which have been mobilised by feminist critics to enable reassessments of Carter's work have shaped the contemporary critical consensus on the author's fiction and 'facilitated a kind of feminist "recovery" of Carter's work since the novelist's death in 1992'.[4] However, Trevenna is one of a number of critics who have questioned the ways in which Butler's theories of performativity have been interpreted and applied, arguing that 'divergences between Carter's overtly theatrical presentation of "gender as performance" and Butler's theories of "gender as performative"'[5] have been overlooked in readings which seek to assimilate queer concepts within pre-existing feminist frameworks. As we have seen, the uses to which transgender bodies and identities have been put in popular accounts of performativity and queer theory have been problematised by transgender theorists. In *Second Skins: The Body Narratives of Transsexuality*, Jay Prosser foregrounds the ways in which the transgender subject has been figured as a 'key queer trope',[6] serving as a defining signifier of queer theory's 'aptly skewed point of entry into the academy'.[7] The transgender figure, it seems, has come to stand for queer theory and, hence, the presence of transgender themes within a literary text has sometimes been read as shorthand for a queer intent. *The Passion of New Eve* is no exception to the trend identified by Trevenna and its critical reception illustrates the ways in which motifs of gender crossing and 'sex change' have come to be equated both with Butler's theories of performativity and – as if by extension – with a queer sensibility. The exemplary role often attributed to the transgender figure in relation to theories of performativity is evoked by Bristow and Broughton when they suggest that in *The Passion of New Eve* 'transsexuality holds the clue to the constructedness of all gendered identities'.[8] Indeed, in *Angela Carter: Writing from the Front Line* (1997), Sarah Gamble reads Tristessa as 'the book's most striking example of gender configured as performance', arguing that 'both [Tristessa] and Eve, in the words of Judith Butler, represent the subversive potential of drag'.[9] Elsewhere, Catrin Gersdorf pronounces the eponymous protagonist 'perfectly queer in that s/he embodies the disparity between physiological sex and psychological gender',[10] and Heather L. Johnson contributes to the perception of Carter's writing as queer *avant la lettre* when she proposes that the novel 'seems to pre-empt, by nearly two decades, recent developments in the discipline of gender studies'.[11] However, to read the transgender subjects in *The Passion of New Eve* simply as queer tropes of gender performativity is to risk overlooking the complex – and often fraught – history of the relationship between feminism and transgender. In her now notorious 1979 polemic *The Transsexual Empire: The Making of the She-Male*, Janice G. Raymond's provocative assertion that 'all transsexuals rape women's bodies'[12] was explicitly grounded in a radical feminist standpoint. Raymond's book can be seen as symptomatic of a mode of reaction to the emerging visibility of transgender women in the Second Wave of the women's movement, especially (but not exclusively) in US contexts, which is historically and culturally specific and whose critical legacy has proved persistent and problematic.

Raymond's book inadvertently inspired some of the founding texts in a new activist and theoretical movement, including Sandy

Stone's 'The Empire Strikes Back: A Posttranssexual Manifesto', first published in 1987, in which she writes:

> Here on the gender borders at the close of the twentieth century . . . we find the epistemologies of white male medical practice, the rage of radical feminist theories and the chaos of lived gendered experience meeting in the battlefield of the transsexual body . . .[13]

Angela Carter's 1977 novel *The Passion of New Eve* is one of her most combative texts and one in which motifs of civil insurrection and sexualised violence are rife; situated in a dystopian American landscape ravaged by guerrilla warfare, the transgender body becomes the site on which violent conflicts are waged.[14] The initially male narrator's involuntary sex reassignment and her subsequent sexual servitude – inflicted by matriarchal and patriarchal autocrats respectively – are made to stand for the war between the sexes. This chapter aims to situate Carter's novel within the context of Second Wave feminist attitudes to male-to-female transsexuals – including the 'radical feminist rage' to which Stone refers – and to examine the way in which these attitudes have shaped the reception of Carter's novel. It proceeds from the premise that it is important for feminist scholars to examine the more troubling legacies of Second Wave feminism and their sometimes unacknowledged consequences. It is vital to note that *The Passion of New Eve* features not one but two characters who might be described as transgender: Eve and Tristessa. However, while the two figures are in many ways mirrored in the narrative – a strategy culminating in their 'double wedding'[15] – they ultimately experience very different fates. The eponymous narrator of Carter's novel is subjected to sex reassignment surgery against her will, transforming her without her consent from Evelyn, an expatriate Englishman whose masculinity is firmly rooted in patriarchal privilege and power, to Eve, whose sexed body is fashioned in the image of normative male heterosexual desire.[16] By contrast, Tristessa, the Hollywood icon of Evelyn's adolescent dreams, is subject to a violent exposure: the apparent disparity between sexed body and gender identification which it reveals triggers a sequence of violent humiliations.[17] Crucially, Tristessa is denied gender reassignment treatment by the very surgeon who imposes it on Evelyn.[18] However, despite these very different depictions of agency in relation to gender identity, a distinction is implicitly drawn in the novel – and explicitly in its critical reception – whereby the involuntary transsexual, Eve, emerges as the more 'authentic' woman against whom the inauthenticity of the elective transgender woman, Tristessa, is contrasted. Moreover, this authenticity rests on the criteria of reproductive sexuality, the keystone of heteronormative constructions of sexuality: Eve's implied pregnancy at the end of the novel seems to implicitly validate her biological womanhood, whereas Tristessa's 'exposure' as a 'passing' male inaugurates a series of assaults which ultimately result in her death. *The Passion of New Eve* dramatises what Stone refers to as the 'textual violence inscribed in the transsexual body'[19] and in doing so raises questions about the mobilisation of metaphors of violence in relation to transgender bodies in feminist contexts, whether political activism, literary fiction or cultural criticism and theory. Indeed, it seems deeply ironic that when Eve refers to a 'violent operation'[20] she has in mind not her own coercive surgery but Tristessa's gender identification as a woman: she invites us to see Tristessa as the agent of self-inflicted mutilation, not as the victim of social violence. This chapter will examine the ways in which Eve's coerced sex reassignment surgery and Tristessa's elective gender identification are depicted in the novel, and its critical reception, by situating both within the context of the critical legacy of Second Wave feminist critiques of male-to-female transsexuals.[21]

Transsexual Empires: Second Wave Feminism and *The Passion of New Eve*

As Joanne Hollows has written, 'for many second-wave feminists femininity was self-evidently problematic' and its critique was 'fundamental to understanding women's oppression'.[22] Indeed, the exposure of femininity as a patriarchal construction is widely recognised as a defining concern in Angela Carter's writing. In her 1975 essay on fashion and femininity, 'The Wound in the Face', Carter uses the figure of the male transvestite to satirically express her bemused alienation from the 'female impersonation' which normative femininity requires of women, noting that 'fashionable women now tend to look like women imitating men imitating women'.[23] The prominence of the figure of the male-to-female transsexual in a number of widely read Second Wave feminist cultural critiques is striking, as is the recurring confusion of this figure with the male transvestite. While female-to-male gender crossing – whether historical or metaphorical – has traditionally been seen by feminist critics as subversive, male-to-female gender crossing is often viewed in these studies with suspicion, as potentially complicit in dominant patriarchal regimes of gender. The male transvestite and male-to-female transsexual are not only problematically conflated but widely understood as agents of gender normativity, perpetuating – rather than transgressing – stereotypes of femininity in ways which are deemed to be inadvertently parodic at best and at worst insidiously misogynist.

Anticipating Carter's conceit concerning 'women imitating men imitating women', UK-based Australian feminist Germaine Greer gave expression to the alienation which many women experience in the face of dominant versions of femininity in her bestselling 1970 book *The Female Eunuch* by comparing the '"normal" sex roles that we learn to play from our infancy' with the 'antics of a transvestite'.[24] Greer declared: 'I'm sick of being a transvestite. I refuse to be a female impersonator. I am a woman, not a castrate.'[25] Central to *The Female Eunuch* is a powerful critique of the denial of sexual freedom to women, underlined by Greer's understanding of sexuality as a source of knowledge of both self and world:

> The acts of sex are themselves forms of inquiry, as the old euphemism 'carnal knowledge' makes clear: it is exactly the element of quest in her sexuality which the female is taught to deny. She is not only taught to deny it in her sexual contacts, but . . . in all her contacts, from infancy onward, so that when she becomes aware of her sex the pattern has sufficient force of inertia to prevail over new forms of desire and curiosity. This is the condition which is meant by the term *female eunuch*. [emphasis in original][26]

Contributing to the ideological critiques of femininity which characterised Second Wave feminism, Greer argues that women are constructed as sexual objects and that their 'sexuality is both denied and misrepresented by being presented as passivity'.[27] The use of 'castration' as a metaphor for the suppression of female sexuality may seem surprising, especially given Second Wave feminist critiques of Freud's theories. Greer acknowledges that the 'corner-stone of the Freudian theory of womanhood is the masculine conviction that a woman is a castrated man'[28] but her analysis does not so much contest this explicitly phallic definition of sexuality as suggest that the fantasy has become reality through the effects of patriarchal social conditioning. Moreover, the analogy between femininity and female impersonation (equated with the male transvestite and the male-to-female transsexual alike) conspires to construct the male-to-female transsexual as both victim and agent of patriarchal ideology. The motif of 'castration' is central to Greer's analysis of the position of women in a male-dominated society in *The Female Eunuch* and relies on arguments by analogy with the historical figure of the eunuch, whose meaning in Western culture has also been shaped by colonial and Orientalist discourses.[29] A servant or slave who served in royal courts, including in the Byzantine and Ottoman Empires, the eunuch showed great loyalty to his master, thought to be ensured by his castration, which removed him from the bonds of family and kinship ensured by the imperatives of normative masculinity. Kathryn Ringrose has challenged the common interpretation of the figure of the eunuch as a despised and feared symbol of emasculation, arguing that the social status of eunuchs was complex and ambivalent, rather than simply inferior.[30] However, it is clear that for Greer the eunuch represents an abject form of servility premised on desexualisation. In the 2006 foreword to Paladin's 21st Anniversary Edition of *The Female Eunuch*, Greer comments on what she calls the 'many new breeds of woman ... upon the earth' including 'men who mutilate themselves and are given passports as statutory women'.[31] The foreword is testament to the persistence of the trope of the male-to-female transsexual as a self-mutilated man which was first given expression in Greer's treatment of the British-born transgender woman April Ashley in *The Female Eunuch*. Ashley's career as a model and actor following her gender transition was brought to a premature end when her transsexual status was revealed without her consent by the British press in 1961. Greer represents Ashley's transition in terms of self-inflicted mutilation:

> He did not think of himself as a pervert, or even as a transvestite, but as a woman cruelly transmogrified into manhood. He tried to die, became a female impersonator, but eventually found a doctor in Casablanca who came up with a more acceptable alternative. He was to be castrated ... He would be infertile, but that has never affected the attribution of femininity.[32]

Having declared 'April's incompetence as a woman', Greer adds that this is 'what we must expect from a castrate, but it is not so very different after all from the impotence of feminine women'.[33] Here it is the transgender woman who functions as the epitome of the ideological internalisation of femininity, her elective 'castration' serving as an ironic counterpoint to the symbolic castration of all women. Greer depicts Ashley as a man whose assigned sex at birth irrevocably determines his gender and whose transition is expressive of an internalisation of ideological constructions of femininity:

> April Ashley was born male. All the information supplied by genes, chromosomes, internal and external sexual organs added up to the same thing. April was a man. But he longed to be a woman. He longed for the stereotype, not to embrace, but to be.[34]

Greer's depiction of Ashley is symptomatic of an emerging stereotype of the male-to-female transsexual as what Cressida Heyes has termed the 'dupe of gender'.[35] This motif was given its most extensive and provocative treatment in Janice Raymond's 1979 polemic *The Transsexual Empire: The Making of the She-Male*, a book which significantly extends Mary Daly's assertion, in her 1978 book *Gyn/Ecology*, that 'transsexualism is an example of male surgical siring which invades the female world with substitutes'.[36]

Central to *The Transsexual Empire* is Raymond's ideological denunciation of what she terms 'man-made "she-males"',[37] arguing that the 'artifactual femaleness' of the male-to-female transsexual is 'constructed, fashioned, and fabricated'[38] through medical technology. Raymond posits 'a society that produces sex-role stereotyping' as the 'primary cause of transsexualism',[39] defining it as a 'social problem whose cause cannot be explained except in relation to the sex roles and identities that a patriarchal society generates'.[40] In other words, medically assisted sex reassignment is seen not as a means through which male-to-female transsexuals express and embody their gender identity but rather as a procedure complicit in the ideological perpetuation of patriarchal 'sex roles'. In this context, the transsexual subject is depicted as a naive hostage to gender ideology and a victim – but also perpetrator – of false consciousness. Indeed, Jack Halberstam observes that transgender identity is often 'dismissed' as 'a form of false consciousness which circulates through the belief that genders can be voluntary and chosen'.[41] A term originating in Second Wave feminist appropriations of Marxist definitions of ideology, 'false consciousness' serves to describe the condition of women who have internalised patriarchal constructions of gender and who are unable to recognise themselves as members of a class defined by their systematic oppression. Hence, the transsexual is assumed to have fully subscribed to dominant ideas about gender identity, including its biological determination by sex, and is reduced to what Prosser terms the 'pawn, victim or dupe of medical technology'.[42] Moreover, Raymond argues that transsexuals are 'living out two basic patriarchal myths: single parenthood by the father (male mothering) and the making of woman according to man's image'.[43] This assertion brings together two otherwise opposing positions, biological essentialism (women are defined by their reproductive capacities) and social construction (gender is culturally constructed), to ridicule the transsexual's aspirations as deluded and unachievable. The charge that male-to-female transsexuals are intent on 'usurp[ing] female biology'[44] not only attributes a sinister intent to their transition but also posits biology as the source of women's identity. The accusation that male-to-female transsexuals 'objectify their own bodies'[45] imputes the persistence of a male consciousness in the transsexual body and implies that maleness cannot be eradicated. Like Greer, Raymond equates male-to-female gender reassignment surgery with mutilation, denying transsexual subjects' agency and instead depicting them as victims of a self-imposed surgical violation: 'Transsexual surgery, first of all, is the most recent brand of medicalized female castration.'[46]

Raymond's book and the opinions which it expressed can be placed in a wider context of ideas and actions at work within some branches of the Second Wave of the women's movement. Raymond credits the author of a letter to the publication *Sister* as a formative influence on her assertion that 'all transsexuals rape women's bodies',[47] revealing the ways in which this critique was shaped by collective activist discourse, rather than being the unique perspective of a single individual. Indeed, her book can be seen as an extended exposition and rationalisation of opinions which had been expressed via public platforms and circulated through feminist networks during the 1970s. *The Transsexual Empire* opens with the following assertion:

> Within the last five years, a number of transsexually constructed lesbian-feminists have appeared within the feminist community. By assuming the identity of feminist and lesbian, these transsexuals give the impression that they are fighting on both the personal and political fronts against stereotyped limitations, while also challenging the basic sex-role constructs of a patriarchal society.[48]

The roots of this preoccupation with the idea of the 'transsexually constructed'[49] lesbian feminist infiltrating women's communities can be attributed to a series of incidents which attracted significant attention in the early 1970s. In 1972, Beth Elliott, a singer and activist who had served as vice president of the San Francisco chapter of the lesbian organisation the Daughters of Bilitis, was expelled from the same group when some members questioned her status as a woman. When Elliott was invited to perform at the West Coast Lesbian Feminist Conference in Los Angeles in 1973, her presence attracted protest and the keynote speaker, Robin Morgan (author, activist and editor of the 1970 publication *Sisterhood Is Powerful: An Anthology of Writings from the Women's Liberation Movement*), denounced her as 'an opportunist, an infiltrator, and a destroyer – with the mentality of a rapist'.[50] Morgan's words clearly anticipate the inflammatory rhetoric of Raymond's book. In 1977, the employment of Sandy Stone as a recording engineer at Olivia Records, a collective formed to promote women in the music industry, attracted opposition and the threat of a boycott; while her colleagues resisted this pressure, Stone felt compelled to leave for the sake of the collective's work.[51] These incidents occurred at a time when the imperative of 'woman-identification' was serving to galvanise arguments for alliances between women beyond differences of sexuality, class and race.[52] However, despite the feminist critique of dominant forms of femininity as ideological constructions, this public policing of identity and community boundaries suggests that for some activists gender identity continues to be equated with sexed identity and sexed identity understood to be fixed and immutable. The 'entitlement' of transgender women to identify as women – and as feminists – was questioned on the grounds that they could not share the experiences of menstruation, pregnancy and childbirth which were seen as uniquely 'female'. While a minority position in contemporary feminist scholarship, Raymond's standpoint continues to be advanced, most notably in Sheila Jeffreys's *Unpacking Queer Politics: A Lesbian Feminist Perspective* (2003) and *Gender Hurts: A Feminist Analysis of the Politics of Transgenderism* (2014). In the former she diagnoses an 'epidemic of female-to-male (FTM) transsexualism', depicting medically assisted transition as 'surgical mutilation'.[53] Jeffreys argues that transsexualism is in 'direct opposition to lesbian survival'[54] and that 'transgender theory and practice contradict the very basis of feminism since feminism is a political movement based on the experience of persons who are women, born female and raised in the female sex caste'.[55] In this context, Carter's novel and its critical reception provides a valuable opportunity to track the persistence of these discourses in women's writing and feminist criticism.

'Violent Operations': Elective and Coercive Transition in *The Passion of New Eve*

The motif of the male-to-female transsexual as a 'man-made woman' – both literally in terms of surgical intervention and politically in terms of ideological internalisation – is clearly evoked by the representation of both Eve and Tristessa in Angela Carter's 1977 novel *The Passion of New Eve*. Eve's body is surgically constructed in the parodic image of normative male heterosexual desire and, on first encountering her new image in a mirror, she comments: 'They had turned me into a Playboy center fold. I was the focus of all the unfocused desires that had ever existed in my own head. I had become my own masturbatory fantasy.'[56] Indeed, Eve later identifies herself as 'a man-made masterpiece of skin and bone, the technological Eve in person'.[57] Carter lends a characteristically satirical twist to this trope by having the surgery performed as an act of feminist revenge by the matriarch of a women's commune, but this depiction of male-to-female sex reassignment as an act of retributive violence arguably reinforces its association with 'castration' and 'mutilation'. When Evelyn discovers the surgical fate planned for him by Mother, he asks, 'of what crime had I been guilty to deserve such punishment?'[58] Later she concedes that 'somewhere, in the darkness and confusion of the city, I had transgressed and now I must be punished for it'[59] and, deducing that the pregnant and abandoned Leilah may have played a witting role in her abduction, wonders whether 'my body [was] her revenge'.[60] When, having escaped from Beulah, Eve is abducted by Zero and repeatedly raped, she interprets her suffering as a realisation of Mother's intention, reflecting that she may have been 'selected ... to atone for the sins of my first sex vis-à-vis my second sex via my sex itself'.[61] At each of these 'violations' Eve understands herself as a former (male) 'violator',[62] thereby depicting her victimisation as an extension of Mother's punishment: she is raped as a woman, but seemingly punished for the man that she was. The way in which sex reassignment is depicted as a punishment for Evelyn's transgressions against women as a man has important implications for the ways in which transgender identity is constructed in *The Passion of New Eve*. If the construction of the sexualised female body through the agency of ideology and the vehicle of medical technology is emphasised in the figure of Eve, Tristessa is arguably intended to represent the cultural construction of femininity.

In *The Passion of New Eve*, Tristessa de St Ange is a screen icon of a bygone age – billed as '"the most beautiful woman in the world"'[63] – whose films are enjoying a 'cult revival'[64] among the art house cinemas frequented by Evelyn both in England and in America. Tristessa's retirement from the industry and withdrawal from the public gaze to a retreat in the Arizona desert only serves to enhance her status as an enigmatic legend of the golden age of Hollywood. The combination of screen charisma and private solitude is reminiscent of Greta Garbo (1905–90); indeed, the actor John Gilbert (1897–1936) – one of Garbo's on- and off-screen romantic partners – is counted as one of her fictional co-stars. Tristessa's star persona is associated with period narratives of transgression, tragedy and untimely death: her distinctly literary repertoire includes Edgar Allen Poe's Madeline Usher, Emily Brontë's Catherine Earnshaw and Gustave Flaubert's Emma Bovary. Indeed, Evelyn declares that: 'Tristessa's speciality had been suffering. Suffering was her vocation. She suffered exquisitely until suffering became demoded: then she retired . . . put herself away tidily in a store-house for worn out dreams.'[65] The uses to which Tristessa's screen image are put in the novel are diverse. According to Evelyn, she is one of a 'queenly pantheon of women'[66] whose memory is cherished by the 'pairs of sentimental queers who, hand in hand . . . come to pay homage'[67] during the 'camp renaissance'[68] of her films and by the 'drag-artiste[s]' who feel their 'repertoire [in]complete without a personation of her magic and passionate sorrow'.[69] By contrast, her image is later commandeered by Mother as part of Eve's gender 'programming'; as Eve recalls: 'old Hollywood provided me with a new set of nursery tales . . . Our Lady of the Sorrows, Tristessa; you came to me in seven veils of celluloid and demonstrated, in your incomparable tears, every kitsch excess of the mode of femininity.'[70] Finally, for Zero she represents the emasculating potential of women's power; he attributes his impotence to a hallucinatory experience during a screening of *Emma Bovary* when, under the influence of mescaline, he felt that 'Tristessa's eyes . . . had fixed directly upon his . . . [and] consumed him in a ghastly epiphany'.[71] In other words, her image is appropriated in ways which are various and contradictory. Through an act of subversive cross-gendered identification, Tristessa becomes an icon for her implicitly male 'queer' audience, her stylised suffering on screen giving coded expression to their experience as an oppressed sexual minority. However, the depiction of her popularity amongst female impersonators within a gay male subculture could also be interpreted as attributing an element of pastiche to her expression of femininity. By contrast, in Mother's commune at Beulah, Tristessa is assumed to represent dominant modes of femininity and her image employed in service to Eve's psychological induction. However, Tristessa is in many ways a peculiar choice, given her apparent disinterest in romance, marriage or motherhood; a video tape featuring mothers and infants from the animal kingdom which is intended to 'subliminally instil the maternal instinct'[72] in Eve implicitly compensates for this deficit, which only draws attention to the arguably transgressive nature of Tristessa's fiercely defended autonomy. Finally, Tristessa is far from the sexually voracious or maternally overbearing female figures who are more traditionally depicted as activating unconscious anxieties about 'emasculation', yet it is she who becomes the target of Zero's irrational hatred. Indeed, the fact that he persecutes her as a presumed 'dyke'[73] indicates that he targets her for her perceived deviance as a woman, not for her normativity. If the complex and contradictory relationship between Tristessa's screen image and gender and sexual norms is often overlooked in readings of the novel, the relationship between this image – mediated by the technology of film and by the dynamics of audience identification and projection – and her own gender identification is equally elided. When an apparent disparity between her screen image and her sexed body is discovered, the possibility of continuity between her on-screen and off-screen gender identification is rarely considered. Following the forcible exposure of Tristessa's sexed body, Eve abruptly shifts pronouns and pronounces her identity a figment of male fantasy in terms which mirror her own reconstruction by Mother. Indeed, she attributes Tristessa's femininity to what she now understands as its male authorship:

> That was why he had been the perfect man's woman! He had made himself the shrine of his own desires, had made of himself the only woman he could have loved! If a woman is indeed beautiful only in so far as she incarnates most completely the secret aspirations of man, no wonder Tristessa had been able to become the most beautiful woman in the world, an unbegotten woman who made no concessions to humanity.[74]

For Eve, the self-appointed arbiter of gender identity in the novel, Tristessa's femininity, while still seductive, is imitative and her gender identity illusory: she pronounces her a 'female impersonator ... forever cheated of experience'[75] and is insistent that while 'he had been she ... she had never been a woman'.[76] If Evelyn's punishment takes the form of enforced sex reassignment surgery, Tristessa's punishment begins with its refusal. Tristessa seeks treatment from Mother, in the latter's former capacity as a cosmetic surgeon, but, as Mother's daughter Lilith recalls: '"Mama told me, he was too much of a woman, already, for the good of his sex; and, besides, when she subjected him to the first tests, she was struck by what seemed to her the awfully ineradicable quality of his maleness."'[77] When Eve's 'ineradicable maleness' is suggested by reference to the 'cock in her head', which 'twitches'[78] at the sight of her new body in the mirror, this vision of a male-to-female transsexual sexually objectifying her own body arguably echoes Raymond's depiction of the transsexual as a man intent on colonising the female body. By contrast, Mother's refusal of Tristessa's request inaugurates a denial of her elective gender identity and a coercive imposition of maleness (inflicted not only by Mother but also by Zero and Eve) which persists, often in violent form, throughout the novel. Here it is interesting to note that Eve is spared the exposure which Tristessa suffers. While the reader is party to her history, Eve is never made vulnerable to the consequences of public knowledge. So convincing is Eve's newly sexed body in this speculative novel that the question of her capacity to 'pass' as a woman, even in the absence of a correspondingly gendered subjectivity, is effectively suspended. Eve seems to emerge as the more authentic transsexual on the basis of her sexed identity alone; her forcible reassignment is privileged over Tristessa's elective transgender agency.

Contemporary feminist scholarship on Carter's novel can be seen as reflecting Second Wave concerns in its recurring analysis of Eve as a satirical representation of ideological constructions of femininity. Linden Peach argues that Evelyn 'fails to make a distinction between transvestism and female masquerade. In other words, he fails to distinguish between a man dressed as a woman and a man dressed as a woman masquerading as Woman.'[79] For Aidan Day, Mother 'reconstructs Evelyn as a woman in the same manner as she constructed herself: that is, effectively as a reflection of masculine images of the female',[80] and Jean Wyatt goes on to suggest that, as '"the perfect woman"', Eve is 'constructed according to the specifications of male desire'.[81] Indeed, the motif of the male-to-female transsexual as a 'castrated man'[82] is evoked in more than one reading of Eve: as Wyatt puts it, 'becoming a woman requires, in *The Passion of New Eve*, a literal castration'.[83] This reading is also extended to Tristessa but she is read not only as revealing the cultural construction of femininity but also as being complicit in the patriarchal construction of femininity – as a kind of 'patriarchal stooge',[84] to use Prosser's words. Roberta Rubenstein writes that when 'Tristessa's true biological sex is unmasked ... Carter exposes the lie at the base of male romantic fantasies of femininity'.[85] Moreover, Merja Makinen claims that 'Tristessa's cross-dressing is a male appropriation of femininity, not a radical form of gender-bending'.[86] Here, Tristessa is depicted as suffering from a form of false consciousness in succumbing to a 'lie' of femininity, but as a sexed male she is also regarded as an agent of male colonisation of female experience in terms which are reminiscent of Raymond's critique. There is no evidence in the narrative of *The Passion of New Eve* that Tristessa derives sexual satisfaction from dressing as a woman (as a transvestite might), nor that her 'cross-dressing' is temporary and provisional (whether for the purposes of pleasure or screen performance). Nevertheless, a recurring motif in scholarship on this novel is the interpretation of the revelation of Tristessa's sexed body as the 'exposure' of Tristessa as a 'male cross-dresser' rather than as a transgender woman. Christine Britzolakis argues that Tristessa 'turns out to be a transvestite',[87] and Claire Westall refers to her as 'the former Hollywood starlet exposed as a transvestite'.[88] Elsewhere Tristessa is described as a 'transvestite' and a 'drag queen',[89] 'a man masquerading in drag'[90] and a 'drag artist',[91] and Makinen asserts that 'Tristessa is in fact a male cross-dresser who has no experience whatsoever of being a real woman. Not only that, Tristessa has little sexual experience of women . . .'[92] Similarly, Rubenstein argues that Tristessa is 'unmask[ed] as a transvestite who has successfully disguised his male sex throughout 'his'/her Hollywood career'.[93] Moreover, this categorisation is made by way of contrast with Eve, whose designation as a 'transsexual' is grounded in her sexed body rather than her gender identity. Rubenstein refers to Eve and Tristessa as 'the transsexual and the transvestite who have inhabited both genders',[94] Johnson remarks on a 'distinction . . . between the treatment of the transvestite and that of the transsexual'[95] and Westall contrasts 'Tristessa, the male-to-female transvestite, and Eve/lyn, the male-to-female transsexual'.[96] This widely drawn distinction suggests that despite feminist critiques of biological essentialism, Eve's and Tristessa's gender identity is ultimately attributed to their sex: Eve merits the title 'transsexual' because she has undergone sex reassignment surgery, albeit against her will, while Tristessa's gender identity is denied despite her lived experience as a woman. The legacy of Second Wave critiques of male-to-female transsexuals has arguably played its part in the genesis of a tendency to read male-to-female gender transition in terms of ideological complicity with patriarchal constructions of femininity. Indeed, in *The Passion of New Eve*, the suggestion that Eve's gender identity is more authentic than Tristessa's relies on themes central to Second Wave feminist politics: the centrality of rape to women's oppression and the significance of reproductive sexuality for women's identity.

'Immune to rape': The Passion of Tristessa de St Ange

When Janice Raymond declared that 'all transsexuals rape women's bodies' she was mobilising one of the most powerful and emotive metaphors for women's oppression in Second Wave contexts. Rape is repeatedly depicted as a weapon of sexualised violence in *The Passion of New Eve* and the prominence of this motif would seem to locate Carter's 1977 novel firmly within the sexual politics of its time. Radical feminist critiques of rape have been central to Second Wave frameworks for the analysis of sexuality and violence; as Vikki Bell has noted, 'sexuality has been posited as a, if not the, central site of women's oppression'.[97] This understanding of sexual violence as playing a key role in the induction of women into patriarchal roles is both reflected and challenged in Carter's fiction. In their introduction to *Rape and Representation*, Lynn A. Higgins and Brenda R. Silver write that 'rape and rapability are central to the very construction of gender identity'.[98] In *The Passion of New Eve*, Eve suffers 'marital rape[s]'[99] by Zero so 'furious' that she fears 'I would die of it'.[100] Moreover, she describes this regime of sexual terror as as 'savage an apprenticeship in womanhood as could have been devised for me'.[101] The extent to which the feminist recognition of the reality of sexual violence might inadvertently serve to reinforce the construction of women as victims has subsequently been the subject of much scrutiny. For example, in her article 'Toward a New Feminist Theory of Rape', Carine M. Mardorassian foregrounds the 'need to resist the facile opposition between passivity and agency that has motivated popular and academic discussions of violence against women'.[102] This opposition is challenged in Carter's audacious imagining of female-perpetrated rape in *The Passion of New Eve*, which is symptomatic of her complex relationship to emerging feminist orthodoxies. Evelyn claims to have been 'unceremoniously raped'[103] by Mother whilst still biologically male. Where Zero's penetrating body is an 'instrument of torture'[104] for the female Eve, Mother is an agent of emasculating humiliation when she 'grasp[s]', 'engulf[s]' and 'expel[s]'[105] Evelyn's penis. In 'Sexual and Textual Aggression in *The Sadeian Woman* and *The Passion of New Eve*', Makinen suggests that such reversals of gendered paradigms of oppression challenge 'passive stereotypes that uphold suffering and eroticise victimisation',[106] arguing that *The Passion of New Eve*, among other texts, demonstrates 'the exhilarating thrill of women's sexual and textual aggression'.[107] The violence exercised by Mother on behalf of the community of women at Beulah is certainly provocative; however, I want to examine what becomes of the male-to-female transgender body in a context where textual violence is waged in terms which rely on binary categories of sex.

Where the 'rape' of Evelyn by Mother reverses hierarchies of gendered power, Tristessa's 'rape' arguably serves to reinforce sexed categories of identity. Eve's conviction that Tristessa 'had never been a woman'[108] is little different to Zero's, whose exposure of Tristessa's biological sex is the impetus for a terrorising ordeal. Here symbolic violence joins forces with material violence which, much like Evelyn's sex reassignment surgery, seems to have a punitive, corrective function: namely, to forcibly inscribe on Tristessa both a biological maleness and a male heterosexuality, the latter constructed as an inevitable consequence of the former. In order to compel the consummation of the forced marriage between Eve and Tristessa, Zero instructs one of his wives to arouse Tristessa with her mouth. Staring in amazement at her own erection, Tristessa falls against Eve's body, to whom she whispers: '"I thought . . . I was immune to rape. I thought that I had become inviolable, like glass, and could only be broken."'[109] In an act which echoes that of Leilah – who 'tears'[110] an orgasm from the barely conscious Evelyn – Eve now 'draws'[111] Tristessa into her, where the latter ejaculates. On one level this scene seems to be offered by the text as 'proof' of what Mother diagnosed as her 'ineradicable maleness'.[112] This maleness is assumed to reside in the fact of her penis, and her arousal and ejaculation are then taken as evidence of the restoration of her (male) heterosexuality. In this sense Carter's narrative trajectory and Zero's homophobic mania seem to be fellow travellers. At the same time, however, this is an act of specifically transphobic violence in that it is designed to violate Tristessa's integrity as a transgender person. Tristessa is coercively inscribed into an identity other than the one with which she identifies: her forced sexual intimacy violates her gendered identity not because it is with a woman – a same-sex encounter would not necessarily negate her gender identity – but because she is made to be intimate as a sexed male. For Zero, Tristessa's rape is a punishment for her gender transgression and an attempt to enforce a normative role on to her. Uneasily, this text also seems to offer this 'rape' as a corrective and one which reveals the 'truth' of sex: namely, that Tristessa cannot be permitted to be a woman. Eve – the 'new' woman – is complicit in this lesson, becoming once more the violator. Eve and Tristessa's enforced 'double wedding'[113] is followed by a consensual encounter in the desert in which the 'interpenetrating, undifferentiated sex'[114] which they experience seems to dispense with sexed identity as a determinant of sexual identity. However, the motif of the restitution of Tristessa's maleness through heterosexuality persists: 'the glass woman I saw beneath me smashed under my passion and the splinters scattered and recomposed themselves into a man who overwhelmed me.'[115] Indeed, an insistence on binary categories serves to contain Eve and Tristessa's union within heteronormative terms when they are described as 'Eve and Adam both, on a mission to repopulate'.[116] At the end of the novel, Eve remarks that '[Lilith] took it for granted that I was pregnant' and Lilith speculates '"What if Tristessa made you pregnant?"', proposing that '"Your baby will have two fathers and two mothers'".[117] The status of Eve's pregnancy is not resolved at the end of the novel, but the possibility that she may have conceived serves an important symbolic purpose in distinguishing her from Tristessa. Pregnancy, as a narrative device, is often used to provide an implicitly redemptive closure, as if the conception of a child inevitably vindicates what has gone before. As such, this device often disregards the realities of pregnancy, birth and motherhood for women, reducing the pregnant body to a vehicle to carry the narrative's promise of a projected future. In *The Passion of New Eve*, Eve's possible pregnancy promises to authenticate her status as a biological woman, problematically reviving motherhood as the final sanction of 'true' femininity. However, it simultaneously acts to affirm Tristessa's maleness – and by implication her heterosexuality – and in doing so invalidates her transgender identity. As Michel Foucault has demonstrated in his *History of Sexuality*, reproductive sexuality was the benchmark by which the legitimacy of sexual desires and practices was judged in late-nineteenth-century sexological discourses. Indeed, Michael Warner gives the name 'reprosexuality' to the conflation of 'heterosexuality, biological reproduction, cultural reproduction, and personal identity', arguing that 'reprosexuality involves more than reproducing, more even than compulsory heterosexuality: it involves a relation to the self that finds its proper temporality and fulfilment in generational transmission'.[118] In this context, Eve's conception is especially charged, and even more so because of the prominence given to the theme of fertility in *The Passion of New Eve*. Evelyn is held indirectly accountable for Leilah's dangerous and damaging abortion and his punishment entails his planned impregnation, by artificial insemination, with his own sperm – a fate which Eve flees and the narrative evades. Zero's pathological hatred of Tristessa is founded on his irrational conviction that she is the cause of his infertility. Both Mother's and Zero's eugenic ambitions are thwarted and yet the fantasy of a post-apocalyptic repopulation is fulfilled in Eve when she announces: 'I myself will soon produce a tribute to evolution.'[119] In this way, the narrative arguably concludes with the triumph of what Lee Edelman has described as 'reproductive futurism'[120] in the form of the anticipated birth of Eve's child.

It is important to note that Tristessa's identity in *The Passion of New Eve* is always mediated by Eve's narrative perspective, one which combines dogmatic denunciations of Tristessa's gender identity with a desire which is sometimes tenderly expressed. Indeed, where Eve's suffering is treated with irreverent humour in the novel, Tristessa is often depicted as a figure of pathos and dignity whose 'passion' evokes the tragic register of martyrdom. In other words, Tristessa is not the transsexual phantom of Raymond's dystopian vision. Indeed, Eve is in some ways a parody of Raymond's conspiratorial theory, given that this 'man-made woman' is the intended agent of a radical feminist plot, rather than the product of patriarchal technology.[121] Nevertheless, as this chapter has demonstrated, there remains a persistent critical tendency to read Tristessa as exemplifying the 'false consciousness' of femininity, a default position which may be an unacknowledged legacy of Second Wave critiques of male-to-female transsexuals. In her critical reflection on this legacy, in her 2003 essay 'Feminist Solidarity after Queer Theory: The Case of Transgender', Cressida J. Heyes observes that the 'approaches I have criticised may say more about non-trans feminists' failure to interrogate our own identities and our comfort with our own gender, than they do about the realities of trans communities or political movements'.[122] The 'disparaging'[123] tradition of feminist attitudes to transgender people is similarly examined in Patricia Elliot's 2010 book *Debates in Transgender, Queer, and Feminist Theory*, where she suggests that

> Transsexuals pose a challenge, intentionally or not, to mainstream feminist conceptions of sex as a stable and immutable basis of gender, a challenge which raises questions about the presumed 'authenticity' of identity and about the inclusiveness of feminist politics.[124]

There is a long tradition of questioning the very category of 'woman' within feminist theory, from Denise Riley's *'Am I That Name?' Feminism and the Category of 'Women' in History* (1988) onwards. Indeed, this questioning was foundational for Judith Butler's *Gender Trouble*, in which she called for a 'new form of feminist politics', which would not only 'contest the very reifications of gender and identity' but also 'take the variable construction of identity as both a methodological and normative prerequisite, if not a political goal'.[125] By revisiting the doubling of an involuntary male-to-female transsexual with an elective transgender woman in a novel which has come to be seen as a feminist classic in traditions of women's writing and feminist literary criticism, this chapter has sought to embrace the challenge which Elliot describes, a challenge which entails acknowledging and addressing the more troubling legacies of the Second Wave era in order to forge renewed forms of feminist cultural politics.

Notes

1. Bristow and Broughton, 'Introduction', in Bristow and Broughton (eds), *The Infernal Desire Machines of Angela Carter*, p. 14.
2. See also Westall, '"His almost gendered voice": Gendering and Transgendering Bodily Signification and the Voice in Angela Carter's *The Passion of New Eve*', in Kim and Westall (eds), *Cross-Gendered Literary Voices: Appropriating, Resisting, Embracing*, p. 131.
3. Bristow and Broughton, 'Introduction', p. 19.
4. Trevenna, 'Gender as Performance', p. 267.
5. Trevenna, 'Gender as Performance', p. 268.
6. Prosser, *Second Skins*, p. 5.
7. Prosser, *Second Skins*, p. 22.
8. Bristow and Broughton, 'Introduction', p. 4.
9. Gamble, *Angela Carter: Writing from the Front Line*, p. 125.
10. Gersdorf, 'The Gender of Nature's Nation: A Queer Perspective', p. 50.
11. Johnson, 'Unexpected Geometries: Transgressive Symbolism and the Transsexual Subject in Angela Carter's *The Passion of New Eve*', in Bristow and Broughton (eds), *Infernal Desire Machines*, p. 167.
12. Raymond, *The Transsexual Empire*, p. 104.
13. Stone, 'The Empire Strikes Back: A Posttranssexual Manifesto', in Stryker and Whittle (eds), *The Transgender Studies Reader*, p. 230.
14. Evelyn's transformation takes place against a distinctly racialised landscape, where the violent disintegration of American society is attributed to both gendered and racial revolt, with 'the blacks' of Harlem 'abandoning dandyism and narcotics' to assume battledress 'to a man'. Carter, *The Passion of New Eve*, p. 17. Mother and Leilah/Lilith are women of colour but their racial identity is principally represented through the alchemical symbolism of old Europe, by which Leilah is described as 'softly black in colour – nigredo, the stage of darkness' (p. 14). Moreover, when the sexual 'slavery' and rape to which Eve is subject as Zero's property is presented as a unique outcome of a violently dysfunctional state it is implicitly constructed as a crime against white women, erasing the long American history of the sexual expropriation of black women's bodies.
15. Carter, *The Passion of New Eve*, p. 135.
16. This depiction of forcible sex reassignment as a vehicle for revenge can also be found in other cultural narratives, from Gore Vidal's *Myra Breckinridge* (1970) to Pedro Almodóvar's 2011 film *The Skin I Live In*, adapted from Thierry Jonquet's 1995 novel *Tarantula*.
17. I will refer to the pre-operative protagonist as 'Evelyn' and the post-operative as 'Eve' to indicate the differently sexed positions to which the narrator is assigned at specific temporal locations in the text. I will refer to Tristessa as 'she' throughout in recognition of her elective gender identification.

18. I use the term 'gender reassignment treatment' in relation to Tristessa only since Eve's experience of medical technology is neither elective nor therapeutic.
19. Stone, 'The Empire Strikes Back', p. 230.
20. Carter, *The Passion of New Eve*, p. 144.
21. This chapter is a revised and expanded version of an article which was first published as '"Violent Operations": Revisiting the Transgendered Body in Angela Carter's *The Passion of New Eve*', *Women: A Cultural Review*, 22:2–3 (September 2011), pp. 241–55 [DOI: 10.1080/09574042.2011.587246]. This article is available in print and online.
22. Hollows, *Feminism, Femininity and Popular Culture*, p. 14.
23. Carter, 'The Wound in the Face', in Uglow (ed.), *Shaking a Leg: Collected Journalism and Writings*, p. 110.
24. Greer, *The Female Eunuch*, p. 33.
25. Greer, *The Female Eunuch*, p. 70.
26. Greer, *The Female Eunuch*, p. 78.
27. Greer, *The Female Eunuch*, p. 17.
28. Greer, *The Female Eunuch*, p. 104.
29. See Gannon, 'Exclusion as Language and the Language of Exclusion: Tracing Regimes of Gender through Linguistic Representations of the "Eunuch"'.
30. See Ringrose, 'Eunuchs in Historical Perspective', p. 501.
31. Greer, *The Female Eunuch*, p. 9.
32. Greer, *The Female Eunuch*, p. 71.
33. Greer, *The Female Eunuch*, p. 72.
34. Greer, *The Female Eunuch*, p. 70.
35. Heyes, 'Feminist Solidarity after Queer Theory: The Case of Transgender', p. 1,095.
36. Daly, *Gyn/Ecology: The Metaethics of Radical Feminism*, p. 71.
37. Raymond, *The Transsexual Empire*, p. xvii.
38. Raymond, *The Transsexual Empire*, p. xvi.
39. Raymond, *The Transsexual Empire*, p. xviii.
40. Raymond, *The Transsexual Empire*, p. 16.
41. Halberstam, 'Telling Tales: Brandon Teena, Billy Tipton, and Transgender Biography', in Sánchez and Schlossberg (eds), *Passing: Identity and Interpretation in Sexuality, Race, and Religion*, p. 14.
42. Prosser, *Second Skins*, p. 8.
43. Raymond, *The Transsexual Empire*, p. xx.
44. Raymond, *The Transsexual Empire*, p. 31.
45. Raymond, *The Transsexual Empire*, p. 29.
46. Raymond, *The Transsexual Empire*, p. xxiv.
47. Raymond, *The Transsexual Empire*, p. 104.
48. Raymond, *The Transsexual Empire*, p. xix.
49. Raymond, *The Transsexual Empire*, pp. xix, 100, 102.

84 Transgender and the Literary Imagination

50. Stryker, *Transgender History*, p. 105.
51. The expulsion of Nancy Jean Burkholder from the Michigan Women's Music Festival in 1991 (Salamon, *Assuming a Body*, 2010; Sreedhar and Hand, 'The Ethics of Exclusion', 2006) and the 1995 legal dispute over Kimberly Nixon's right to train as a counsellor at the Vancouver Rape Relief Centre (Elliot, *Debates in Transgender, Queer, and Feminist Theory*, 2010; Karaian, 'Strategic Essentialism on Trial', 2006) demonstrate that 'women only' cultural spaces continue to be the object of controversy.
52. See Rubin, *Self-Made Men: Identity and Embodiment among Transsexual Men*, pp. 63–92.
53. Jeffreys, *Unpacking Queer Politics*, p. 122.
54. Jeffreys, *Unpacking Queer Politics*, p. 143.
55. Jeffreys, *Gender Hurts*, p. 36.
56. Carter, *The Passion of New Eve*, p. 75.
57. Carter, *The Passion of New Eve*, p. 146.
58. Carter, *The Passion of New Eve*, p. 68.
59. Carter, *The Passion of New Eve*, p. 74.
60. Carter, *The Passion of New Eve*, p. 172.
61. Carter, *The Passion of New Eve*, p. 107.
62. Carter, *The Passion of New Eve*, p. 102.
63. Carter, *The Passion of New Eve*, p. 5.
64. Carter, *The Passion of New Eve*, p. 15.
65. Carter, *The Passion of New Eve*, p. 8.
66. Carter, *The Passion of New Eve*, p. 6.
67. Carter, *The Passion of New Eve*, p. 5.
68. Carter, *The Passion of New Eve*, p. 8.
69. Carter, *The Passion of New Eve*, p. 6.
70. Carter, *The Passion of New Eve*, p. 71.
71. Carter, *The Passion of New Eve*, p. 104.
72. Carter, *The Passion of New Eve*, p. 72.
73. Carter, *The Passion of New Eve*, p. 91.
74. Carter, *The Passion of New Eve*, p. 129.
75. Carter, *The Passion of New Eve*, p. 144.
76. Carter, *The Passion of New Eve*, p. 152.
77. Carter, *The Passion of New Eve*, p. 173.
78. Carter, *The Passion of New Eve*, p. 75.
79. Peach, *Angela Carter*, p. 115.
80. Day, *Angela Carter: The Rational Glass*, p. 116.
81. Wyatt, 'The Violence of Gendering: Castration Images in Angela Carter's *The Magic Toyshop*, *The Passion of New Eve*, and "Peter and the Wolf"', in Easton (ed.), *Angela Carter: Contemporary Critical Essays*, p. 62.
82. Wyatt, 'The Violence of Gendering', pp. 62, 77; Makinen, 'Sexual and Textual Aggression in *The Sadeian Woman* and *The Passion of New Eve*', in Bristow and Broughton (eds), *Infernal Desire Machines*, p. 156.

83. Wyatt, 'The Violence of Gendering', p. 77.
84. Prosser, *Second Skins*, p. 90.
85. Rubenstein, 'Intersexions: Gender Metamorphosis in Angela Carter's *The Passion of New Eve* and Lois Gould's *A Sea-Change*', p. 110.
86. Makinen, 'Sexual and Textual Aggression', p. 158.
87. Britzolakis, 'Angela Carter's Fetishism', in Bristow and Broughton (eds), *Infernal Desire Machines*, p. 50.
88. Westall, '"His almost gendered voice"', p. 132.
89. Gamble, *Angela Carter*, p. 127.
90. Palmer, 'Gender as Performance in the Fiction of Angela Carter and Margaret Atwood', in Bristow and Broughton (eds), *Infernal Desire Machines*, p. 30.
91. Hanson, '"The red dawn breaking over Clapham": Carter and the Limits of Artifice', in Bristow and Broughton (eds), *Infernal Desire Machines*, p. 61.
92. Makinen, 'Sexual and Textual Aggression', p. 157.
93. Rubenstein, 'Intersexions', p. 107.
94. Rubenstein, 'Intersexions', p. 111.
95. Johnson, 'Unexpected Geometries', p. 175. The distinction drawn by Johnson is particularly striking since it is situated within a critical framework explicitly aligned with transgender theory. Drawing on Sandy Stone's concept of 'posttranssexual' identity, Johnson applies it to Eve, rather than Tristessa, on the grounds that the former discloses rather than conceals her pre-operative sexed history.
96. Westall, '"His almost gendered voice"', p. 142.
97. Bell, *Interrogating Incest: Feminism, Foucault and the Law*, p. 5.
98. Higgins and Silver, 'Introduction: Rereading Rape', in Higgins and Silver (eds), *Rape and Representation*, p. 3.
99. Carter, *The Passion of New Eve*, p. 102.
100. Carter, *The Passion of New Eve*, p. 107.
101. Carter, *The Passion of New Eve*, p. 107.
102. Mardorassian, 'Toward a New Feminist Theory of Rape', p. 771.
103. Carter, *The Passion of New Eve*, p. 64.
104. Carter, *The Passion of New Eve*, p. 86.
105. Carter, *The Passion of New Eve*, pp. 64–5.
106. Makinen, 'Sexual and Textual Aggression', p. 163.
107. Makinen, 'Sexual and Textual Aggression', p. 163.
108. Carter, *The Passion of New Eve*, p. 144.
109. Carter, *The Passion of New Eve*, p. 137.
110. Carter, *The Passion of New Eve*, p. 27.
111. Carter, *The Passion of New Eve*, p. 138.
112. Carter, *The Passion of New Eve*, p. 173.
113. Carter, *The Passion of New Eve*, p. 135.
114. Carter, *The Passion of New Eve*, p. 148.
115. Carter, *The Passion of New Eve*, p. 149.

116. Carter, *The Passion of New Eve*, p. 165.
117. Carter, *The Passion of New Eve*, p. 187.
118. Warner, 'Introduction: Fear of a Queer Planet', p. 9.
119. Carter, *The Passion of New Eve*, p. 186.
120. Edelman, *No Future: Queer Theory and the Death Drive*, p. 2. Edelman writes that the figure of the child, including the unborn child, has 'come to embody for us the telos of the social order and come to be seen as the one for whom that order is held in perpetual trust' (p. 11).
121. Bristow and Broughton have observed that 'much of *The Passion of New Eve* is given over to travestying the radical feminism of the 1970s' ('Introduction', p. 11). The figure of Mother can be understood as a satirical comment on the preoccupation with matriarchal mythology in some strands of Second Wave feminist thinking.
122. Heyes, 'Feminist Solidarity after Queer Theory', p. 1,117.
123. Elliot, *Debates in Transgender, Queer, and Feminist Theory*, p. 18.
124. Elliot, *Debates in Transgender, Queer, and Feminist Theory*, p. 21.
125. Butler, *Gender Trouble: Feminism and the Subversion of Identity*, p. 9.

Chapter 3

Playing the Breeches Part: Feminist Appropriations, Biographical Fictions and Colonial Contexts in Patricia Duncker's *James Miranda Barry* (1999)

In a founding essay on transgender life narratives in contemporary fiction and film, 'Telling Tales: Brandon Teena, Billy Tipton, and Transgender Biography', Jack Halberstam demonstrates why this genre of representation has proved so fraught and contested. Examining how the lives of transgender subjects have been 'dismantled and reassembled through a series of biographical inquiries', Halberstam proposes that transgender biography can be understood as 'a sometimes violent, often imprecise project, one which seeks to brutally erase the carefully managed details of the life of a passing person and which recasts the act of passing as deception, dishonesty, and fraud'.[1] The eponymous protagonist of Patricia Duncker's 1999 novel *James Miranda Barry* was subject to a form of posthumous 'exposure' which can be seen as characteristic of the ways in which potentially transgender lives have been depicted in biographical narrative and historical fiction. Historical records indicate that Barry (c. 1799–1865) lived much of his youth and all of his adult life as a man, from his enrolment as a medical student at the University of Edinburgh in 1809, through a notable colonial career as a military surgeon, to his death in London. However, Barry's public memory was irrevocably changed when reports that his body had been discovered on his deathbed to be female were published in the Irish and British press. Barry's life presents a range of narrative possibilities for the historian, biographer or novelist engaged in the project of imagining his experience of his sexed, gendered or sexual identity and its impact on both his personal and his professional identity. However, the narrative most commonly adopted in historical reconstructions of Barry's life is one which depicts him as a woman cross-dressing as a man. This motif is evident in historical biographies including Isobel Rae's *The Strange Story of Dr James Barry: Army Surgeon, Inspector-General of Hospitals, Discovered on Death to Be a Woman* (1958) and June Rose's *The Perfect Gentleman: The Remarkable Life of Dr. James Miranda Barry, the Woman Who Served as an Officer in the British Army from 1813 to 1859* (1977) and in cultural histories such as Julie Wheelwright's *Amazons and Military Maids: Women Who Dressed as Men in Pursuit of Life, Liberty and Happiness* (1989). These works can be considered revisionary histories which seek to claim Barry for a history of women. In doing so they contest the 'deception, dishonesty, and fraud' often attributed to transgender lives, but achieve this by substituting an emancipatory or subversive intent grounded in an identity position in which gender is determined by sex. By contrast, Duncker's *James Miranda Barry* departs significantly from established narratives by refusing to define Barry's sexed or gender identity in categorical terms. Indeed, despite the extensive opportunities for personal revelation offered by its partial use of the first-person narrative form, the novel declines to resolve questions to do with Barry's gender identification. Jana Funke applauds what she interprets as Duncker's principled refusal to retrospectively impose binary categories of sexed or gendered identity on to this historical figure. Acknowledging that the novel may have 'disappoint[ed] some feminist readers',[2] Funke argues that its 'supposed shortcoming – its failure to provide insight into Barry's inner life as a woman – can also be read as one of the text's main achievements'.[3] This chapter will explore questions of authorship and agency in the writing of historical transgender lives, with a focus on Duncker's novel and its biographical intertexts. Firstly, it will argue that while a feminist narrative of subversive gender crossing is implicitly complicated by Duncker's depiction of James Miranda Barry, this motif nevertheless emerges in displaced form through the lives of female characters whose aspirations to greater liberty are acted out vicariously through Barry: namely, his mother, Mary Ann, and his childhood sweetheart and lifelong love, the fictional Alice Jones. Secondly, it will question the exclusive attention given to gender as the primary category of identity in historical and fictional reconstructions of Barry's life through a specific focus on the colonial contexts in which his life story unfolds. It will examine the uses to which the theatre of empire is put in accounts of Barry's life, investigating the relationship between gender norms and racialised hierarchies in historical conditions where the latter is arguably privileged over the former.

'A Mystery Still': The Afterlives of James Miranda Barry

In an important intervention in transgender historiography, David J. Getsy has argued for the importance of 'making visible, bringing into experience, or knowing genders as mutable, successive, and multiple'.[4] For Getsy, a recognition of what he terms 'transgender capacity' is essential to the historical project of acknowledging 'all of the ways in which self-determined and successive genders, identities, and bodily morphologies have always been present throughout history as possibilities and actualities'.[5] Similarly, K. J. Rawson has argued that, in the absence of documented life narratives, historical traces of transgender lives may nevertheless be 'glimpse[d]'[6] through careful reading of a range of archival sources. Details of the public and professional life of James Miranda Barry – a colonial military surgeon of Irish heritage and Scottish education – are not lost to history; his professional service and social standing in settler communities in South Africa, the West Indies and Canada are indeed 'glimpsed' in both public and private records of the period. However, these historical accounts were overwritten in the years following his death in London in 1865 when press reports of disputed revelations about his sex prompted the production and publication of 'new' private and public memories which retrospectively rewrote his previously accepted gender identity in changed terms. The passage of Barry's life into fiction – and moreover into romantic and sensational speculation at increasing remove from the known facts of his life – seems to have been rapid and long lasting. In 1867, two years after his death, Barry appeared in Charles Dickens's popular periodical publication *All the Year Round* in an anecdotal story entitled 'A Mystery Still'. Depicted as 'frail in body, unique in appearance and eccentric in manner',[7] Barry is remembered for his 'queer ways and irritable temper' which, somewhat paradoxically, 'rather increased than diminished his prestige'.[8] The anonymous author contributes to the speculation about a mysterious period of absence without leave taken by Barry from his posting at the Cape in 1829 by reproducing the legend that he had undertaken the arduous journey to England for a haircut, a story which reflects the posthumous perception of Barry as an idiosyncratic dandy.[9] Barry's painted portrait was encountered by Mark Twain during his travels in the Southern Cape and recalled in his 1897 travel memoir *Following the Equator: A Journey around the World*. The portrait in question was commissioned by James Barry Munnik, the child Barry delivered in 1820 in what is thought to have been the first successful caesarean section; the family expressed their gratitude to Barry by naming all of their first-born males in his honour. Twain reproduces the popular legend of the former medical inspector as a 'wild young fellow' guilty of 'various kinds of misbehaviour' but peculiarly immune to punishment, an 'imposing and uncanny wonder to the town', a 'marvel' and a 'puzzle'.[10] Twain's unfounded assertion that Barry was the 'daughter of a great English house' who had 'disgraced herself with her people' and sought a 'new start in the world'[11] is symptomatic of the emergence of more sensational narratives of sexual and moral scandal, including Ebenezer Rogers's 1881 three-volume novel *A Modern Sphinx*. Barry was sufficiently well remembered in the Cape to feature in caricature form in a 1910 pageant marking the Union between the four provinces[12] – an appearance which inspired one eyewitness, Olga Racster, to co-author with Jessica Groves a new romantic novel based on Barry's life, entitled *Dr James Barry: Her Secret Story*, published in 1932.

While neither forgotten nor undocumented, by this point in the early twentieth century the life of a reforming medical professional had been posthumously rewritten. James Miranda Barry's life had passed from the annals of public biography, via the storytelling channels of anecdote, legend and speculation, into the realms of romantic and popular fiction. Barry has subsequently been the subject of a number of historical biographies (including Rae's *The Strange Story of Dr James Barry*, Rose's *The Perfect Gentleman* and Rachel Holmes's *The Secret Life of Dr James Barry*, 2002), as well as Duncker's historical fiction. Indeed, Isobel Rae's and June Rose's historical biographies can be considered 'corrective' interventions which seek to remedy the falsifications of Barry's life in fictional accounts through reference to newly assembled historical evidence. In her 1958 book Rae articulates clearly the transformation which she expects her research to effect in popular perceptions of Barry's life:

> The temperamental, hysterical girl of high degree, who joined the Army Medical Service for love of an army surgeon, and who was protected in all her escapades by powerful, but unknown, authorities in high places, becomes instead the brilliant student, the dedicated doctor, the dauntless reformer of abuses; a different, but no less interesting character.[13]

Writing in the post-war decades, which saw the memory of women's service in the war effort subsumed under a socially conservative directive to reinstate the home and family as women's appropriate sphere, Rae claims Barry as an unacknowledged pioneer in the history of women's professional emancipation. Rose's 1977 biography shares in this project of revisionary historiography and underlines the point with dramatic irony by opening in the year of Barry's death:

> It was 1865 – the year the 'first' woman doctor in Great Britain, Elizabeth Garret Anderson, graduated. And yet another woman – James Barry – had already served with distinction as physician and surgeon for forty-six years in the British Army.[14]

Writing in the context of the Second Wave of the women's movement, with its political campaigns for workplace equality, its historical reconstruction of women's history and its ideological critique of 'woman' as a category of oppression, Rose depicts Barry as a significant predecessor who proved that, 'given the opportunity, a woman could become the intellectual equal of a man'.[15] While neither biographer adopts explicitly feminist methodologies or frameworks of analysis – Rae depicts an act of loyalty to the Governor of the Cape as a 'feminine action'[16] and Rose assumes that Barry 'almost certainly . . . must have sometimes longed to be a private person, a woman able to express her femininity'[17] – both reclaim Barry for a history of women. The assumption that Barry 'exchanged skirts for breeches'[18] in order to realise his ambition to enter the medical profession is one which is cited in Holmes's more recent biography, where she suggests 'the bondage and trappings of petticoats' were exchanged for 'education, the self-sufficiency of a profession, and liberty of mind'.[19] In her influential study *Vested Interests: Cross-Dressing and Cultural Anxiety* (1992), Marjorie Garber places Barry in the company of 'dozens, probably hundreds, of such stories of lifelong cross-dressers whose "true" gender identities were disclosed only after death'.[20] Julie Wheelwright similarly attributes this mode of gender expression to a strategic motivation in her cultural history of women's military gender crossing, *Amazons and Military Maids*, describing Barry as 'a woman who cross-dressed to graduate from the University of Edinburgh's medical school in 1812'.[21] While the dramatic impact of Rae's, Rose's and Holmes's biographical narratives is premised on the exceptional nature of Barry's life, Wheelwright incorporates his life story into a much larger historical narrative, mobilising a feminist narrative of female-to-male gender crossing as subversive and empowering. As Wheelwright explains, women's historic gender crossing has been understood as a means to 'gain access to male social privileges, to escape poverty by entering a male occupation, to travel safely or to avoid an arranged marriage'.[22] The progressive counter-narratives constructed by Rae and Rose – which have significantly influenced subsequent reconstructions of Barry's life – seek to reinstate some dignity, credibility and historical accuracy to a life arguably travestied and trivialised in popular memory and fiction. They successfully restore Barry to visibility in public life but not as the man who served with fellow officers and socialised with their wives and families, but as a woman. The possibility of a transgender life is obscured by the emancipatory feminist narrative of a gender-crossing woman. In this way, Rae's and Rose's biographies are symptomatic of one of the dominant twentieth-century strategies for reading the lives of transgender people thought to have been assigned female at birth. While Barry is exonerated of accusations of 'deception, dishonesty, and fraud' through reference to a noble and progressive motivation, his life as a man is retrospectively 'dismantled' and 'reassembled'[23] as the life of a masquerading woman.

In her 2005 book *The Woman's Historical Novel*, Diana Wallace notes that the cross-dressed heroine has been a recurring motif in women's historical fiction:

> The motif of masquerade, especially of a girl dressing in a boy's clothing, is a recurring one in women's historical novels and it connects in an especially suggestive way to feminist theories of gendered subjectivity as socially, culturally and, above all, historically constructed.[24]

In *James Miranda Barry*, Duncker's use of the first-person narrative grants the reader unique imaginative access to Barry's interiority. However, it is notable that this access is not employed to disclose the kind of strategic motivation which classic feminist readings of gender crossing imagine. In refusing to deliver such an 'explanation' Duncker can be understood as departing from some of the dominant conventions of narrative representations of gender crossing, which depict it as a mystery to be solved or an aberration to be explained. In this way, Duncker's novel resists a reductive reading of Barry's life and in some ways preserves – rather than forecloses – its narrative possibilities. However, what is just as striking in Duncker's narrative is its treatment of authorship and agency: namely, the way in which Barry's gender identity is authored by others to the effect that his gender expression is emptied of personal agency. The following two sections will explore Duncker's treatment of two key motifs in biographical accounts of Barry's life: the purported role of powerful male patrons in enabling his life as a man and the contribution of a working-class woman in originating the legend of his concealed sexed identity. In both cases Duncker introduces a powerful female character as a source of dramatic agency, a strategy which has two principal effects: reviving feminist narratives of gender crossing in displaced form while simultaneously depriving Barry of agency in relation to his own gender identity.

Being a Boy Forever: Rewriting Childhood in *James Miranda Barry*

Barry's early childhood until his enrolment at Edinburgh University in 1809 remains beyond the historical record. Born in an era predating the civil registration of births (1837 in England and 1864 in Ireland), Barry's date of birth is itself contested, with Rae and Rose opting for 1799 but Holmes locating it between 1790 and 1795. In a formal letter to General Francisco de Miranda written as a student in 1810, Barry refers to James Barry as his uncle, to a 'Mrs Bulkley' (generally thought to be his mother) as an aunt and to himself as a 'nephew'.[25] In her 1977 biography Rose provides some further family context, in the form of Mrs Bulkley's journey from Cork, on the south west coast of Ireland, to London to seek support from her artist brother for herself and her two daughters, fifteen-year-old Margaret and an unnamed younger child. In 2002 Holmes further elaborates on Mrs Bulkley's plight, explaining that she and her husband had been made destitute as a consequence of their efforts to free their eldest son from his debts. Remaining close to their historical sources, Barry's biographers do not attempt to imagine his unrecorded childhood in Ireland and England. By contrast – and in a bold departure made possible by the licence of historical fiction – Duncker places very considerable emphasis on Barry's childhood. In her 1999 novel Barry is the only child of Mary Ann, a widow who is the long-term lover of the General as well as an artist's model (and possible lover) to her brother James Barry and recipient of the hospitality of David Steuart Erskine, the Earl of Buchan. Erskine's home is relocated in Duncker's novel from Dryburgh in the Scottish Borders to Shropshire, where it plays host to radical political sympathies, unorthodox sexual arrangements and eccentric personalities. In this liberal and permissive atmosphere Barry and his mother enjoy class privileges through association with their wealthy patrons. Pivotal scenes in Barry's childhood take place in Erskine's residence, a location in which key characters can plausibly be gathered and a milieu in which gender norms are suspended without penalty. It is here that Barry benefits from a classical education of the kind usually reserved for boys; privately tutored by Francisco in his extensive library, he learns Italian, French and Latin, studies mathematics, history and botany, and reads Rousseau, Voltaire and Milton. Indeed, there is a marked degree of indeterminacy in how Barry's sex and gender are both perceived by others and experienced by himself during his sojourns at Erskine's residence. First introduced to the household as an infant, when Barry returns to Erskine's country house as an older child he habitually wears a 'vest and short trousers'[26] and his own mother refers to him as 'he'[27] on occasion, if not consistently. The mistress of the houses observes that '"You've grown into something quite different from what I expected"'[28] but there is no sense of censure or disapproval in her comment. Barry's own sense of gender identity seems principally informed by a desire to continue to enjoy his current freedoms and an understanding that this liberty would be curtailed should he become a woman in adulthood. When one of Erskine's servants reminisces about hearing 'the most famous castrati of his age'[29] (presumably the eighteenth-century singer Farinelli, reputed to have cured King Philip V of Spain of melancholy), Barry articulates a revealing identification:

> He explained to me in great detail what a castrato was. It sounded wonderful. You were specially chosen, then you remained a boy forever with a voice borrowed from God and became famous, fat and rich. You never turned into a woman, nor did you die in childbirth.[30]

The idea that a castrato – a person defined by the surgical removal of some of the signifiers of the male sex – could evade 'turning into a woman' suggests that a causal relationship between sex and gender is not fixed in this child's mind. Moreover, gendered identity for adult women is equated with reproductive sexuality and hence 'remain[ing] a boy forever'[31] seems to be posited as a means of escaping its sometimes fatal consequences. The analogy with the castrato suggestively implies a desire for a social masculinity which is not defined by sex. Elsewhere, the child Barry smarts when his gender is misread but struggles to find the language to express his sense of self in his own terms. In his first encounter with Alice Jones, a young kitchen maid in Erskine's household, she gives uninhibited voice to the speculation which attends his paternity by asking if he is James Barry's 'natural son'.[32]

> I flushed bright red with embarrassment and shouted, 'It's not true. My father's dead. He died before you or I were born. And now we live with the General and I'm not a son.'
> I hesitated. I had never been dressed as daughters usually were and was therefore swaying in limbo between the safe worlds of either sweet ribbons or breeches.[33]

Barry passionately rejects the social slight implied by not only illegitimacy but illegitimacy born of incest, a subject he has already sought reassurance on from his mother. However, his discomfort with the denomination 'son', and admission that he is not dressed as most daughters are, is a more qualified negotiation of gendered address: 'son' and 'daughter' are relational terms which privilege the binary identity designated at birth, but a person might be born a daughter and grow up to be a man. Barry's desire to be 'a boy forever' and his recognition that he is not a son suggest a sense of being at odds with gender norms which is later confirmed by his assertion that 'I felt myself to be outside every system'.[34] Duncker's depiction of Barry's desire to be 'a boy forever' powerfully suggests that his social identity as a man in adulthood might be understood to be an expression of his own gender identification, rather than a strategic subterfuge as implied by feminist narratives of women's gender crossing. However, this potential narrative of transgender agency is quickly overtaken by competing narratives of 'authorship' which attribute the origins of his gender identity to other agents.

A recurring theme in speculative and anecdotal accounts of Barry's life, including those published by Dickens and Twain, is the imagined role of unidentified but powerful patrons in his professional career. Both Dickens and Twain contribute to the popular deduction that a public figure without the advantage of birth or name must have enjoyed the patronage and protection of interested parties, especially given his widely recorded conflicts with military and colonial authority. This theme is taken up by Barry's earliest biographers who transform the suspicion of a hidden and perhaps undeserved influence into a kind of enlightened conspiracy. When Barry submitted his thesis to the University of Edinburgh in 1812 it bore a dedication to General Francisco de Miranda (1750–1816), an exiled Venezuelan revolutionary, and David Steuart Erskine, 11th Earl of Buchan (1742–1829), a Scottish antiquarian and political reformer. Both were in turn patrons of James Barry (1742–1806), the Irish neoclassical and proto-Romantic painter who was Barry's maternal uncle. Rae identifies James Barry and Francisco as advocates of women's education, who

> held strong views not only on the value of education, but on the value of female education, the artist being sufficiently advanced to be a follower of Mary Wollstonecraft and to express the belief that women should be the 'well instructed companions and confidential associates of man'.[35]

Rose attributes similar sentiments to Erskine, who is quoted as observing that '"[t]he men of Europe have crushed the heads of women in their infancy and then laugh at them because their brains are not so well ordered as they desire"'.[36] Indeed, Rose asserts that Erskine and Francisco's support for James Barry extended to his sister's child: 'They had decided that Mary Anne Bulkley's younger daughter, whose outstanding intellectual abilities were by now obvious, should have an education worthy of her.'[37] Rose depicts James Barry and Francisco acting in concert with their associate, Dr Fryer, but Duncker – and Holmes after her – incorporates James Barry himself into the conspiratorial trio. Indeed, Holmes attributes not only his name – James Miranda Barry – but a campaigning vocation for enlightened reform to his triple paternity: 'Fostered by a romantic painter, a progressive aristocrat, and a revolutionary, James Barry was cultivated into a radical tradition.'[38]

Duncker's novel seems to follow Rae's and Rose's lead in its depiction of Barry's gender identity as the outcome of a progressive plot, of which Barry is the intended beneficiary. At the climax of Part One of *James Miranda Barry*, the child Barry is taken late at night to the heart of an ornamental maze which appends Erskine's family home where he and his mother are guests; here he finds a 'triumvirate of cigars'[39] – namely, James Barry, Erskine and Francisco – looking 'very powerful and very drunk'.[40] Barry's gender identity is quite explicitly authored by these three men in an action in which progressive philanthropy and personal hubris are uneasily combined; their agency is stamped in his new name as he is conscripted into their gender:

> 'From now on you're going to be a boy. And then a man. Your uncle and I are giving you our names. And David's volunteered to be your patron and your guardian.'
> David Erskine laughed hoarsely. It was a wonderful idea. A trick, a masquerade. A joke against the world. . . .
> 'Welcome aboard, James Miranda Barry. You'd be wasted as a woman. Join the men.' Then they all laughed.[41]

This scenario would seem to sit rather uneasily within a feminist narrative of women's gender crossing; while the plot is hatched in defiance of conventions which deny women access to education and the professions, it is nevertheless enabled by male social and economic privilege. However, in Duncker's narrative a plot revelation later identifies Barry's mother, Mary Ann, as the originator of the conspiracy, employing her influence over the men in her life to engineer a radical change in her child's fortunes. After Mary Ann's death

Francisco reveals her role to the adult Barry: "'She was the source of the plot, soldier. It was her idea. She was the woman who held all the cards and the dice. She set the rules of the game. It was a game worth playing, don't you think so soldier?'"[42] In this way, female agency is restored, but Barry is revealed as the vehicle through which Mary Ann vicariously realises her own thwarted aspirations. The experience which has motivated Mary Ann's pivotal intervention in her child's gender identity is revealed in two ways: firstly, in coded form through the symbolic content of her brother's canvases, whose meaning is intuited but incompletely understood by Barry as a child, and secondly, after her death through the testimonies of her lover, Francisco, and her confidante, Louisa Erskine, Lord Buchan's sister.

As a child, Barry's perception of the gendered role which he seeks to escape is significantly shaped by his uncle and namesake James Barry, whose art is characterised by a preoccupation with culturally legitimated scenes of sexualised violence and whose intimate relationship with his sister, Barry's mother, has sinister undercurrents. The historical James Barry has been seen as an important precursor of Romanticism, not least in his rejection of patronage in favour of individual artistic freedom. However, while not artistically bound to the influence of a single patron he was nevertheless reliant on the support of advocates and friends. In Duncker's novel, Erskine's home serves as a gallery in which his work is exhibited and provides space for the studio in which it is produced. Barry's encounter with these canvases as a child seems to play a formative role in shaping his perception of the relationship between the sexes. The appearance of his mother's face in his uncle's paintings could be attributed to Barry's obsessive childhood love for his mother. However, it becomes clear that this presence has its origins in a relationship of ambiguous and disturbing sexuality; the implications of these symbolic narratives begin to reveal themselves, and the canvases that provide the backdrop to an apparently idyllic childhood of liberty and indulgence start to tell a different story. That story centres on Mary Ann and her position as the possible object of a complex economy of male favour, sexual access and economic support. Her role as her brother's model symbolises the ambiguities of agency at work in her position: an economic dependant whose only currency is her sexuality, she is enlisted to serve the fantasies of heterosexual men in such a way as to appear complicit in her own exploitation.

The mythology, literature and art of ancient Greece and Rome has played a pivotal role in shaping Western perceptions of the idea of changing sex or crossing gender, from Hermaphroditus to Tiresias.

However, these narratives of desire, enchantment and metamorphosis are not the subject of James Barry's canvases, which seem more concerned with epic motifs to do with the role of power, violence and sexuality in the founding of civilisations. Barry's *Jupiter Beguiled by Juno on Mount Ida* (1790–9) appears on the staircase of Erskine's country home in Duncker's novel where the sheer scale of these 'giants on Olympus' terrifies the three-year-old Barry, who sees Francisco and his mother embodied in 'two solid masses of pink and gold' and transformed into 'monsters'.[43] When Barry requests the story of the 'picture on the staircase',[44] his mother's lover Francisco attempts to mitigate the horror of the scene it portrays by depicting Juno as the seducer of Jupiter, 'playing a very clever game'[45] in order to achieve a political and military end to a conflict triggered by the abduction of Helen of Troy. However, Francisco initially mistakes Barry's request as a reference to another painting and informs him: '"You're not old enough for The Rape of Lucrece."'[46] The content of this narrative is more typical of Barry's canvases than the story of triumphant female cunning which Francisco seeks to tell. Indeed, when a young Barry pays an uninvited visit to his uncle's studio he is engaged in a painting of the rape of the Sabine women, a topic which seems symptomatic of his uncle's view of the fate of women. The seizure of the Sabine women by the founding fathers of Rome establishes the violent assertion of men's sexual access to women as an enabling myth for the history of Rome. Indeed, when asked by Barry to explain what rape is, he replies: '"All societies are based on the seizure, slaughter and slavery of women, child. You ask your mother."'[47] Returning to this theme, he claims: '"I made her what she is, child. But I never made her a whore. She did that all by herself."'[48] James Barry's vicious words position Mary Ann both as a victim of sexual objectification and violence and as a morally culpable woman complicit in her own exploitation. The possibility that Mary Ann might exercise control over her own reproductive sexuality is imagined by James Barry in terms which could only be deeply hurtful to his child audience: '"Always finds a way out, your mother does. Surprised she got caught pregnant with you, really. Or that she didn't put paid to you with pointed twigs or by swallowing cockroaches."'[49] The force of James Barry's words and the sexualised nature of his language suggest an attitude of propriety to his sister's body. Indeed, his possessive impulse towards Mary Ann is expressed in open rivalry with his sister's child, whom he declares a '"jealous little bastard"',[50] boxing his ears and holding him by his belt over an open fire. Barry's identification of his mother and Francisco in his uncle's canvases seems prompted by a child's intuition that there is a connection between the apparent struggle he had inadvertently witnessed as an infant in a scene of sexual intimacy between them ('I love her. And he is killing her'[51]) and his uncle's depiction of heterosexual desire as a battle for power. However, the revelation that his mother has served as a life model for her brother's art – and that she continues to do so – serves to suggest an unsettling proximity between life and art: 'Then, unclothed, but perfectly at ease, as graceful as if she were entering a ballroom, the woman walked across the floor and stood beside James Barry. . . . It was my mother.'[52] By the time the older Barry recalls his uncle's rendering of the myth of Vertumnus and Pomona, in which a 'seduction' achieved through dissimulation can be read as an act of sexual violence, the relationship between the women depicted in his uncle's art and his mother's experiences has become firmly forged: 'I remember the woman's face, my mother's face, open-mouthed in fear, confronting the satyr's treacherous, leering grin.'[53] The 'classical rapes'[54] with which James Barry seems so preoccupied implicitly posit women's experiences of male violence and sexual exploitation as the driving force behind a narrative of gender crossing in which a mother's desire for freedom is acted out vicariously through her child.

The passion with which Mary Ann expresses her aversion to the prospect of marriage as her child's fate combines with other narrative hints to suggest that this conviction may be rooted in personal experience: 'Mrs Booth said that there were only two authorities to whom women were accountable: God and their husbands. I repeated this. My beloved exploded. "You must never marry! Never! I forbid it."'[55] It is only after Mary Ann's death that the deep feeling underlying this injunction is explained, when Barry seeks out his mother's lover, General Francisco de Miranda, and her friend Louisa Erskine (Lord Buchan's sister) in an attempt to reconcile himself with a once beloved mother from whose memory he has become estranged. Louisa is depicted as an accomplice and ally in Mary Ann's ambitions for her child, moving with Barry and his mother to Edinburgh when he takes up his place at medical school. It is Louisa who reveals that Mary Ann's husband was a 'drunken' and 'abusive' man who 'wanted her to be his private possession'.[56] The theme of women as men's property is echoed in Mary Ann's own words, as recalled by Francisco after her death. Mary Ann and Francisco spend their final years together in the West Indies, where their residence is within sight of the trading blocks of a slave port. This prompts Mary Ann to draw a provocative analogy, as recounted by Francisco: '"I could not imagine being owned ... when I said as much to Mary Ann she declared that women's bodies are always for sale, to the highest bidder. But that only harlots manage to keep the cash.'"[57] When Francisco discloses Mary Ann's motives to Barry after her death it becomes clear that his mother was compelled by a desire to remove her child from the market of sexual exchange to which she felt herself captive:

> "'I was always a man's possession. Even yours. That's why I asked you [Francisco] to do it. You were the three men I had every right to command. I asked you to give my child the life I never had. My child has a position in the world. She will be respected, remembered. My child will have the freedom I never enjoyed.'"[58]

However, Louisa's insistence on Mary Ann's role as the instigator of the plot ostensibly undertaken by the 'triumvirate of cigars' uneasily implies that the child Barry has himself become incorporated into a kind of sexual economy of favour and patronage, in which he figures as a symbolic substitute for his mother's sexualised body:

> 'She loved two men, James. My brother and Francisco de Miranda. But they all loved you. David's opinions of the education of women were very advanced for the times. It's true that he had always wanted a son. But he didn't want you to be wasted. So they decided to share you too, as they shared Mary Ann, and to invest in you together.'[59]

In Duncker's novel, the revelation that a woman Barry loves has served as model – and possibly more – for his predatory uncle occurs not once but twice. Like Mary Ann before her, Barry's childhood sweetheart, Alice Jones, is discovered in James Barry's canvases. However, where Mary Ann seems symbolically and materially trapped in baleful narratives of women's sexual exploitation, Alice's access to James Barry's studio serves to launch her path towards fame and success as a professional performer on the popular stage. In Duncker's novel Alice's life and art emulate a comic dramatic structure, in which a low-born heroine defies social disadvantage through wit and cunning to achieve wealth and fame. Alice, like Mary Ann, is deeply invested in Barry's gender transformation and in these two characters the feminist narrative of women's gender crossing is not only displaced but doubled. If Mary Ann's tragic narrative testifies to the sexual oppression and individual alienation which women have historically struggled to escape, Alice's represents the comic triumph of subversive defiance over gender and class hierarchies. Both women appropriate the narrative of James Miranda Barry's life but in different ways. If Mary Ann provides the motive to animate an enlightened conspiracy of powerful men then Alice provides the meaning to make sense of Barry's experience. However, as a consequence Barry himself is reduced to a vehicle for the desires of others, his gender identity not an expression of his own agency but a channel through which other women's narratives can be acted out.

Playing the Breeches Part: Posthumous Performances

Biographical accounts of James Miranda Barry's life routinely attribute the 'truth' of his sex to a posthumous revelation. However, the source of this disclosure was not a figure of medical authority. Indeed, no post-mortem was undertaken following Barry's death and hence no medical record exists testifying to his sexed identity. Rather it is the reported eyewitness testimony of a female domestic servant, engaged in the act of preparing Barry's corpse for burial, which forms the basis of this retrospective reversal of his gender identity. Her evidence was recorded in writing by Staff Surgeon Major D. R. McKinnon, who had originally signed the death certificate as male, and her statement is cited by Rae, Rose and Holmes in their respective biographies:

> 'She then said that she had examined the body and it was a perfect female and farther that there were marks of her having had a child when very young. I then enquired how you have formed this conclusion? The woman pointing to the lower part of her stomach, said, "From marks here, I am a married woman, and the mother of nine children. I ought to know."'[60]

In her later biography Rose identifies the servant as an Irishwoman, Sophia Bishop, and Holmes puts her testimony in the context of the working woman's pursuit of an unpaid fee. The role of a migrant working-class woman in 'authoring' James Miranda Barry's sex testifies to an era in which the vernacular knowledge and expertise of mature women in relation to the female body had yet to be overruled. Barry's biographers have been intrigued by evidence that he studied dissection and midwifery at Edinburgh (the latter under Dr James Hamilton, an advocate of female midwives), practices which were not formally examined and whose status in legitimate medical practice and education was not yet assured. Indeed, Holmes observes that the mid eighteenth century saw the emergence of the 'man-midwife' and the beginnings of a 'fight for territorial rights over the reproductive female anatomy [which] became one of the longest-running medical conflicts in history'.[61] However, in this instance Bishop's authority is guaranteed by her experience of maternity which empowers her to act as an arbiter of sexed and gendered identity in pivotal moments such as birth and death. Bishop has the last word on Barry's sex, setting in motion a narrative by which he will be known posthumously. Indeed, Rae defers to her non-expert judgement as incontrovertible: 'She gave proofs, which appear physiologically correct and irrefutable, for this statement, and I accept it as the final answer.'[62] The unexpected power with which a working-class woman is invested is taken up in a playful and provocative way by Duncker through the creation of a character – Alice Jones – who has no apparent origin in historical record but whose role in Barry's narrative mimics that of Bishop. Alice begins her working life as a servant in Erskine's household, and her childhood friendship with Barry proves the catalyst for a rapid ascension to wealth and fame, fuelled by personal ambition and made possible by skill as an actor on the popular stage. Duncker's novel concludes with a revelation that sets in motion the historical rewriting of James Miranda Barry's gender identity, when Alice furnishes an American journalist, Miss Stackpole, with a 'marvellous narrative'[63] flagrantly at odds with the truth as she knows it:

> 'And not only was it the perfect body of a woman, Miss Stackpole, but a woman who had borne a child. Of this I am quite certain.'
> Alice had invented the stretch marks. She had them on her own belly and did not see why James should get away with being so handsomely preserved at nearly seventy.[64]

At this point, James Miranda Barry's narrative passes decisively into Alice's hands as a 'revelatory angel'[65] who exchanges her storytelling flair as a 'professional performer' in return for the 'highest possible price'.[66] Alice's cavalier attitude to the truth and irreverent treatment of the reputation of a devoted friend is in keeping with the comic and subversive register in which her character is presented and can be aligned with the postmodern sensibility with which the novel approaches the writing of history. However, her role in 'authoring' the life of James Miranda Barry in Duncker's novel is also indicative of the ways in which feminist narratives of women's gender crossing can have the effect – however inadvertently – of erasing transgender narratives. Moreover, Alice's authorship of Barry's gender identity in Duncker's novel extends significantly beyond her posthumous pronouncements.

Barry's relationship with Alice drives the romantic plot of mutual attachment but unrequited desire which dominates Duncker's fictional account of Barry's life. Indeed, Barry's devotion to Alice is given as a possible motivation for his earliest acts of cross-dressing. When planning how to dress for a ball as a child, Barry gives his desire to partner Alice as his motivation to wear trousers: "'I can't ask Alice if I don't wear trousers,' I protested. 'We'd be two girls.'"[67] However, Barry's first encounter with Alice reinforces the narrative of Barry as a person whose gender is authored by others and specifically by women. When Alice demands that the young Barry prove he is a girl he is at a loss to know how to do so. Impatient at the slowness of his response to her demand to see his genitals, Alice takes command and subjects him to an impromptu examination:

> she pushed my muddling fingers aside and thrust her hand down my pants. It was a most perturbing sensation. For a second she looked at me, puzzled and amazed, her fingers moving on an exploratory voyage between my legs. Then she burst out laughing, withdrew her hand and kissed me.[68]

The child servant of an unmarried mother here assumes the authority to adjudicate on Barry's sex; her authority has its origins in her knowledge of, and pride in, her own sexed identity as an adolescent female and mobilises the lay authority of reproductive women which professionalised medicine has historically sought to discredit or undermine. Hence, this most intimate form of self-knowledge is delivered by another and Barry's own understanding and experience of his sexed identity plays no further part in his narrative. Moreover, whereas Mary Ann's motives are only posthumously revealed to an adult Barry, Barry's childhood friend and lifelong love Alice is an open and enthusiastic champion of his cause, always ready to provide a narrative rationale for the life which Barry is living and articulating on his behalf the advantages which he will enjoy. When Barry returns to Erskine's country house from his studies in Edinburgh it is Alice who assumes the authorship of his life, projecting on to it her own aspirations and ambitions:

> Alice talked, invented, dreamed. And Barry clasped her version of the world to his breast, like a shipwrecked sailor. He felt that he had been locked up in a box. She made him understand the ways in which he had been set free.[69]

Alice is disadvantaged not only by gender but also by class and Barry's social privilege becomes the channel through which she plots her escape, in the first instance by commandeering Barry to teach her to read and write. This desire is given a history and heritage in the form of Alice's mother, a woman without literacy who champions both her daughter's and Barry's education. When Barry equivocates in response to the question of whether his unofficial stepfather (Francisco) will continue his education, Alice's mother adeptly appropriates discourses of gendered entitlement in the name of female education:

> Suddenly she blazed up and spoke very sharply. 'Your mother must insist upon it. You're dressed up like his son, not his daughter. You can claim a son's privilege.'
> She spoke with the same passion, the same gestures, Alice had when she asked me to teach her to read.[70]

Hence, Alice's desire for literacy is rooted in a history of female and working-class disenfranchisement and Barry becomes the vehicle through which these injustices can be redressed. Alice is impatient with Barry's doubts about his own identity and insistent on the power of social position: '"You are who the world says you are. And the world says you're a man."'[71] It is Alice who asserts Barry's gender identity without equivocation:

> 'Look, when we first met I wanted to know what you were, because I wasn't certain. But now I am. Now you're really a man. Soon you'll be a real doctor. You can be a gentleman. Last year was a game. It isn't a game anymore. Now it's the real thing. Games are all finished.'[72]

Significantly, Alice's ambition to act can be dated to Barry's faltering attempts to articulate his discomfort with the plot hatched by his patrons. When Barry discloses that '"it's like being two people"', one '"out there"' and the other '"crouching underneath, all tensed up, waiting to spring"',[73] Alice interjects: '"Now that's what I've always wanted to do. Act in a real theatre. Not just charades. Dress up like a lady. Or be a soldier."'[74] Barry's anguished sense of a divided self is transformed by Alice into a licence for liberty. A key scene in the novel occurs when Erskine's household elects to stage scenes from Shakespeare to mark James Barry's departure. The initial plan is to perform the last act of *A Midsummer Night's Dream*, with 'the boy'[75] – that is, Barry – in the role of Robin Goodfellow. However, when

Barry makes his appearance in costume and begins to recite his lines it becomes apparent that this casting was misguided:

> As soon as all eyes were fixed upon his tiny pallid face and open mouth and once the assembled household, radiant with expectation, leaned forwards to hear him, he was metamorphosed into a wooden mannikin, whose clockwork innards were on the brink of extinction.[76]

In the face of an audience, Barry is found wanting: he becomes uncanny, imitative and inauthentic. Instead, Alice is enlisted to play the cross-dressed heroine Rosalind, from Shakespeare's *As You Like It*, to Barry's largely mute Orlando:

> The household was bewitched. O Alice, thou art translated. A glamorous boy looked her public in the eye, tweaked the nose of her plain little coz . . . Barry, languishing on moss, was merely a foil, an occasion for this boy-girl's barefaced offering of sex to every member of the audience . . .[77]

In *Vested Interests* Marjorie Garber observes that 'Shakespeare's cross-dressing female characters were often seen in the early years of feminist criticism as role models for modern (and postmodern) women'.[78] Moreover, she notes the particular recurrence of allusions to Rosalind, a character who (unlike Viola) returns to the stage dressed as a woman. Garber suggests that '"Rosalind" appears, in fact, in a surprising number of modern texts as a kind of shorthand for the cross-dressed woman, or the enigma that she represents'.[79] Theatrical motifs feature prominently in Duncker's novel, from the domestic dramatic entertainments staged in English country houses and colonial mansions, to the professional theatres of Edinburgh and London and the popular performances by travelling players in the pleasure grounds of Greenwich Fair. Alice's career as a celebrated performer – whether as an artist's model, stage actor or spirit medium – provides the narrative thread which links many of these scenes. It is not in the legitimate theatre that the adult Barry, returned to England from an overseas posting, discovers Alice pursuing her ambition but amidst the heavily painted travelling players who perform melodramas, pantomimes and comic songs for the entertainment of fair-going crowds. When Alice plays Cassandra in an ensemble production depicting the siege of Troy and the massacre of Hecuba and her children, the topic echoes James Barry's taste for classical slaughter. However, it is in a breeches part that Alice takes centre stage, performing love songs as Viola from *Twelfth Night*: 'A gasp goes up. Her tunic clings tight to her bosom and her fine legs are displayed for all the world to see. Natural and at ease in her buckskin boots.'[80] Alice attempts to extend her rationalisation for her reliance on role-playing in her professional and personal life to Barry when she argues: '"You act out different roles. I've acted every minute of my life. I'm always on stage. We all are. It's all a performance . . . We're on stage now. This is it. And you got the breeches part, James."'[81] However, the prominence of metaphors of theatricality, role-playing and disguise in this narrative is potentially troubling given that these same motifs have often been used to challenge the authenticity of the transgender subject and to forcefully reveal a sexed or gender identity as the hidden or concealed 'truth' of identity. Duncker's narrative does not expose Barry as a fraud or a fake but it does rely on the conceit of gender as theatrical performance to advance a narrative about women's gender identity; in doing so it arguably reduces Barry's gender identity to little more than a mask behind which the faces of his mother, Mary Ann, and childhood sweetheart, Alice, are concealed. When Alice absconds with a jewellery box belonging to the dying artist James Barry, Barry – now a medical student in Edinburgh – searches for her in the London theatres. While Alice herself is not found, one of the more comic and dashing performers in a Gothic drama of ill-fated passions seems to speak strongly of her presence. Mary Ann has noted that the play features a 'stunning breeches part'[82] and that the production will host the debut of a new actress; the 'loving friend' of the heroine, disguised as a woodcutter and sporting 'such shapely legs and such a daringly short green tunic', is 'the star of the evening, the real heroine'.[83] The same might be said of the role of Alice Jones in Duncker's novel; she appears in pivotal scenes in the 'breeches part' which ostensibly belong to Barry, and it is her desire and aspirations which animate the narrative and her presence (or absence) around which the drama revolves.

While Duncker is careful not to unequivocally claim James Miranda Barry for a feminist history of women's gender crossing, this narrative nevertheless returns in displaced form through the figures of Mary Ann and Alice Jones. Moreover, at pivotal moments in Barry's life, Mary Ann and Alice author his gender identity, appropriating it to serve their own ambitions. Despite Alice being his self-proclaimed champion in childhood, her role in the narrative effectively serves to contest, challenge or compromise Barry's lived gender identity in different ways in the novel. More fundamentally, her 'authorship' of Barry's sexed and gendered identity in life and after death – echoing the role of Sophia Bishop in biographical narratives – serves to reinforce the construction of reproductive heterosexuality as the defining criterion of authentic womanhood, one which empowers women to adjudicate on other people's gender status. One evident effect of interpretations of James Miranda Barry's life influenced by narratives of women's gender crossing is the foregrounding of gender as the defining category of identity. It can be observed that other constructions of identity have received much less attention in biographical and fictional accounts of his life: principally, those to do with 'race' in colonial contexts. James Miranda Barry's life took place in the theatre of empire; the final section of this chapter examines the metaphors, omissions and analogies which characterise the treatment of racial and colonial constructions of identity in reconstructions of Barry's life and career.

Whiteness, Race and Empire in Narratives of the Life of James Miranda Barry

In an essay on Christine Jorgensen, Susan Stryker argues that the post-war fame of this 'first global transsexual celebrity'[84] should be understood as a 'white (post)colonial phenomenon',[85] examining the 'processes through which her presence racializes others while rendering opaque her own racialisation'.[86] In other words, Stryker demonstrates how Jorgensen's whiteness was integral to her gender identity and in doing so makes visible an identity position whose universality has historically been granted the privilege of invisibility. Moreover, she explores the implications of this whiteness for those who are constructed as racial 'others'. From his posting to the Cape in 1816 until his retirement by the army on medical grounds in 1859 Barry lived much of his life abroad, from South Africa to the West Indies and Canada. Even when he did retire he elected to return to Jamaica (1860–1), visiting Josias Cloete, a man with whom he had fought a duel during his posting to the Cape. One of the most reproduced images of Barry is a photographic portrait taken in a studio in Jamaica in this period; Barry is depicted in formal civilian dress standing by a cane chair, one hand resting on the head of his seated pet dog Psyche and the other hooked at his hip. He is flanked by an unidentified man of colour, also formally dressed in a suit with a white scarf at his neck and a watch chain at his waistcoat. Both men stand, with Barry's age and health offset by the figure of his companion whose height, breadth and posture – his hands need no support – suggest greater vigour. Whether a former comrade in the army, manservant, friend or companion, the individual nicknamed 'Black John'[87] by the Victorian British press silently testifies to the integral role played by the British Empire in Barry's life. Often overlooked in a portrait whose ostensible subject is Barry, he represents those whose lives and histories are neither recorded nor told. In biographies and fictions of Barry's life a number of significant motifs emerge in relation to the depiction of the British Empire, the history of colonialism and slavery, and the politics of race; indeed, colonial subjects and spaces are often made to serve as metaphorical vehicles for Barry's experience, their own historical reality obscured or erased as a result.

The British Empire is repeatedly depicted, in biographical and fictional narratives of Barry's life, as an arena in which social mobility and professional advancement can be pursued, implicitly by white European men. For example, Rae draws attention to the 'promise of interesting professional experience in the maladies of Jamaica'[88] and Holmes observes that the Caribbean 'offered not merely escape but an opportunity for adventure and advancement of his knowledge of tropical medicine',[89] noting that Barry's posting to Jamaica had positioned him 'at the frontier of tropical medicine'.[90] Indeed, Barry's biographers attribute some of his greatest achievements to his modernising efforts in colonial contexts. These achievements were less to do with breakthroughs in medical science than with the management of populations – including soldiers, prisoners and lepers – subject to colonial administration. Whether as a laboratory of tropical medicine or a scene for social experiment, the Empire becomes a space in which knowledge and power can be exercised by British subjects empowered by race and gender. Barry's biographers – whether in fiction or non-fiction – depict him as a progressive thinker, radical reformer and champion of the oppressed while all the time serving as an agent of Empire. Rose depicts Barry as an active reformer motivated by a sense of sympathetic solidarity with other oppressed or marginalised groups: 'this small and curious person raised the standards of medicine and touched the public conscience about the condition of the most degraded members of society – the prisoners, the pauper, the blacks and the lunatics – wherever she went.'[91] Barry's reputation as a radical sympathiser is illustrated with reference to individual acts of defiance or charity throughout his career: in the Cape, disputing a post-mortem which declared that a slave owned by Dr Robert Shand of Aberdeen who had been flogged to death had died of bulimia; in Jamaica, purchasing the freedom of two slaves, Sanna, who was reputed to be a hermaphrodite, and Hermes, who became a servant in the household of the abolitionist Sir Jahleel Benton; in St Helena, hiring a 'respectable woman of colour'[92] as a Matron to attend to female patients. When the inequalities and oppressions of Empire are acknowledged they serve to provide biographers and novelists with categories of people with which to compare Barry's position: in other words, analogies of oppression between race and gender are mobilised to make sense of Barry's position.

Duncker's treatment of James Miranda Barry's historical role as an agent of Empire has three notable features: firstly, an emphasis on Englishness; secondly, the omission of Barry's posting in the Cape, arguably the most significant in his career; thirdly, its representation of the 1831 rebellion in Jamaica as a backdrop for Barry's personal despair. It is striking that four of the six parts of Duncker's dense and richly imagined historical novel are set in Britain, with lengthy narrative passages dedicated to scenes in Shropshire and London which represent imaginative departures from the historical record. It has already been noted that Duncker places particular emphasis on the least documented part of Barry's life: his childhood. It can also be observed that Barry's childhood takes place in locations and contexts which mobilise powerful and persistent ideas about Englishness, at the expense of both Barry's Irish heritage and Scottish education.[93] The possibility of an Irish childhood is not imagined in the novel and the reality of Barry's Irish heritage is only acknowledged in passing, and mostly in derogatory terms. The 'red'[94] hair which Barry and his uncle share draws repeated comment and might be seen as a coded allusion to Irish origin but is stereotypically associated with quick temper. In the closing stages of the novel when Barry attempts to suggest a different way of expressing his gender, Alice briskly dismisses his suggestion: '"Are you out of your senses? Do you think that your pension would be paid to some nameless Irish woman who'd hoodwinked the army all her life?"'[95] This is the first time in the novel that Barry has been explicitly identified as Irish and it seems clear that his nationality might be a source of disqualification as much as his sex. The erasure of Barry's Irish heritage is also an erasure of a colonial history and instead Barry is placed at the heart of a very specific mythology of Englishness. The Earl of Buchan's home is relocated from Dryburgh Abbey in the Scottish Borders to a rural Shropshire redolent with rural and class signifiers of Englishness; the idyllic summers which Barry spends at his patron's country house serve to establish key signifiers of national identity against which Barry's future travels are tested. As a powerful and persistent symbol of Englishness the country house forges close connections between national identity, inherited wealth, class hierarchy and agrarian landscapes. The neoclassical design of Erskine's home and gardens extends to the depiction of social relations between the landed gentry and the working poor; labour and poverty are not prominently depicted but rather the working people appear principally as actors in a vision of social harmony and bucolic pleasures. The fact that the house serves as a refuge for political exiles and artists further acts to promote an idea of Englishness which is equated with traditions of liberty and tolerance. By contrast, even Edinburgh – whose reputation as the Athens of the North is strongly evoked by Barry's biographers[96] – is depicted as a place of chilly exile whose 'clear, hard, and very cold'[97] air is in contrast to the endless 'extraordinary summer'[98] which seems to reign in Shropshire. Barry enrolled as a literary and medical student at the University of Edinburgh in 1809, an institution which had welcomed Sir Walter Scott and David Hume before him at a similarly tender age (both enrolled at the age of twelve). Edinburgh is an interesting choice for a student who is not Scottish by birth: the university was not subject to the Test Act and so admitted Catholics who would have been debarred from English universities. It is here that the motif of the 'ice-cold doctor'[99] with his hands which are 'always so cold', 'frosty'[100] and like 'chilled swabs'[101] is established, as if the Scottish air has imparted a chill which no amount of travel in warmer climates can remedy. Moreover, with the balance of the novel very markedly situated in England, it is striking that Barry's experiences in the Cape – his first posting, the scene of his professional elevation and witness to his most public and longstanding intimate attachment – are almost entirely omitted from the narrative.

Having passed an army medical board examination and enlisted as a hospital assistant in 1813, Barry was posted to the Cape in 1816 and was appointed Colonial Medical Inspector in 1821. During his term in the Cape Barry acquired a reputation as a progressive medical reformer, seeking to regulate the control of patent medicines and enacting improvements to the conditions in which both lepers and prisoners were confined. Rose suggests that Barry was pioneering 'preventive medicine'[102] before the term had been coined; hygiene, ventilation, drainage, the relief of overcrowding, diet and exercise all featured in his endeavours. This period was also marked by his close relationship with the incumbent Governor, Lord Somerset. Indeed, in 1824 the two men were subject to a libellous claim when a placard was displayed in a public place accusing them of an immoral relationship, namely sodomy. Where Barry's politics are thought to have been radical Somerset's were reactionary; the placard libel reflected, in satirical terms, public comment on the apparent intimacy between the two men, but may also have been intended as an intervention in the debate about press freedom, which Somerset was intent on suppressing. However, Barry's posting to the Cape is represented only indirectly in Duncker's novel, through the medium of anecdote and gossip, pertaining to the more colourful society legends rather than his medical career, and reported via indirect speech at Barry's arrival at his next posting. The location of this commission is never explicitly identified. Part Four of the novel is entitled 'The Colony' and while the references to Greek place and personal names might suggest that it should be identified as Corfu (where Barry served in the 1840s and 1850s) the title of this section seems to suggest that it is intended to serve as a generic representation of Barry's colonial postings. Barry is attended by a 'tiny, swarthy'[103] servant and causes outrage when he brings a 'half-caste hospital orderly'[104] to act as his second in a duel; it is clear that racial and colonial hierarchies are at work on this island, with its Turkish and Moorish influences, but in this European location the more starkly racialised dynamics of slavery are evaded and the narrative emphasis turns to the internal dynamics of the settler community – political, social, sexual and romantic – rather than the structural inequalities between colonising and colonised subjects. By contrast, these inequalities cannot be avoided in Part Five, which is set in Jamaica where Barry witnessed the 1831 slave rebellion led by Sam Sharpe, a Baptist preacher, and the brutal retribution which many enslaved people suffered after its suppression.

Interestingly, Jamaica is depicted more than once in Duncker's novel, including in Francisco's retrospective narrative embedded in Part Five. At first sight Jamaica is something of a paradise for Francisco and Mary Ann as they are able to live there openly as lovers, despite the existence of Francisco's wife and children elsewhere. Mary Ann's assured and 'fair-minded'[105] interaction with two 'inherited' female household servants – Immaculata and True Repose – and her ability to communicate without words with the 'giant freed slave'[106] who makes his living as a fisherman are offered as evidence of an instinctual spirit of equality. However, the site of the former slave market, which Francisco imagines witnessing from their 'front verandah',[107] prompts Mary Ann to expound on not racial but gender exploitation; she declares that 'women's bodies are always for sale',[108] using chattel slavery as an analogy for gender oppression and offering (white) women as the true victims of an ongoing injustice. Francisco explains that he was investigating the conditions of the slaves and bemoans the '"difficult[y]"' in '"find[ing] blacks who were willing to talk to me"'.[109] He reports that '"the prospect of emancipation made little difference"'[110] and that '"those whose old masters had been declared bankrupt were the most unfortunate"'.[111] Despite his revolutionary credentials, Francisco's words are suggestive of a paternalism which depicts the fate of former slaves as always mortgaged to white prosperity; his political disillusion is the prerogative of the powerful, a symptom of a sense of entitlement to act as an agent of historical change underlined by a sense of responsibility to redress its shortcomings. If Jamaica provides a very comfortable refuge for two social exiles from British society and a canvas for political philosophy, Barry himself presents it as a scene of utter personal misery: 'This is unhappiness.'[112] Part Six is the penultimate section of the novel, prior to Barry's reunion with Alice Jones in London. Its title – 'Tropics' – ascribes a climactic, rather than historical or political, character to the location of the action:

> Life is of little value here. The days too hot, too bright, the rain too rapid and powerful, the vegetation renews itself too rapidly. The tropics may resemble paradise, at a glance, from a great distance, but living here I can never rid my nostrils of the smell of putrefaction.[113]

Indeed, Barry claims to have been 'defeated' by the 'place' itself: 'this sweating humid bush, jiggers in the dust, white nights drenched in stars and the clinging yellow fever.'[114] Here Barry is placed in a specific tradition of colonial representations of the Caribbean, one driven by the craving for the '"wind fresh from Europe"'[115] which promises to bring '"purity"' and release for Rochester from his '"filthy burden"'[116] in Charlotte Brontë's 1848 novel *Jane Eyre*. The Caribbean is depicted as a place of degeneracy, disease and madness, and European civilisation prescribed as the antidote, rather than the cause, of it horrors. In Barry's Jamaica, plantation owners are 'indolent creatures',[117] including Edward Ellis (named after a famous family of plantation owners on the Montpelier Estate) whose deficiencies place him 'at the mercy' of his 'ruthless black servant'[118] Newton; wearing his former master's signet ring and carrying the keys to the armoury, Newton's competence is depicted as implicitly usurping his master's rightful inheritance. When Barry visits his mother's grave in Port Royal, children 'grinning like mad masks on All Hallows' desecrate Mary Ann's memory by pronouncing her a '"duppy woman"'.[119] Tending the sick child of one of 'these women' – '[t]he thing is dying'[120] – Barry is moved to disabuse the reader of any sentimental illusions: 'Don't forget, these people whom you serve sell their children too, sell them . . . as workers, prostitutes, servants.'[121] Barry's reforming spirit has given way to fatalism: 'If they live, they live. If they must die, then nothing I can do will save them.'[122] The ambiguous nature of the identity of 'these people' and the cause of their suffering in Barry's account suggests a slippage between a doctor's expression of despair in the face of overwhelming conditions and an abdication of responsibility with political overtones. Indeed, special contempt is reserved for those people whose existence blurs the boundaries between Europe and its '"filthy burden"',[123] with the spectre of miscegenation bringing with it sexualised discourses of moral and physical corruption: 'The Creoles were deeply inbred. Inherited diseases were rife within their families. The women were addicted to pleasure and demonstrated a loose sensuality that was shockingly overt.'[124] The novel nevertheless seeks to protect Barry's credentials as a political radical and natural sympathiser and this is achieved not through the evidence of his actions or express convictions but through the witness of other characters.

In the days leading up to the slave rebellion of 1831, members of the servant household concerned for Barry's safety seek reassurance that he will be absent from the plantation during the Christmas period when the mass withdrawal of labour is due to take place. When Barry encounters Jessica – the woman whose child he had buried – in the cane fields with other rebels her loyalty to him protects him from any possible harm from the 'black shadows'.[125] Moreover, she invites him to join the rebellion:

> They had justice on their side, if not the law . . . Jessica must have read my thoughts. She held the bay's bridle firmly and peered up into my face.
> 'Den come wid us, Doctor.'
> 'I will tend the wounded of both sides, Jessica. Both sides. And I urge you to spare as many lives as possible. A man's life lost is the only thing he can never regain.'[126]

Barry's lofty and didactic response places him in a position above politics, a position not available to those who are not privileged by race. Duncker's ingenious response to the problem of squaring Barry's reputed abolitionist convictions with his role as an agent of Empire during a period of brutal suppression is one not available to the biographer since it is such a bold departure from historical plausibility, but Holmes's response to this same dilemma shares some similarities with Duncker's strategies. Like Rae and Rose before her, Holmes consistently portrays Barry as a 'champion of the socially marginalised and economically dispossessed'[127] in her biography. She grounds this assertion in the legacy of the 'humanitarian education bequeathed by his mentors'[128] but also attributes his commitment to a personal investment in the form of sympathetic identification: 'Barry always identified with the plight of the dispossessed.'[129] However, this presents a challenge when dramatising Barry's role in Jamaica at the time of the slave uprising. Holmes claims that his 'abolitionist views were well-known'[130] and she is fully alert to the paradoxes of his position: 'Pro-emancipation, Barry had gone into the field of battle to restore and protect the lives of soldiers whose job it was to destroy the lives and spirits of the slaves whose bid for freedom Barry so keenly understood.'[131] Holmes deals with this paradox by emphasising Barry's powerlessness rather than his agency: 'Barry was witness to cases of extreme brutality in which he had no power to intervene.'[132] If Barry's actions in the Caribbean do not quite live up to his image as a champion of the oppressed, the islands nevertheless offer metaphors which can be mined to fashion his life narrative in particular ways. Holmes depicts the Caribbean not only as a place of 'opportunity for adventure and advancement'[133] for agents of Empire but also as a place with a reputation for gender transgression. She prefaces her chapter on Barry's experience in Jamaica with a passage on piracy and its 'tradition of cross-dressing and effeminacy', arguing that 'the pirates of the Caribbean West Indies were famed for being dandies who adored ornate, satirical, unconventional dress'.[134] This nautical motif is extended to incorporate a popular history of female-to-male gender crossing: 'In the eighteenth century, cross-dressed female sailors, soldiers, warriors, and cabin boys were a favourite theme in the pages of broadsides, and celebrated in ballads and folk songs.'[135] In this way, the history of the Caribbean in the era of slavery is deployed as a trope in service to metaphors of gender. Elsewhere, Holmes refers to slavery more directly, quoting from Alexis de Tocqueville's observations on slavery in *Democracy in America* (1835): '"He remains halfway between . . . two communities, isolated between two races, sold by one, repulsed by the other; finding not a spot in the universe to call by the name of country, except the faint image of a home which the shelter of his master's roof affords."'[136] However, Holmes proposes an analogy which suggests an affinity between the condition of slavery and 'Barry's own condition of being halfway between'.[137] Indeed, it is as if the Caribbean and its enslaved populations are being employed to metaphorically foreshadow a revelation yet to come. Barry did not choose his postings to 'the islands of the Indian Ocean, the Atlantic, and the Mediterranean'[138] but Holmes interprets them as if they were expressive of a quality of his own identity: 'All of these islands were hybrid, creolised places. Barry liked his islands of indeterminacy.'[139] The geography and history of colonialism is appropriated as a metaphor for the life history of the transgender subject with tropes of migration and hybridity mobilised to convey by analogy the narrative of someone who is perceived (in rather contradictory fashion) both to have 'crossed' from one sexed or gendered category to another and to have assumed an identity which is not reducible to a single binary category. Indeed, the symbolic significance of Holmes's 'islands of indeterminacy'[140] is not fully revealed until the end of her biography, and I would like to end this chapter with a postscript which will serve as a bridge to the next.

Postscript – James Miranda Barry, Transgender Narratives and Intersex Lives

The possibility that the historical Barry may have been an intersex person is acknowledged by all three of the biographies examined in this chapter. When pressed by the Registrar General to respond to Sophia Bishop's claims that Barry was a woman, Staff Surgeon Major D. R. McKinnon, who attended Barry in his final illness, asserted that he had 'never had any suspicions that Dr Barry was a female' during their acquaintance in the West Indies and England but also that 'it was none of my business whether Dr Barry was a male or a female', going on to suggest that he may have been an 'imperfectly developed man'.[141] Expressing doubts about Bishop's motives, he proceeded to disclose his own personal impressions:

> 'The woman seemed to think that she had become acquainted with a great secret and wished to be paid for keeping it. I informed her that all Dr Barry's relatives were dead, and that it was no secret of mine, and that my own impression was that Dr Barry was a Hermaphrodite.
> 'But whether Dr Barry was male, female or hermaphrodite I do not know . . .'[142]

This possibility is also acknowledged early on in the narrative of Patricia Duncker's novel, when Alice Jones – like Sophia Bishop – adjudicates on Barry's sex following an intimate investigation: '"Well, you're a sort of girl I suppose. But definitely not like me. Perhaps you're a girl dressed up as a boy? Or a boy that's got enough girl for it not to matter too much either way."'[143] It is both ironic and typical that Alice later 'hotly denie[s]' the rumour initiated by the household cook 'that Barry was in fact a hermaphrodite'[144] given that she is the only person, other than Barry, to be in a position to confirm it.

However, when Alice assumes her role as 'author' of Barry's posthumous legend, the sexed identity which she elects to 'reveal' is unambiguously female.

For some of his biographers, the assertion that Barry was a 'hermaphrodite' and not a woman (the two are assumed to be incompatible) is seen as a ruse by which to entrench male privilege and deny female achievement. Rose is suspicious of this reading, describing the 'obsession with the specifically sexual identity' as 'typical of a common – and predominantly male – assumption that a woman by nature would have been incapable of sustaining the masquerade and attaining such professional prominence'.[145] In contrast to Rae's or Rose's much earlier works, Holmes's biography employs the male pronoun when referring to Barry; in this way it appears to accept Barry's lived gender identity in a style which is in keeping with more contemporary perspectives. However, the narrative dynamic of revelation which Holmes seems so conscientiously to avoid in her retelling of Barry's life is dramatically revived in the denouement of her biography, which concludes with the assertion not that Barry was 'really' a woman but that he was 'really' an intersex person. This revelation is foreshadowed by some carefully placed narrative insinuations: 'For Barry had secrets. Barry's secrets were of a nature that placed him beyond the understanding of the society in which he moved. They were also the secrets of the imposter.'[146] Holmes's biography is distinctive in its use of the techniques of creative non-fiction to imagine the life of her biographical subject. Through the insertion of narrative vignettes, often at the start of a chapter detailing a new stage in Barry's life, Holmes is able to introduce the reader to Barry as a character in the life she is reconstructing. For example, when Holmes imaginatively reconstructs a scene in which Barry works on his thesis in Lord Buchan's library at Dryburgh Abbey, he emerges sympathetically as an earnest young scholar working hard to vindicate the faith placed in him by others:

> James Barry sat writing, his back rounded over his desk like a question mark ... Absorbed in his thoughts, Barry was unaware of the figure framed by the full-length cheval mirror standing in the corner of the room; but if he had paused for self-reflection, he would have seen the very picture of a young nineteenth-century gentleman at study.[147]

However, there are metafictional motifs at work here and it is the authorial point of view which dominates: a privileged and ironic perspective is foregrounded and the 'question mark' which Barry's body unwittingly forms is one which only the author can discern. This is one of a number of embedded details which combine to suggest the presence of another narrative, and which activate in subtle fashion the dynamics of suspense and revelation. The Scottish Gothic is mobilised to full effect when Barry recalls his first dissection like a 'demonic dream' situated in a 'room of instruments and shadows, the temperature of a meat locker, somewhere between an artist's studio and a butcher's shop'.[148] In the climax of a vividly recreated scene, in which the 'chaotic topography' of the interior of the body is memorably visualised, Barry's encounter with the object of the exercise is charged with foreshadowed meaning:

> Barry's startled attention was drawn to the face of the corpse. Stripped of the animation of everyday life, it was a face unsexed. ... Barry was looking at the inverted mirror of a woman's body. A life anatomised. The scalpel cut a swath through the history of the corpse, revealing its physiological secrets to the students. Barry discovered things unknown to the woman during her recently ended life.[149]

The narrative motif of posthumous exposure which recurs in narratives of transgender lives is evoked in an indirect way in this scene. Indeed, at the climax of this biography, the desire to evade a similar exposure is suggested as the primary motivation for Barry's gender identification:

> From the point that Barry became aware that his body was a strangely sexed anomaly, he would have understood that he must hide himself in order to live a normal life, and not be turned into a medical freak. Safer by far to become a medic himself and hide behind the guise and growing professional authority of the scholar-gentleman-surgeon than run the risk of becoming a specimen, exposed to the curiosity of medical science. It was the perfect disguise.[150]

Despite the apparent acceptance of Barry's gender identity as a man at the outset of the biography, the narrative structure of revelation is fully mobilised at the end of the biography. The particular significance of the scene in which Barry works on his thesis becomes clear with hindsight when Holmes remarks upon the 'uncommon coincidence' that 'Barry, whose life turned out to be so ambiguous after his death, chose to write on the one condition that led most consistently to the discovery of an error of sex definition'.[151] Holmes observes that the diagnosis and treatment of hernias has played a 'key role in the drama of revelation'[152] and it is on this basis that she proceeds to read his medical thesis as autobiography: Barry becomes 'the unnamed subject of this startling document of the problems of sexual differentiation'.[153] The metaphor which Holmes uses to dramatise her own role as a writer in the arbitration of Barry's sexed and gendered identity is striking: 'As Barry's biographer . . . I felt like a midwife confronted by expectant parents who wanted the clear, incontrovertible answer to the question that accompanies the birth of all lives: is it a boy or a girl?'[154] This scene of medical adjudication has become a very charged one for intersex activists and theorists since it has often served as a prelude to 'corrective' cosmetic surgery on intersex infants, a practice which has been subject to extensive critique.[155] Instead of conducting a post-mortem over Barry's death, as the documented speculation following his demise invites us to do, Holmes positions herself as a key actor in his birth, mobilising the long history of lay expertise associated with this explicitly gendered profession, just as Sophia Bishop had done before her. Holmes's presumption that Barry's life constitutes a question which requires an answer is projected on to the reader and her elaborate narrative manipulations are attributed to the biographer's need to meet the expectations of the reader. While the imagining of this possibility presents an important departure from the biographical and fictional tradition of reading Barry as a gender-crossing woman, the narrative structure to which this possibility is subjected perpetuates the construction of the transgender life as 'double, duplicitous, deceptive',[156] to use Halberstam's words, and reinstates the biographer as the knowing subject who authors the transgender life retrospectively. Moreover, the presumption that Barry will be inevitably transformed into a 'medical freak . . . exposed to the curiosity of medical science'[157] is one which historians of the period have questioned. Some intersex people did make a living through exhibition in medical schools, including Gottlieb Göttlich (born 1798), whose audience included Sir Astley Cooper, one of Barry's tutors.[158] However, in *Doubting Sex: Inscriptions, Bodies and Selves in Nineteenth-Century Hermaphrodite Case Histories* (2012), Geertje Mak challenges the perception that an intersex person's life would inevitably be marked by encounters with the medical profession. Mak argues that prior to the advent of concepts of the sexed self at the turn of the twentieth century, 'the rationale of sex was primarily its being inscribed in the social, economic, moral and ultimately legal fabric of the community.'[159] Cases of 'doubtful sex', as she puts it, were only considered problematic if they presented a challenge to this social order; in the event of such a challenge a medical expert might be called upon as an expert witness but adjudication would reside with the courts and legal authority. Mak observes that 'in many cases of hermaphroditism until around the 1860s and 1870s, the initial response was not to disclose the sexual body to a physician in order to have it examined objectively',[160] acknowledging that in 'cases of publicly visible sexual ambiguity, the modern reader unfamiliar with medical history is surprised by the lack of urgency to have the body examined'.[161] Moreover, this was the era of 'bedside medicine' in which medical examination was limited to the external and visible aspects of the body; more intimate or internal contact with the naked body, especially the female body, was not considered within the proper realm of respectable medicine. The case studies which Mak analyses come from largely rural, rather than urban or industrial, communities and while tolerance of intersex people is not universal there is evidence of their integration as individuals: 'There might be something odd or idiosyncratic about them, but they were no threat to the social or moral order because they had more or less *grown into* the community in the way they had turned out to be' [emphasis in original].[162] In this context, I will conclude by returning to an eyewitness testimony published in *The Lancet* in 1895 by a Captain who had seen Barry in Trinidad in 1844: '"The impression and general belief was that he was a hermaphrodite and as such escaped much comment or observation in places where everyone was used to him."'[163] This account (which finds echoes in later testimonies by Billy Tipton's friends and family) punctures the anticipation of scandal or sensation which narratives of revelation seek to generate by depicting Barry as an individual integrated into a community, his identity impervious to posthumous revelations bringing 'news' that has no currency or purchase for those who knew him.

The complex relationship between transgender history, public memory and heritage practice is exemplified in the very different ways in which James Miranda Barry is remembered in twenty-first-century contexts. A commemorative plaque situated near Old College in the grounds of the University of Edinburgh honours Barry as an alumnus who is 'believed to be the first woman graduate of the University' and this interpretation is reinforced by the university's website, which (at the time of writing) describes his gender crossing as an act of 'deception' undertaken to overcome barriers to a medical career.[164] By contrast, in July 2017 Barry's grave in Kensal Green Cemetery, London, was relisted as part of Historic England's 'Pride of Place', a project which seeks to 'uncover new locations associated with England's LGBTQ past'.[165] The fiftieth anniversary of the partial decriminalisation of homosexuality in England and Wales provided the impetus for both 'Pride of Place' and the National Trust's 'Prejudice & Pride'[166] project which mark a significant turning point in the work of public bodies and charities charged with both conserving and promoting access to historical environments. In this way, the LGBT umbrella has served as a vehicle through which some historical figures with transgender potential can gain a renewed visibility (such as the soldier and diplomat the Chevalier d'Eon (1782–1810), who features in both campaigns). The relisting of Barry's grave acknowledges that his life might have meanings which exceed those recorded in the plaque which marks the location of his education; however, caught between historical frameworks which foreground either gendered or sexual categories of identity, neither narrative accommodates the possibility that Barry may also have been an intersex person. The competing claims to James Miranda Barry's memory in contemporary heritage practice point to the importance of a transgender historiography which acknowledges the particular challenges of interpreting the relationship between perceived acts of gender crossing and possible experiences of gender identification in changing historical contexts, while at the same time 'making visible, bringing into experience, [and] knowing'[167] the gender diversity of the past in all its variety and complexity.

Notes

1. Halberstam, 'Telling Tales: Brandon Teena, Billy Tipton, and Transgender Biography', in Sánchez and Schlossberg (eds), *Passing: Identity and Interpretation in Sexuality, Race, and Religion*, pp. 13–14.
2. Funke, 'Obscurity and Gender Resistance in Patricia Duncker's *James Miranda Barry*', p. 224.
3. Funke, 'Obscurity and Gender Resistance', p. 215.
4. Getsy, 'Capacity', *TSQ: Transgender Studies Quarterly Special Issue – Postposttranssexual*, p. 47.
5. Getsy, 'Capacity', p. 48.
6. Rawson, 'Archive', *Postposttranssexual*, p. 24.
7. 'A Mystery Still', *All the Year Round*, Volume XVII (18 May 1867), p. 493; Dickens Journals Online, <http://www.djo.org.uk/all-the-year-round.html> (last accessed 15 January 2018).
8. 'A Mystery Still', p. 492.
9. Some suggest that Barry was attending his close friend Lord Somerset in his illness, while others populate this absence with the pregnancy which Sophia Bishop attributed to him after his death.
10. Twain, *Following the Equator: A Journey around the World* (1897), Project Gutenberg, <http://www.gutenberg.org/files/2895/2895-h/2895-h.htm> (last accessed 15 January 2018).
11. Twain, *Following the Equator*.
12. See Holmes, *The Secret Life of Dr James Barry: Victorian England's Most Eminent Surgeon*, pp. 157–8.
13. Rae, *The Strange Story of Dr James Barry*, p. v.

14. Rose, *The Perfect Gentleman*, p. 12.
15. Rose, *Perfect Gentleman*, p. 27.
16. Rae, *Strange Story*, p. 63.
17. Rose, *Perfect Gentleman*, p. 102.
18. Rose, *Perfect Gentleman*, p. 21.
19. Holmes, *Secret Life*, p. 274.
20. Garber, *Vested Interests*, p. 67. Garber describes Barry as a 'famous lifelong female-to-male transvestite' (p. 288).
21. Wheelwright, *Amazons and Military Maids*, p. 69.
22. Wheelwright, *Amazons and Military Maids*, p. xii.
23. Halberstam, 'Telling Tales', pp. 13–14.
24. Wallace, *The Woman's Historical Novel: British Women Writers, 1900–2000*, p. 21.
25. Rae, *Strange Story*, p. 4; Rose, *Perfect Gentleman*, p. 24; Holmes, *Secret Life*, pp. 29–30. To avoid confusion, James Miranda Barry will be referred to as 'Barry', his uncle as 'James Barry' and General Francisco de Miranda as 'Francisco' (the usage employed in Duncker's novel).
26. Duncker, *James Miranda Barry*, p. 28.
27. Duncker, *James Miranda Barry*, p. 27.
28. Duncker, *James Miranda Barry*, p. 39.
29. Duncker, *James Miranda Barry*, p. 10.
30. Duncker, *James Miranda Barry*, pp. 10–11.
31. Duncker, *James Miranda Barry*, p. 11.
32. Duncker, *James Miranda Barry*, p. 35.
33. Duncker, *James Miranda Barry*, p. 35.
34. Duncker, *James Miranda Barry*, p. 48.
35. Rae, *Strange Story*, pp. 6–7.
36. Rose, *Perfect Gentleman*, p. 20.
37. Rose, *Perfect Gentleman*, p. 21.
38. Holmes, *Secret Life*, p. 33.
39. Duncker, *James Miranda Barry*, p. 59.
40. Duncker, *James Miranda Barry*, p. 60.
41. Duncker, *James Miranda Barry*, p. 60.
42. Duncker, *James Miranda Barry*, p. 277.
43. Duncker, *James Miranda Barry*, p. 11.
44. Duncker, *James Miranda Barry*, p. 12.
45. Duncker, *James Miranda Barry*, p. 3.
46. Duncker, *James Miranda Barry*, p. 2.
47. Duncker, *James Miranda Barry*, p. 31.
48. Duncker, *James Miranda Barry*, p. 33.
49. Duncker, *James Miranda Barry*, p. 32.
50. Duncker, *James Miranda Barry*, p. 17.
51. Duncker, *James Miranda Barry*, p. 6.
52. Duncker, *James Miranda Barry*, p. 47.
53. Duncker, *James Miranda Barry*, p. 352.
54. Duncker, *James Miranda Barry*, p. 331.
55. Duncker, *James Miranda Barry*, p. 25.

56. Duncker, *James Miranda Barry*, p. 345.
57. Duncker, *James Miranda Barry*, p. 268.
58. Duncker, *James Miranda Barry*, p. 277.
59. Duncker, *James Miranda Barry*, p. 349.
60. Rae, *Strange Story*, pp. 115–16. See also Rose, *Perfect Gentleman*, p. 13, and Holmes, *Secret Life*, pp. 243–4.
61. Holmes, *Secret Life*, p. 20.
62. Rae, *Strange Story*, p. vi.
63. Duncker, *James Miranda Barry*, p. 371.
64. Duncker, *James Miranda Barry*, p. 370.
65. Duncker, *James Miranda Barry*, p. 371.
66. Duncker, *James Miranda Barry*, p. 371.
67. Duncker, *James Miranda Barry*, p. 55.
68. Duncker, *James Miranda Barry*, p. 35.
69. Duncker, *James Miranda Barry*, p. 91.
70. Duncker, *James Miranda Barry*, p. 54.
71. Duncker, *James Miranda Barry*, p. 359.
72. Duncker, *James Miranda Barry*, p. 94.
73. Duncker, *James Miranda Barry*, p. 93.
74. Duncker, *James Miranda Barry*, p. 93.
75. Duncker, *James Miranda Barry*, p. 104.
76. Duncker, *James Miranda Barry*, p. 105.
77. Duncker, *James Miranda Barry*, p. 108.
78. Garber, *Vested Interests*, p. 72.
79. Garber, *Vested Interests*, p. 73.
80. Duncker, *James Miranda Barry*, p. 163.
81. Duncker, *James Miranda Barry*, p. 358.
82. Duncker, *James Miranda Barry*, p. 146.
83. Duncker, *James Miranda Barry*, p. 147.
84. Stryker, 'We Who Are Sexy: Christine Jorgensen's Transsexual Whiteness in the Postcolonial Philippines', p. 80.
85. Stryker, 'We Who Are Sexy', pp. 81–2.
86. Stryker, 'We Who Are Sexy', pp. 81–2.
87. See Holmes, *Secret Life*, pp. 235–6.
88. Rae, *Strange Story*, p. 66.
89. Holmes, *Secret Life*, p. 159.
90. Holmes, *Secret Life*, p. 177.
91. Rose, *Perfect Gentleman*, p. 120.
92. James Miranda Barry quoted in Rae, *Strange Story*, p. 73, and Holmes, *Secret Life*, p. 197.
93. Barry's Irish origin plays an important role in Sebastian Barry's reimagining of his encounter with Florence Nightingale in his stage play *Whistling Psyche*, in which the impact of famine on the people and landscape of his native Cork is depicted as a formative memory: 'And in that change I think I trace the beginnings of my true story. For necessary then to all Irish persons was subterfuge and subtle guiles, things not unknown to me now and long since' (p. 15).

94. Duncker, *James Miranda Barry*, pp. 61, 197, 353.
95. Duncker, *James Miranda Barry*, p. 357.
96. See Rae, *Strange Story*, p. 8, and Holmes, *Secret Life*, p. 15.
97. Duncker, *James Miranda Barry*, p. 69.
98. Duncker, *James Miranda Barry*, p. 92.
99. Duncker, *James Miranda Barry*, p. 236.
100. Duncker, *James Miranda Barry*, p. 83.
101. Duncker, *James Miranda Barry*, p. 115.
102. Rose, *Perfect Gentleman*, p. 41.
103. Duncker, *James Miranda Barry*, p. 183.
104. Duncker, *James Miranda Barry*, p. 217.
105. Duncker, *James Miranda Barry*, p. 270.
106. Duncker, *James Miranda Barry*, p. 271.
107. Duncker, *James Miranda Barry*, p. 268.
108. Duncker, *James Miranda Barry*, p. 268.
109. Duncker, *James Miranda Barry*, p. 273.
110. Duncker, *James Miranda Barry*, p. 273.
111. Duncker, *James Miranda Barry*, p. 273.
112. Duncker, *James Miranda Barry*, p. 281.
113. Duncker, *James Miranda Barry*, p. 284.
114. Duncker, *James Miranda Barry*, p. 282.
115. Brontë, *Jane Eyre*, p. 355.
116. Brontë, *Jane Eyre*, p. 356.
117. Duncker, *James Miranda Barry*, p. 295.
118. Duncker, *James Miranda Barry*, p. 295.
119. Duncker, *James Miranda Barry*, p. 299.
120. Duncker, *James Miranda Barry*, p. 281.
121. Duncker, *James Miranda Barry*, p. 282.
122. Duncker, *James Miranda Barry*, p. 282.
123. Brontë, *Jane Eyre*, p. 356.
124. Duncker, *James Miranda Barry*, p. 285.
125. Duncker, *James Miranda Barry*, p. 311.
126. Duncker, *James Miranda Barry*, p. 312.
127. Holmes, *Secret Life*, p. 7.
128. Holmes, *Secret Life*, p. 189.
129. Holmes, *Secret Life*, p. 189.
130. Holmes, *Secret Life*, p. 182.
131. Holmes, *Secret Life*, p. 186.
132. Holmes, *Secret Life*, p. 184.
133. Holmes, *Secret Life*, p. 159.
134. Holmes, *Secret Life*, p. 164.
135. Holmes, *Secret Life*, p. 164.
136. Tocqueville cited in Holmes, *Secret Life*, p. 189.
137. Holmes, *Secret Life*, p. 189.
138. Holmes, *Secret Life*, p. 191.
139. Holmes, *Secret Life*, p. 191.
140. Holmes, *Secret Life*, p. 191.

141. Rae, *Strange Story*, p. 115; Rose, *Perfect Gentleman*, p. 13; Holmes, *Secret Life*, p. 241.
142. As transcribed in Holmes, *Secret Life*, p. 244, but also reproduced in Rae, *Strange Story*, p. 116, and Rose, *Perfect Gentleman*, p. 13.
143. Duncker, *James Miranda Barry*, p. 35.
144. Duncker, *James Miranda Barry*, p. 90.
145. Rose, *Perfect Gentleman*, p. 153.
146. Holmes, *Secret Life*, p. 119.
147. Holmes, *Secret Life*, p. 35.
148. Holmes, *Secret Life*, p. 12.
149. Holmes, *Secret Life*, p. 14.
150. Holmes, *Secret Life*, p. 289.
151. Holmes, *Secret Life*, p. 278.
152. Holmes, *Secret Life*, p. 277.
153. Holmes, *Secret Life*, p. 293.
154. Holmes, *Secret Life*, p. 298.
155. See Chase, 'Hermaphrodites with Attitude: Mapping the Emergence of Intersex Political Activism'; Fausto-Sterling, *Sexing the Body: Gender Politics and the Construction of Sexuality*; Morland, '"The Glans Opens Like a Book": Writing and Reading the Intersexed Body'.
156. Halberstam, 'Telling Tales', p. 24.
157. Holmes, *Secret Life*, p. 289.
158. Dreger, *Hermaphrodites and the Medical Invention of Sex*, p. 15.
159. Mak, *Doubting Sex*, p. 41.
160. Mak, *Doubting Sex*, p. 17.
161. Mak, *Doubting Sex*, p. 29.
162. Mak, *Doubting Sex*, pp. 27–8.
163. Rae, *Strange Story*, p. 92; Rose, *Perfect Gentleman*, p. 123.
164. University of Edinburgh website, <https://www.ed.ac.uk/about/people/plaques/barry> (last accessed 15 January 2018).
165. *Pride of Place: A Guide to Understanding and Protecting Lesbian, Gay, Bisexual, Transgender and Queer (LGBTQ) Heritage*, Historic England (23 September 2016), p. 1, <https://historicengland.org.uk/images-books/publications/pride-of-place-guide-to-understanding-protecting-lgbtq-heritage/> (last accessed 15 January 2018).
166. 'Prejudice & Pride' is a programme of 'celebrations and commemorations' designed to 'mark the lives of people who challenged conventional notions of gender and sexuality'. Oram and Cook, *Prejudice & Pride: Celebrating LGBTQ Heritage*, p. 4.
167. Getsy, 'Capacity', p. 47.

Chapter 4

Two Beings/One Body: Intersex Lives and Transsexual Narratives in *Man into Woman* (1931) and David Ebershoff's *The Danish Girl* (2000)

Autobiography has proved a key genre for the representation of transgender lives, especially in relation to narratives of medically or surgically assisted gender transition. In *Second Skins: The Body Narratives of Transsexuality*, Jay Prosser describes narrative as 'a kind of second skin: the story the transsexual must weave around the body in order that this body may be "read"', declaring every transsexual an autobiographer, '[w]hether s/he publishes an autobiography or not'.[1] At the same time, autobiography is recognised as a 'fraught practice',[2] to use Kadji Amin's words, because of its complex relationship to dominant discourses of sex and gender and the clinical contexts in which they prevail. David Ebershoff's 2000 historical novel *The Danish Girl* is a late-twentieth-century reworking of the life story of Lili Elbe (1882–1931), whose reputation as one of the first people to undergo gender reassignment treatment was assured by the 1931 publication of *Man into Woman: An Authentic Record of a Sex Change, the True Story of the Miraculous Transformation of the Danish Painter Einar Wegener (Andreas Sparre).*[3] Indeed, *Man into Woman* has assumed a significant place in the history of transsexual life writing, acting as a generic precedent for authors of subsequent autobiographies.[4] However, *Man into Woman* is a 'memoir' whose status within the canon of transsexual autobiography is complicated in two ways: firstly, by its generic hybridity as a narrative composed by an author other than its subject, and secondly, by the fact that its subject may have been an intersex person. In *Man into Woman* the discovery of ovarian tissue in Elbe's abdomen is offered as proof of her female sex; her subsequent surgeries are then presented as correcting a disparity between sex and gender and, in doing so, preserving the categories of identity which her ambiguously sexed body might otherwise challenge. Underlying this rationale is an evident presumption that sex has a causal relationship to gender and that both sex (male or female) and gender (masculine or feminine) are binary constructions. *Man into Woman* is an important historical source text for *The Danish Girl*, which reproduces its recurring motif of 'two beings' competing for 'possession of one body'.[5] This motif of self-division depicts Elbe's body as a site of contest between two mutually exclusive entities: one male and one female, one masculine (an artist and intellectual) and one feminine (an aspiring wife and mother). This chapter is concerned with the uses to which narratives of intersex bodies are put in nominally 'transsexual' narratives, including auto/biographies and historical fiction. Two key issues are at stake here. The first concerns the way in which binary constructions of sex and gender might be reinforced in representations of intersex as a condition in need of 'correction', an assumption which intersex activists and theorists have done much to challenge. Iain Morland defines intersex bodies as having 'genetic, hormonal, and anatomical configurations that cannot be adequately apprehended by hegemonic discourses of sexual difference'.[6] Indeed, the discursive construction of sexed categories of identity and the ideological motivation underpinning the medical management of intersex bodies are concerns which are central to intersex studies. The second issue is to do with the ways in which the categorisation of some life narratives as 'transsexual' may serve to inadvertently obscure or conceal the history of intersex lives. This chapter does not aim to suggest that Elbe's life is the exclusive 'proper subject'[7] of either transsexual or intersex genres of representation but it does intend to draw attention to the 'intersex capacity' (to paraphrase David Getsy)[8] of Elbe's life story as constructed in auto/biographical and fictional narratives. Contemporary intersex activists and theorists have been keen to emphasise the differences, as well as affinities, in the respective histories and experiences of intersex and transsexual people. In this context this chapter examines the ways in which intersex and transsexual narratives have sometimes been conflated in retellings of Elbe's life, an enterprise which has been given renewed significance by the 2016 film adaptation of Ebershoff's novel, which brought Elbe's life story to a significantly expanded audience. While the first part of the chapter examines the relationship between *The Danish Girl* and its source text with a focus on discourses of intersex, the second examines the implications of binary thinking for the depiction of gender and sexuality in Ebershoff's novel. The title's emphasis on nationality is especially significant because in Ebershoff's novel the Danish-born artist who became Einar Wegener's wife, Gerda Gottlieb, is transformed into an American woman of Danish descent, Greta Waud. Motifs of modernity, mediated by discourses of race, class and mobility, are foregrounded in the figure of Greta, whose white, American femininity provides a crucial counterpoint to Lili's gender identity in this novel.[9] If the substantial expansion of Greta's character in Ebershoff's novel is one of the most notable departures from the narrative of *Man into Woman*, the focus on sexuality in *The Danish Girl* constitutes another. While the conventions of heterosexual romance play an important role in Lili's expression of her gender identity as depicted in *Man into Woman*, in *The Danish Girl* heterosexual desire is granted a pivotal role in the narrative discovery of a 'true' sex and gender. A sympathetic portrait of a historical subject, *The Danish Girl* largely avoids pathologising or sensationalist narrative tropes. However, through the introduction of scenes in which questions of sexuality are explored in illicit contexts, *The Danish Girl* places considerable emphasis on heteronormative constructions of sexuality in shaping Elbe's understanding of her gender identity. The retelling of Elbe's life in *Man into Woman* and *The Danish Girl* exemplifies the ways in which transgender – and intersex – lives have been 'authored by others'; this chapter will examine the narrative imperatives at work in biographical and fictional reconstructions of Elbe's life, with a particular focus on their investment in normative constructions of sex, gender or sexuality.

'A person of my own kind': Auto/biographical Narratives in *Man into Woman*

An autobiographical account of the life story of an early-twentieth-century pioneer of gender reassignment treatment is likely to invite particular expectations on the part of the reader, especially in relation to first-hand experience and authentic testimony. A potential antidote to the absence of historical record, such a narrative might also be approached as a credible corrective to accounts which medicalise or sensationalise transgender subjects. Einar Wegener was a Danish-born artist who met and married a fellow artist, Gerda Gottlieb, while studying in Copenhagen. Following a series of pioneering surgeries between 1930 and 1931, first in Berlin and then in Dresden, a new passport was issued to Lili Ilse Elvenes (who came to be known as Lili Elbe) and her marriage to Gottlieb was annulled. Elbe died in 1931 following complications arising from an attempt to transplant a uterus into her body. *Man into Woman* takes as its focus Elbe's own account of the events leading up to and following the medical operations which are often identified as constituting the first successful gender reassignment surgery. As such, this publication has taken its place in the canon of transsexual life writing, foregrounding as it does the experience and perspective of its transsexual subject. However, its status as a 'memoir' is complicated by its generic hybridity as auto/biography, drawing on the conventions not only of the memoir but also of biography and the novel. Moreover, its self-conscious reflexivity draws attention from the outset to the ways in which Elbe's life story is mediated by narrative.

First published in Danish in 1931 and translated into English (from the German) by H. J. Stenning in 1933, *Man into Woman* includes extracts from letters and diaries written by Elbe (and her former wife), compiled by an editor, Niels Hoyer, and published posthumously after Elbe's death. In an editorial note which prefaces the first chapter, Hoyer declares a commitment to honouring Elbe's intentions: 'In accordance with Lili Elbe's last wishes, I have arranged the papers she left behind in the form of this book. It is a true life story . . .'[10] However, the 'arrangement of papers' extends beyond the more conventional processes of chronological ordering and thematic selection. Indeed, *Man into Woman* is a non-linear narrative whose protagonist appears as a character in a distinctly novelistic story. Andreas Sparre – a pseudonym for Einar Wegener – is first introduced to the reader in the third person in a fictionalised scene in which Andreas and his wife are socialising with a fellow expatriate married couple in Saint Germain, Paris. A solicitous reference to 'Lili' anticipates Andreas's transformation and indicates that the narrative is situated at a pivotal point in Elbe's life. The story of Andreas's earlier years is recounted retrospectively on the eve of his first operation and inserted into the narrative in the guise of a transcribed conversation with his host in Berlin. This attribution gestures to oral testimony and historical record but the positioning of this passage is arguably novelistic in motivation, designed as it is both to quell the curiosity which has been cultivated in the reader and to heighten the dramatic tension at this crucial moment in Elbe's transition. Indeed, techniques of characterisation, anticipatory suspense and temporal manipulation are all employed in this narrative. Hoyer's deference to Elbe's intentions is indicative of the sympathy and respect with which the volume depicts her experience but his modest presentation of his editorial role does not obscure the extent to which this non-fiction narrative is shaped by the conventions of storytelling.

The status of *Man into Woman* as an auto/biographical source text is further complicated by its self-reflexivity. When Andreas recalls his childhood on the eve of his first surgery, he announces to his new acquaintance that he will '"tell you the story of my life, like an accurate chronicler"'.[11] His host 'complete[s] the sentence' by adding, '"I will run my blue pencil through it afterwards, as your Tacitus."'[12] This allusion evokes classical traditions of historiography but qualifies those same traditions by drawing attention to their literary status. Moreover, the readiness of the 'blue pencil' of editorial intervention acknowledges that this history cannot be unmediated. Andreas's interlocutor is named Niels but is not to be mistaken for the actual editor (Ernst Ludwig Harthern Jacobsen), who wrote under a pseudonym and who enters the narrative in a much later diary entry in the guise of an unnamed 'new friend who wants to help me collect and collate the loose leaves of my confession'.[13] Indeed, towards the end of the narrative lengthy extracts from Lili's final diary dwell on the form and reception of the book, interrogating her own storytelling in the light of anticipated 'reproach[es]'.[14] The narrative of self which unfolds in *Man into Woman* is both a 'confession'[15] and a vindication: an attempt, in anticipation of her critics, to justify her actions whatever their outcome. Elbe wonders whether she should write a preface explaining why she 'use[s] the third person, as in a novel'[16] when referring to Andreas. In doing so she anticipates one of the distinctive generic features of transsexual autobiography as highlighted by Jay Prosser: 'the split between the "I" of the *bios* and the "I" of the *graph*, the past self written and the present self writing, is heightened by the story of sex change . . . I was a woman, I write as a man' [emphasis in original].[17] Elbe's apologia extends to the format and coherence of a narrative written in difficult circumstances: 'this book, which arose out of diary entries and descriptive extracts and letters, I had to write in such a short time, between late autumn and early spring, between two very serious operations, as if between battles.'[18] These passages give rise to ambiguity and uncertainty about the respective roles of Hoyer as editor and Elbe as author. When Elbe acknowledges that many chapters 'read like a novel',[19] it seems as if she – and not Hoyer – is the originator of the novelistic insertions, in which case the narrative takes on the form of an autobiographical fiction.

Prosser has proposed that 'to be transsexual, transsexuals must be arch storytellers – or if they are not, must learn to become passable ones'.[20] Indeed, the context which shapes the imperative which

Prosser describes has historically been a clinical one: that is, the diagnostic situation in which the life story of a person seeking medically or surgically assisted gender reassignment is tested against the criteria which determine eligibility for treatment. This context necessarily complicates the nature of the story told, given the requirement to comply with what Amin terms the 'diagnostic narratemes'[21] dictated by medical and psychological discourses and the normative constructions of sex, gender or sexuality which they often enshrine. Gayle Salamon describes the 'medical and social histories' produced in these contexts as 'highly scripted and compelled, a set of necessary fictions'.[22] This is not to suggest that these life histories are 'fictional' in the sense of being false or inauthentic but rather that the genre of life story produced in these conditions is one in which dominant narrative tropes are necessarily authored by others. Indeed, Amin describes both the 'medical criteria for diagnosing transsexuality' and the 'generic conventions of written autobiography' as *authorizing transsexual subjects by implanting normative narratives of sexed development, continuity, and coherence*' [emphasis in original].[23] Like other life narratives written from a subject position which is not granted automatic social recognition (whether on grounds of sex, gender, sexuality, race, ethnicity, disability or other 'minority' formation), the transsexual autobiography is not simply a testament to existence but a plea to be permitted to exist: as such its terms are inevitably mortgaged to those of the dominant culture, whether in a relationship of coded resistance, strategic assimilation or aspiring compliance. Indeed, *Man into Woman* (and *The Danish Girl* after it) recounts a quest for medical intervention as a 'corrective' solution to a crisis of gender identity: as such, much of the narrative work can be understood as an attempt to generate a legitimate diagnosis. In this context, encounters with the medical establishment of the period prove pivotal and the forces of incomprehension, resistance and misdiagnosis which Elbe encounters serve as antagonists in both texts until it becomes possible to align medical authority (in the form of a sympathetic diagnosis and willing surgeon) with Elbe's aspirations.

In *Man into Woman*, Lili poignantly reflects on the absence of lives such as her own in the literature that she reads:

> 'Now I never opened a book or a journal. What were the fates of strange persons to me, unless I could find consolation in reading about a person of my own kind? But of such a person no author had been able to write, because it had never occurred to any author that such a person could ever have existed.'[24]

This reflection is underlined by the possibility that Lili's narrative might itself offer 'consolation' to later readers of her 'own kind'. This is one of the few places in the book where Elbe imagines herself as a putative member of a community and the reader is left to ponder with which 'kind' she might identify. Indeed, the possibility that Elbe was an intersex person has significant implications for the way in which this narrative of transition and Elbe's encounters with medical technology are interpreted. Iain Morland has observed that intersex and transsexual people's relationship with medical technology has often been construed as exemplifying opposing positions, with intersex people seeking to end unwanted interventions and transsexual people seeking equality of access to desired treatments: 'where the former shows gender's assemblage by force, and the latter its alteration by free will.'[25] The surgeries which Elbe undergoes acquire different meanings in these contexts; as the vehicle of transsexual transition they are allied with Elbe's agency, but when considered as a 'corrective' intervention to resolve sexed ambiguity they could be seen to reinforce culturally constructed categories of identity which intersex theorists have sought to challenge. A central motif in *Man into Woman* is that of 'two beings' struggling for 'possession'[26] of one body; in the next section I will situate this motif in the history of the medical management of intersex bodies, before considering the implications of its replication in David Ebershoff's 2000 novel *The Danish Girl*.

Two Beings/One Body: Narrative Constructions of Intersex in *Man into Woman* and *The Danish Girl*

It was in the introduction to a new edition of a late-nineteenth-century memoir by an intersex person, Herculine Barbin (1838–68), that Michel Foucault proposed the idea that the binary category of sex which prevails in modern Western European culture is a relative historical novelty. In answer to the question 'Do we *truly* need a *true* sex?' [emphasis in original], Foucault proposes:

> With a persistence that borders on stubbornness, modern Western societies had answered in the affirmative . . . For a long time, however, such a demand was not made, as is proven by the history of the status which medicine and law have granted to hermaphrodites. Indeed it was a very long time before the postulate that a hermaphrodite must have a sex – a single, a true sex – was formulated. For centuries, it was quite simply agreed that hermaphrodites had two.[27]

Subsequent histories of the medical management of intersex bodies by Alice Domurat Dreger (1998), Anne Fausto-Sterling (2000) and Geertje Mak (2012) all observe, with different emphases, the increasing medicalisation of the intersex body over the course of the nineteenth century, with adjudication of ambiguous or contested sex shifting from the courts of law to the doctor's surgery or operating theatre. It is with the advent of the biopolitical state that the intersex body becomes the object of concerted surveillance, regulation and intervention. As Foucault argues:

> Biological theories of sexuality, juridical conceptions of the individual, forms of administrative control in modern nations, led little by little to rejecting the idea of a mixture of the two sexes in a single body, and consequently to limiting the free choice of indeterminate individuals.[28]

In other words, ideological imperatives underlying binary categories of sex were employed in an effort to eliminate the diversity of sexed identity represented by intersex bodies. Critiques of 'normalising' surgery, especially when practised on intersex infants, have been central to leading work in the field of intersex studies since its emergence in the 1990s. Crucial to this critique is the argument that binary categories of sex have been imposed on subjects, including those unable to give consent, in the name of protecting normative ideas about sex, gender and sexuality. Leading intersex theorists have testified to the harmful effects of these surgeries, often undertaken in conditions of secrecy and resulting in experiences of shame and trauma. As Cheryl Chase writes in her landmark 1998 essay 'Hermaphrodites with Attitude: Mapping the Emergence of Intersex Political Activism', 'Pediatric surgeries literalize what might otherwise be considered a theoretical operation: the attempted production of normatively sexed bodies and gendered subjects through constitutive acts of violence.'[29] 'Corrective' surgical intervention has been understood by intersex activists and theorists as motivated by cultural and ideological imperatives to do with maintaining binary constructions of sex (and by extension of gender and sexuality) rather than by medical necessity. Hence, whereas the history of transsexual encounters with medical technology has often been characterised by the pursuit of elective surgery, the history of intersex encounters has been dominated by the discovery and critique of unwanted interventions. As Abby L. Wilkerson has noted, the 'surgical procedures rejected by intersex activists are the very interventions that many transgendered individuals pursue and to which the movement seeks greater access'.[30] Elbe's quest to realise her sense of self through gender reassignment treatment, obtained despite the resistance of the medical establishment, can be seen as enabling an elective transition from one sex and gender to another. From this vantage point, it is easy to see why *Man into Woman* has gained an important position within the canon of transsexual autobiography. However, the uses to which an intersex diagnosis is put in this narrative – and its subsequent retellings – deserve careful thought. It can be argued that the discovery of an intersex condition in *Man into Woman* is presented as providing a legitimate pretext for medical intervention: an appeal to normative discourses of binary sex acts to justify surgery which can then be understood as preserving – not challenging – the causal relationship between sex and gender. This appeal, however strategic, arguably reinforces binary constructions of sex. Moreover, to read *Man into Woman* exclusively as a 'transsexual' narrative is to risk erasing the intersex narratives which it also contains. The absence of 'consoling fictions' with which Lili can identify points both to the importance that such narratives accrue for future communities of readers and to their formative role in the recovery of an unacknowledged history. It is only in the final pages of *Man into Woman* that the figure of the 'hermaphrodite' (the only available term for an intersex body in this period) emerges in a complex passage in which Lili pits the evidence of her ongoing existence against the forces of 'Nature':

> 'If I should succumb spiritually and seek suicide, everybody would be right in saying that what had happened to me had been contrary to Nature, an audacious challenge of the unnatural and the artificial to the natural and to Nature; a creature born as a hermaphrodite must remain an hermaphrodite, especially if it had lived as an hermaphrodite for a lifetime.'[31]

The understanding of the 'hermaphrodite' as a naturally occurring phenomenon seems indebted to the work of Isidore Geoffroy Saint-Hilaire (1805–61), the founder of teratology, which, as Fausto-Sterling argues, 'offered a natural explanation for the birth of people with extraordinary bodies'.[32] However, the objectifying language used in this passage – the hermaphrodite is referred to as 'it' – indicates that no matter how natural her occurrence, she is an abject figure to be spurned. Nevertheless, it is interesting to observe that the defenders of 'Nature' do not charge Lili with being unnatural and artificial because she has changed gender but because she has acted to undo her 'natural' status as a 'creature born as a hermaphrodite'.

Man into Woman can be situated within the prevailing medical discourses of its time, in which categories of sex, gender and sexuality were often conflated but the binary oppositions between male and female and masculine and feminine persistently upheld. In her 1998 book *Hermaphrodites and the Medical Invention of Sex*, Dreger argues that the end of the nineteenth century saw the emergence of what she terms the 'gonadal definition of sex', which she describes as 'a rather extraordinary, uniform sex classification system according to which everybody's "true" sex would be marked by one trait and one trait only, the anatomical nature of a person's gonads: the ovaries or testicles'.[33] This hypothesis privileges the gonads over other markers of sex and insists on a strict binary opposition between male and female, despite evidence to the contrary presented by bodies with intersex variations. Indeed, the discovery of ovarian tissue in Elbe's abdominal cavity in *Man into Woman* is understood by doctor and patient alike as medical evidence of her 'true' sex and vindication of her expressed gender identification. From this point onwards medical opinion (albeit not universal) becomes aligned with Elbe's sense of herself as a woman. Indeed, Elbe anticipates this medical discovery through her intuition that her body harbours internal female anatomy and her deduction that this anatomy must be the cause of the feminising changes to her body and the mysterious periodic bleeding to which she becomes subject. The recurring motif of two beings at war within one body in *Man into Woman* is evidently informed by a binary understanding of categories of sex. As the narrator declares, as a prelude to the narrative which follows: 'Andreas was, in fact, two beings: a man, Andreas, and a girl, Lili. They might even be called twins who had taken possession of one body at the same time.'[34] 'Male' and 'female' are understood as mutually exclusive categories whose presence in a single body gives rise to a struggle for supremacy whose consequences are potentially fatal: Andreas refers to 'this incessant and ruthless inner struggle between Lili and myself' and reflects that 'for a long time it looked as if neither of us would survive the contest'.[35] Indeed, metaphors of sacrifice, suicide and murder are employed to characterise the nature of this contest: as the narrative progresses, each sex is characterised as a separate and rival entity and Andreas's body as a battlefield in which only one can ultimately survive. Andreas predicts that '"it will be Lili who survives"'[36] following his surgery and Grete confesses that if Lili were to '"suddenly vanish, it would seem like a murder"'.[37] Lili is depicted as a being seeking possession of Andreas, who indicts himself as a 'usurper', improperly occupying a body which rightfully belongs to another:

> 'During these nights I was obsessed by the delusion that this body did not belong to me alone, that my share in this body grew less day by day, as it enclosed in its interior a being which demanded its existence

at the price of my existence. I seemed to myself like a deceiver, like a usurper who reigned over a body which had ceased to be his, like a person who owned merely the facade of his house.'[38]

Both Lili and Grete understand the surgery as resulting in the death of Andreas and Lili even experiences guilt at his demise: '"Perhaps I am the murderer of Andreas, and this idea tortures me fearfully, as I surmise that I shall perhaps be of much less value than he."'[39] This feeling is especially pronounced in encounters with those who loved Andreas and who mourn his loss: '"I am so afraid of meeting people who belonged to Andreas, who loved Andreas and whom he loved. It seems as if I have murdered him."'[40] Elbe's life story occupies a significant historical moment in the history of the medical management of intersex bodies. While the medicalisation of the condition is strongly in evidence in Andreas's encounters with authority as an adult, his childhood in rural Jutland suggestively offers evidence of attitudes and practices which are vestiges of an earlier period. Lili's account of her encounter with her sister when she returns to her family home is candid and poignant. The siblings struggle to reconcile one sister's grief at the loss of her brother with another's desire for acceptance: '"It was a terribly hard contest between my sister and me for my recognition as a person, as a sister."'[41] Lili recalls that they held hands in silence while her sister (who is unnamed) 'sought for words'.[42] Elbe's sister is a significant character in *Man into Woman* whose attitude to her younger brother's indeterminacy as a child might be seen as supporting Mak's argument for the existence of 'structural space for people of ambiguous sex'[43] in longstanding communities prior to the medicalisation of intersex bodies in the late nineteenth century. His sister accommodates and even cherishes Andreas's gender ambiguity as a child, allowing him to push a doll's pram but protectively concealing his hand in her own to avert the mockery of others. Indeed, she creates not only space for the child but also a name:

> 'There was never a prettier, sweeter brother than he. He played with my dolls, he pushed my doll's prams. And I called him "Lilleman" – little man. Once when I wrote down the name for Mother and Mother told me that I had spelt "Lilleman" with only one "n" instead of two, I said my brudderkins Andreas was only a "Lilleman" with one "n", for he was not a proper man at all.'[44]

In terms of normative masculinity this denomination may seem belittling, but positioned within a testament of love and devotion – his sister's home is a 'museum'[45] to Andreas's art – it can also be read as an expression of recognition of her sibling's distinctive identity.

Ebershoff's 2000 novel takes from its 1931 predecessor the notion of Elbe as a 'doubled'[46] being whose destiny is to become singular. The motif of two separate and mutually exclusive beings inhabiting one body is replicated in *The Danish Girl*: 'He realized that Lili and he shared something: a pair of oyster-blue lungs; a chugging heart; their eyes, often pink rimmed with fatigue. But in the skull it was almost as if there were two brains, a walnut halved: his and hers.'[47] As in *Man into Woman*, these two beings are depicted as rivals for possession of a single body, with the death of one the necessary condition for the survival of the other:

> When he, Einar, the remote owner of the borrowed body, was about to ask Lili what she was referring to; when he, Einar, floating above like a circling ghost, was about to lean in and ask . . . just then Lili, with her forearms flushed with heat, with chiffon in her fists, her half of the walnut brain electric with the current of thought, felt a warm trickle run from her nose to her lips.[48]

The periodic bleeding to which Einar is subject is depicted as a direct manifestation of Lili's presence; or to put it another way, the possible presence of female (as well as male) reproductive organs is seen as the origin of a distinctly 'feminine' personality at odds with Einar's established gender. The motif of Lili 'stirring'[49] inside Einar is a recurring one in *The Danish Girl* and further reinforces the assumption that the relationship between Einar and Lili cannot be one of continuity: 'Something made him feel as if his soul were trapped in a wrought-iron cage: his heart nudging its nose against his ribs, Lili stirring from within, shaking herself awake, rubbing her side against the bars of Einar's body.'[50] Moreover, the ambiguously sexed body is depicted as contradictory, conflictual and in need of correction. Surgical intervention is anticipated in metaphorical language – 'Once again there were two. The walnut halved, the oyster knifed open'[51] – and Einar's transition into Lili is depicted as self-division rather than self-realisation: 'Einar and Lili were one, but it was time to split them in two.'[52] In *The Danish Girl*, a pivotal scene occurs in the Bibliothèque Nationale in Paris, where Einar consults 'scientific books on sexual problems'[53] in a search for an explanation for his condition. Here he is introduced to terms such as 'sexual pathology' and 'sexual intermediacy',[54] although their actual historical origin, in works such as Richard von Krafft-Ebing's *Psychopathia Sexualis* (first published in 1886), is not acknowledged. More significant than these clinical studies is a life history of a Bavarian aristocrat which provokes feelings of recognition:

'Somehow Einar knew he was reading about himself. He recognised the duality, the lack of complete identification with either sex. He read about the Bavarian, and a dull pang lay at rest in Einar's chest.'[55] Einar makes repeated visits to the library, assisted by a young female librarian whose hand like a 'baby starfish'[56] evokes the 'hermaphrodites' of the natural world, and draws the following conclusion:

> He eventually read enough to become convinced that he too possessed the female organs. Buried in the cavity of his body were Lili's organs, the bloody packets and folds of flesh that made her who she was . . . He imagined a uterus shoved up behind his testicles. He imagined breasts trapped by his ribcage.[57]

This conclusion is worth dwelling on. Einar becomes convinced that he possesses female reproductive organs as well as male, but this does not lead him to deduce that he has an intersex body but rather that he is truly female. The 'buried'[58] and 'trapped'[59] status of the evidence, as opposed to his visible male genitalia, seems to render it more, rather than less, definitive. The existence of female gonadal tissue proves his sex even where it inhabits his body alongside his testicles. Indeed, it is the removal of his testicles (not his penis) which is later presented as the irreversible moment at which Einar's life as a man comes to an end and Lili's life as a woman begins. The binary constructions of sexed identity which *The Danish Girl* inherits from *Man into Woman* have further implications for its depiction of gendered identity (especially femininity) and sexuality (specifically male homosexuality). Moreover, the relationship between femininity and modernity – a topic introduced into *Man into Woman* – is significantly foregrounded in *The Danish Girl* through the transformation of Andreas's wife Grete into an American woman, Greta Waud, whose femininity is implicated in discourses of mobility, race and class.

'I do not want to be an artist, but a woman': Femininity and Modernity in *Man into Woman* and *The Danish Girl*

In *Man into Woman*, Lili undergoes a remarkable change of personality following her first operation, disavowing Andreas's heritage as an artist in emphatic terms: 'I think death would be more welcome to me than, for instance, a life as an artist, even as a great and fêted artist on my own account. For I do not want to be an artist, but a woman.'[60]

Her aspirations cease to be intellectual and artistic and instead become marital and maternal: 'It is not with my brain, not with my eyes, not with my hands that I want to be creative, but with my heart and with my blood. The fervent longing in my woman's life is to become the mother of a child.'[61] While the gender identity which Lili adopts in *Man into Woman* is distinctly traditional, her femininity is not without its critics; a range of women's voices identify a disparity between Lili's attitude to gender roles and the social changes which characterise the early twentieth century. In *The Danish Girl* this contrast is significantly heightened by the transformation of Gerda Gottlieb/Grete Wegener from a Danish citizen to an independently wealthy American, Greta Waud, whose modernity is underlined by motifs of mobility, race and class. However, the proto-feminist voices given expression in *Man into Woman* are absent from *The Danish Girl*, where the forces of modernity are aligned with new discourses of normative power.

In *Man into Woman*, in her first letter following her initial surgery in Berlin, Lili places considerable emphasis on signifiers of feminine glamour and sexual allure, despite the fact that the letter is addressed to a platonic friend and relative, her brother-in-law Christian: '"It is now Lili who is writing to you. I am sitting up in my bed in a silk nightdress with lace trimming, curled, powdered, with bangle, necklace, and rings."'[62] This conception of herself as the sexualised object of men's desire extends to her relationship with her doctor at the Dresden Women's Clinic, which is described in terms of heterosexual romantic subjection. Professor Kreutz's power as a figure of medical authority is eroticised and her willing subjection to his surgical intervention presented as a kind of sexualised thraldom: 'it was the first time her woman's heart had trembled before her lord and master, before the man who had constituted himself her protector, and she understood why she then submitted so utterly to him and his will.'[63] Indeed, Lili's identity as a woman is defined by passivity, compliance and submission: 'Everything in the past belonged to the person who had vanished, who was dead ... Now there was only a perfectly humble woman, who was ready to obey, who was happy to submit herself to the will of another.'[64] There is a Pygmalion quality to the motif of Lili being brought to life through the creative intervention of a male maestro. As Grete puts it in a diary entry:

> 'Hitherto Lili has been like clay which others had prepared and to which the Professor has given form and life by a transient touch ... By a single glance the Professor yesterday awoke her heart to life, to a life with all the instincts of woman.'[65]

However, Grete's comment is made in a narrative context in which the ideological function of Kreutz's interactions with Lili is made apparent: '"what the Professor is now doing with Lili is nothing less than an emotional moulding, which is preceding the physical moulding into a woman."'[66] In other words, Kreutz is inducting Lili into the subordinate role that defines the social position of women by mobilising a heterosexual dynamic of masculine power and feminine submission. However, this process – and Lili's eager subjection to it – is not without its critics. A female friend of a fellow patient at the clinic in Dresden expresses her impatience with Lili's expression of her femininity directly:

> '"You are very coquettish and your head is full of nonsense. I believe you would like the lord of creation to tyrannize over you. But perhaps you achieve more by your methods than we modern women. What we have to fight for you achieve in a twinkling by means of a few tears. You seem to me like a female type of a vanished age ... Women like you are best suited for a – harem."'[67]

Lili's critic is identified as a doctor from Berlin and this professional woman employs racialised discourses of modernity and political struggle to suggest that Lili's femininity is regressive, both historically and politically. The doctor is not alone in this view, which is expressed with humour and exasperation by different members of the female community of the clinic, including the nursing staff and fellow patients. However, later in the narrative, during her return to Jutland and her encounter with her sister, Lili is more reflective about her femininity. Describing herself in terms which are almost identical to those adopted by the Berlin doctor, Lili compares herself unfavourably with Andreas:

> 'He was ingenious, sagacious, and interested in everything – a reflective and thoughtful man. And I was quite superficial. Deliberately so, for I had to demonstrate every day that I was a different creature from him, that I was a woman. A thoughtless, flighty, very superficially-minded woman, fond of dress and fond of enjoyment, yes, I believe even childish. And I can say it calmly now: all this was not merely farcical acting. It was my real character, untroubled, carefree, illogical, capricious, female.'[68]

While concluding with a defence of her femininity as an authentic expression of her 'female' nature, the passage also reveals both an awareness that her femininity might be perceived to be excessive and parodic ('merely farcical acting') and a sense of a gender identity under duress: her daily 'demonstration' of femininity is a labour of proof, by which she asserts a gender identity which cannot be taken for granted. Deviation from gendered norms is presented as a luxury which she cannot risk, since her identity is constantly susceptible to forfeit: '"Other women could be ugly, could commit every possible crime. I, however, must be beautiful, must be immaculate, else I lost every right to be a woman."'[69] In *Man into Woman*, the visiting doctor from Berlin is depicted as a modern woman in somewhat disparaging terms, her censorious attitude to Lili's gender presentation implying that her own femininity has been lost to her modernity. However, Lili's former wife, Grete, is in many ways a living embodiment of the modern woman as an economically independent professional whose attitudes to gender, sexuality and marriage are not dictated by social convention; her support for Einar's transition is consistently sympathetic but she asserts her autonomy and sexual agency by finding another lover in an arrangement which has Lili's blessing. Grete's modernity in *Man into Woman* is significantly foregrounded in the character of Greta in *The Danish Girl*, whose subtly anglicised name is a signifier of her third-generation Danish-American identity. Whereas in *Man into Woman* a diverse range of women's voices, including Lili's, reflect on the political significance of her chosen mode of femininity, in *The Danish Girl* Greta Waud serves as the principal counterpoint to Lili's femininity. She is a much more prominent character in the narrative of *The Danish Girl* (she is furnished with a childhood, a twin brother and a first marriage), and Greta's modernity has national, racial and class undertones which are implicated in her American origin. Rather than serving as a feminist counterpoint to Lili's outdated femininity, Greta's femininity seems to be symptomatic of a modernity which casts the 'vanished age' to which Lili subscribes in an ambivalent and even nostalgic light.

Mobility is an important enabling condition for the narrative recounted in *Man into Woman*; Andreas is a descendant of migrants from Mallorca to Jutland[70] and in the course of the narrative Andreas and Grete live first in Copenhagen and then in Paris, from where they take regular touring holidays in southern Europe. Andreas travels to Berlin and then to Dresden for his surgeries and returns as Lili to visit her family home in Jutland towards the end of the narrative. As members of a cosmopolitan artistic community which crosses national borders, Andreas and Grete are distinctively mobile; they are uniquely able to access transnational networks of like-minded individuals in whichever European metropolis they find themselves. Uprooted by choice from the country of her birth, Lili possesses a national allegiance which is equally mobile; famously, Elbe adopted the name of the river which runs through Dresden as a tribute to the city. While Einar's dark brown eyes – the implied signifier of his Spanish heritage – are retained in *The Danish Girl*, it is Greta in whom the motif of mobility is elaborated. *The Danish Girl* opens in 1925 with Einar and Greta working at their easels under the 'twin skylights'[71] of their attic room, overlooking the harbour in Copenhagen and cooled by the 'chill blowing in from the Baltic'.[72] The flight path of the Deutscher Aero-Lloyd service to Berlin is visible from the window and while Lili will not go to Berlin in this narrative (her operations are all relocated to Dresden), at its conclusion Greta boards this same flight with her husband-to-be, Einar's childhood friend Hans, on the first leg of her return to America. Moreover, Greta has made a pact with Lili that they will meet again in America, as Lili's marriage to Henrik, a fellow painter, is due to take place in New York. In this way America bookends the narrative, as the place from which Greta travels and to which she returns and as Lili's imagined future marital home. Greta Waud is an American of Danish descent, the daughter of a second-generation Danish-American, a Californian landowner and diplomat whose posting to the Danish embassy first brings Greta to Copenhagen. Greta's Danish grandmother is depicted as an intrepid figure whose departure from her homeland is motivated by a spirit of romantic adventure rather than by economic necessity; female, unmarried and apparently unaccompanied, Gerda is not a typical migrant of the period and presents a pioneering precedent in terms of female mobility. Greta and Einar's courtship is interrupted when her family return to America at the outbreak of the First World War; here and elsewhere their transatlantic mobility is material evidence of national and class privilege – they travel by choice and flee to safety at will – and yet Greta exploits the language of displacement and statelessness to express her displeasure at their departure: 'There she was, the freest girl in Copenhagen, if not the whole world, and now that dirty German had just about ruined her life. An exile – that's what she'd become. Banished to California. . . .'[73] The prominence of migration and mobility as thematic concerns in *The Danish Girl* is especially significant given that travel has been identified as a defining motif in transgender, and more specifically transsexual, narratives. In *Second Skins*, Prosser explores how 'transition as a geographic trope applies to transsexual narratives',[74] and in *Assuming a Body: Transgender and Rhetoric of Materiality*, Gayle Salamon observes that it is 'commonplace to speak of gender transition as a border crossing of sorts'.[75] However, the implications of this motif in colonial and racialised discourses have also been recognised by theorists such as Jack Halberstam: 'Myths of travel and border crossings are inevitable within a discourse of transsexuality. But they are also laden with the histories of other identity negotiations, and they carry the burden of national and colonial discursive histories.'[76] Where migration is often compelled or coerced by economic or political forces, mobility – by contrast– can be seen as an expression of class, racial or national privilege. The nature of Greta's status as a white American is revealed through discourses which counterpoint her femininity with that of East Asian women, in both American and European contexts.

In California, the presence of 'Japanese maids', who 'clack' through the Waud family home in their 'geta sandals'[77] is an indication of Greta's class status. Akiko, a maid who is bequeathed to Greta after her first marriage, is instrumental in introducing her mistress to the Pasadena Arts and Crafts Society where she meets her first husband. Her reported speech would seem to suggest that she is a first-generation, or Issei, migrant, whose arrival predates the Immigration Act of 1924. Here a migrant woman, excluded from citizenship by race-based legislation, serves as a foil for the white protagonist, the green jade of the Buddha which Akiko keeps in her private quarters later serving as a colour palette with which to describe the effects of the winter rain.[78] Orientalist connotations are made explicit in a European setting when Greta is depicted as borrowing the 'exotic' status of another East Asian migrant woman: 'In Copenhagen . . . she was more exotic than the black-haired laundresses who had wandered across the earth from Canton . . .'[79] It is striking that following her journey from California to Copenhagen, Greta's femininity continues to be counterpointed with that of non-white women, specifically that of a Chinese woman worker who solicits custom for her laundry business from the streets of Copenhagen.[80] The material artefacts of transcontinental migration provide a literal foundation for Greta's art in her Danish studio: 'The model's platform Greta used was a lacquer trunk bought from a Chinese laundress who would make a pick-up every other day, announcing herself not with a call from the street but with a ping of the gold cymbals strapped to her fingers.'[81] This transaction transforms not only the practical function of the trunk but also its symbolism, from an object testifying to a specific cultural legacy and historical experience to a decorative prop serving to add a touch of chinoiserie to a bohemian interior. Moreover, the sale of the trunk effectively signals that the laundress will not undertake a return journey, as Greta is able to do. The unnamed laundress is silent and her presence signalled by non-verbal sounds which serve to punctuate the narrative. The '*ping*!' [emphasis in original][82] of her finger cymbals is one of the distractions credited with diverting Greta from her ongoing art education under Einar's instruction and by the end of the narrative this same percussive sound has become a synonym for memory itself: 'Standing at her easel, Greta would think about Einar then and Lili today, and Greta would shut her eyes and hear a tinkling bell of memory in her head but then recognise it as the *ping!* of the Cantonese laundress who was still calling from the street.'[83] The chime of the laundress's cymbals serves as an aural signifier of place and past for Greta, confirming the 'exotic' nature of a journey undertaken in defiance of family expectation but ultimately serving as a prelude to her return home and her resumption of the class and racial privilege to which she was born. Indeed, in *The Danish Girl*, Greta's national identity as a white American is central to her characterisation as a woman of energy, will and vitality, often in contrast to the Danish-born 'little Lili'.[84] Greta's convictions and actions are underpinned by a sense of entitlement empowered by economic and political power. Greta and her twin brother Carlisle are depicted as the active agents of Lili's transition, with each sibling competing to demonstrate their capacity for enterprise and achievement by independently investigating the most appropriate medical care. For Greta the possession of a 'western spine'[85] seems to be closely associated with ideas about heredity, normative embodiment and sexual morality. Greta attributes her own dynamic energy to this quality, which is figured as an innate property of the (white) American body: 'sometimes Greta was filled with too much immediate energy to stop and think and plan and plot. The energy was the fluid running up and down her western spine.'[86] Indeed, Greta's exceptional height – she is 'probably the tallest woman [Einar had] ever known'[87] – is remarked upon by her husband, who is repeatedly described in diminutive terms suggesting arrested development.[88] Raised in affluence and comfort, Greta possesses speed and stature which seem indicative of the privileges of prosperity. However, it is not only Einar whom Greta judges as deficient but also her brother Carlisle and her first American husband Teddy. Carlisle's mobility has been impaired following a childhood incident in which Greta 'accidentally nudged her twin brother into the path of a carriage'[89] and her first husband, a potter and son of strawberry farmers, contracts tuberculosis not long after Greta accidentally sets fire to his studio.[90] It is clear that Greta's 'western spine' is deeply encoded with normative assumptions about the body and serves to implicitly reinforce assumptions to do with not only national but also racial hierarchy, underpinned by a conviction in heredity.

Greta's geographical mobility can be seen as an extension of the privilege which she enjoys as a wealthy white American. However, while Greta places herself at significant geographic distance from her family and national origin, she does not renounce the economic privilege which is her inheritance. Unbeknownst to Einar, Greta is in receipt of a private income funded by the profits generated by her father's orange groves in California and, moreover, is the owner of the building in which their attic studio is situated. Greta's class identity is affirmed by her marriage to Einar's childhood friend, Hans. Both are seeking to escape the responsibilities and expectations of inherited wealth, whether it is the 'dead'[91] Danish aristocracy of Hans's family or the new wealth of Greta's family. For Greta and Hans – a commercial artist and international art dealer respectively – social mobility takes the form of rejecting a class position defined by birth and becoming elective members of a new cosmopolitan cultural elite, one whose existence is nevertheless dependent on the purchasing power of an emerging industrial middle class, the 'young industrialists, their money made fast from mass-produced crockery and cooking pans' who attend the artists' ball, at which Lili makes her first public appearance, in the hope of 'mov[ing] themselves up through society'.[92] At the start of the narrative these 'industry titans'[93] are Greta's clients as a portrait artist, providing an income from the production of what she later describes as 'drab commissions'.[94] The capital generated by this class provides Greta with an independent living but the disdain with which its members are regarded is expressed in terms which again conflate heredity, health and sexuality. The clinic of the radiologist Dr Hexler, which Einar attends at Greta's suggestion, is depicted as providing remedies for dysfunctions endemic to this new breed of masculinity: 'After all, the clinic drew the richest men in Denmark, men with bellies loose over their belts who, in their flurry to manufacture rubber shoes and mineral dyes and superphosphates and Portland cement, lost control of all that hung below their belts.'[95] These men are obese and impotent, their energetic investment in the new mass markets of the modern age depicted as being at the price of their sexual vitality; in an era in which ideologies of sexual and racial hygiene resulted in state regulation of the reproductive capacities of targeted populations, this new class employ their wealth to enlist the new medical sciences in restoring their prerogatives as men. Despite Greta's initial distaste for her commercial commissions, her professional success is nevertheless attributed to the new art markets.

In *Man into Woman*, Andreas depicts the couple's move to Paris as motivated by a commitment to his wife's art: 'In Copenhagen he had frequently been obliged to hear how much his pictures were preferred to those of his wife. And that was perhaps the worst thing that could be said to him. In Paris, where the contrary was generally the case, he felt at home for this very reason.'[96] By contrast, in *The Danish Girl*, Greta is explicitly depicted as the inferior artist and Einar's eternal pupil; they first meet not as art student peers, as in *Man into Woman*, but as female student and male professor, and this hierarchy persists in their marriage. Einar's offer to remedy Greta's lack of 'technical skill'[97] through instruction is repeatedly deferred due to domestic interruptions. Greta's paintings fail to sell and her methods are depicted as evoking the impersonal and lifeless qualities of mass-produced objects: 'Greta's paintings were oversized and glossy with a shellacking process she created from varnish. They were so shiny and hard you could clean them like windows.'[98] However, Greta's renewed reputation – fuelled by the commercial success of her portraits of Lili – gives her access to new professional opportunities, principally commissions to illustrate features in the fashionable Parisian press, including *La Vie Parisienne* (1863–1970), a weekly magazine renowned for its full-colour illustrations and often eroticised Art Nouveau and Art Deco aesthetic, and *L'Illustration* (1843–1944), a French newspaper which pioneered colour photographic illustration. Greta's professional life as an artist is marked more by the modernity of the interwar period than the late modernism of the art world; the imperatives of commerce, consumption and leisure which characterise the mass-circulation press also serve to shape and define the specific modernity of Greta's identity as a professional woman.

It is evident that discourses of modernity are used to different effect in *Man into Woman* and *The Danish Girl*. Whereas in *Man into Woman* the 'modern woman' is an economically independent professional who castigates Lili for her regressive femininity, in *The Danish Girl* Greta's 'modernity' is treated in a more ambivalent fashion. Greta is an enterprising individualist; her art is aligned with commerce rather than the avant-garde and her desire for freedom is not understood as part of a collective struggle shared with other women. The narrative's attitude to 'modern women' is itself rather ambivalent: Greta's somewhat hapless role in her brother's injury and her first husband's death seems to suggest that there is something emasculating about the freedoms which she exercises. Moreover, as a white, wealthy, American woman Greta is aligned with futurity in *The Danish Girl*, whereas Lili is implicitly associated with regression. Lili is not able to fulfil the dream of making a new home in New York with her future husband. Indeed, the narrative concludes in 1931 with a fragile Lili, approaching the premature death which the reader will know is her fate, sitting alone in the sun on the famous 'Balcony of Europe' in Dresden, surrounded by courting couples and playing children. In this novel, the insertion of a narrative of an expatriate American in Europe introduces themes to do with mobility underpinned by race and class privilege which are ultimately destined to leave Lili behind; a pioneer of gender transition, Lili could be seen as a figure of futurity, but here she is abandoned to the past of an old Europe.

Red Alcoves and Grey Facts: Male Homosexuality in *The Danish Girl*

A recurring motif in histories of the medical management of intersex bodies is the role played by attitudes to homosexuality in justifying corrective interventions. Dreger (1998), Fausto-Sterling (2000), Matta (2005) and Reis (2007) all identify a close relationship between the biomedical histories of the construction of intersex and of homosexuality, with Matta describing them as 'parallel stories'.[99] The 'prevention of homosexuality'[100] is diagnosed by these scholars as an underlying goal which has played a formative role in the treatment of intersex bodies. As Dreger puts it:

> Even after a cursory study of the phenomenon of sex-sorting, one soon discovers that a significant motivation for the biomedical treatments of hermaphrodites is the desire to keep people straight ... medical doctors, scientists, hermaphrodites' parents, and other lay people have historically been interested in sorting people according to their sexes to avoid or prevent what might be considered homosexuality.[101]

Indeed, Fausto-Sterling asserts that it is 'impossible to understand the continuing arguments over the treatment of intersexuals without putting them in the historical context of highly charged debates over homosexuality'.[102] The relationship between the discursive history and medical management of both intersex and homosexuality is further complicated by the emergence of theories of sexual inversion in the late nineteenth and early twentieth century. As Matt Johnson has written, 'homosexuality was sometimes described as "psychic hermaphroditism," and explained by the existence of a third, intermediate sex.'[103] Indeed, for Richard von Krafft-Ebing (1840–1902) female sexual inversion was characterised by 'the masculine soul, heaving in the female bosom', and for Karl Heinrich Ulrichs (1825–95) male homosexuality was characterised by a 'feminine soul confined by a masculine body'.[104] Borrowing from the ancient cultural symbolism of the hermaphrodite, these theories sought to legitimise same-sex desire. However, Jay Prosser reclaims these case histories as 'foundational' for a 'transsexual historiography' because they provide historical records of individuals 'identifying with, appearing as, living as, and sometimes seeking out the surgical means to aid a transition to the "other" sex'.[105] The concluding section of this chapter examines how the fear of being misrecognised as a male homosexual is presented as significantly shaping Elbe's gender transition in Ebershoff's novel. In this way normative constructions of sexuality – as well as sex and gender – are arguably reinforced in a historical novel set in an era and location which saw the emergence of radical new ways of thinking about sexual identity.

In *Man into Woman*, Lili's heterosexuality is central to her gender identity: following her transition, she quickly finds a new partner, Claude Lejeune, and looks forward to their marriage. Andreas is insistent on the '"healthy and perfectly normal ... emotional life"' of '"each of the beings within me"'[106] and elsewhere expresses distaste for the 'abnormal'[107] or 'unfortunate'[108] individuals he encounters at the clinic in Berlin. However, a significant passage in *Man into Woman* suggests that Einar is not completely indifferent to the historical plight and cultural legacy of sexual minorities. During a stay in a small hotel in Paris, Andreas and Grete find themselves in the rooms in which Oscar Wilde spent his last days: 'He had died in the alcove with the red-diapered curtains.'[109] Inspired by this resonant location, they spend their days immersed in Wilde's words, reading 'page after page of the works of the poet' until they come to 'know *De Profundis* and *The Ballad of Reading Gaol* by heart'.[110] Such a detail might seem too implausibly suggestive to introduce into a fiction had it not had its origins in an auto/biographical source. Indeed, Ebershoff's novel retains the 'curtained alcove' which is 'trimmed in red' and the proprietors' 'proud'[111] claim that it was the scene of Wilde's death. However, the implications of this detail – as a testament to the legal persecution of homosexual people and the creative legacy of gay men and women throughout history – are not pursued. Wilde's former residence is disclosed only to Greta and she declines to share it with Einar, foreclosing possibilities for empathy or identification: 'Greta took little note of this bit of history. It seemed too grey a fact to press on Einar.'[112] By contrast, an aversion to suspicions of homosexuality play a much more prominent role in Einar's quest to make sense of his gender identity in *The Danish Girl* and the distancing strategies practised by Andreas are significantly internalised by Einar.

Einar's revelation in the Bibliothèque Nationale is the culmination of a quest which dominates the second section of Ebershoff's novel. If the first part, entitled 'Copenhagen, 1925', is dedicated to depicting the way in which Lili is 'born on the lacquer trunk'[113] of Greta's studio, the second, 'Paris, 1929', depicts Einar's search for an explanation and a solution to the inner conflict which follows Lili's emergence. The Parisian section of Ebershoff's novel is characterised by two narrative trajectories, each of which constitutes a form of education. The reader is educated in early-twentieth-century medical and psychological discourses of sex, gender and sexuality through the promenade of doctors and diagnoses which Einar experiences under the tutelage of his wife and her brother. These encounters have their origins in *Man into Woman* and serve as a prelude to the arrival of Einar's surgeon, Professor Bolk. However, Einar's private investigations, which take place in the illicit world of sex work as well as the scholarly environment of the library, play a more prominent role in shaping his own sense of identity. Einar's commitment to finding a way to 'split' Lili and Einar 'in two'[114] is made at the start of Part Two, following a visit to the voyeuristic booths of Madame Jasmin-Carton's brothel in Paris. His determination to do so within a year or take his own life is compelled by a sense of sexual shame; sitting in a public park with semen stains drying on his trousers as children play around him, the narrator concludes: 'This was when Einar knew something had to change. Einar had become a man governesses feared in a park.'[115] Experiences of shame play a pivotal role in Einar's narrative as imagined by Ebershoff; moreover, the location of suspected sexual transgression in public places of leisure and recreation has a particular charge, associated as it is in this narrative with male same-sex desire.

Prompted by growing concerns about Einar's declining health and motivated by a desire to secure an appropriate diagnosis and treatment, Greta and her brother Carlisle independently engineer a series of encounters with medical experts, during which Einar is subject to interviews, examinations and treatment. Throughout this process Einar is chaperoned and protected by the American siblings who attempt to shield him from distressing diagnoses and harmful treatments; both act in the name of 'a pretty young lady called Lili',[116] who is the passive recipient of their efforts. Greta's approach is secretive and strategic, approaching doctors privately before she exposes Einar to their methods; by contrast, Einar accompanies Carlisle in their first meetings with the candidates which Carlisle has identified. It is an encounter with Dr Hexler which propels Greta and Einar's move to Paris. The radiologist denounces Einar's '"delusion that he is a woman"', declaring that Einar has forfeited his '"free[dom] to roam"'; when Greta declines Hexler's offer to '"get this demon out of him"'[117] the doctor threatens to report Einar to the health authorities as a '"danger to society"'.[118] Greta conceals the letter and its contents, burning it in the stove and attributing their move to an invitation from Hans. Einar's next three medical encounters occur in Paris under the direction of his brother-in-law, Carlisle: the Irish Dr McBride declares Einar a homosexual and advises him to 'ignore'[119] his desires; the genial Dr Mai discloses a diagnosis of schizophrenia to Carlisle and proposes that Einar be admitted to hospital; Dr Buson prescribes a lobotomy as treatment for a multiple personality disorder, an option which Carlisle suggests Einar consider. A desire to suppress potential homosexuality is a recurring concern in these medical encounters. Indeed, Einar recalls a consultation with a doctor regarding his fertility during the early years of his marriage to Greta when he had indignantly rejected his doctor's enquiries about whether he had desires for men: 'Einar told the doctor that he, too, became disturbed when he saw the men with the quick, frightened eyes and the excessively pink skin loitering near the toilets ... Homosexual! How far from the truth!'[120] In *The Danish Girl* Einar's aversion to homosexuality in other men, despite his close emotional attachment to his childhood friend Hans, is a recurring theme. At crucial points in the narrative, Lili's emergence is counterpointed by textual aspersions of homosexuality; Einar's growing gender identification as a woman is implicitly troubled by a fear that his sexual identity will be categorised as homosexual as a consequence.

The existence of subcultures of homosexual men in major European cities in the interwar period is acknowledged in Ebershoff's novel through allusions to coded forms of self-presentation and behaviour and through depictions of the sexual appropriation of public places associated with recreation or culture. Insinuating language works to suggest that this community exists on the margins, beneath the surface or in disguise. On their way to the artists' ball in Copenhagen – Lili's first public engagement – Greta and Lili pass through a cobblestone street 'dark and safe enough ... for the privacy of a secret transaction'.[121] The street hosts a Turkish coffee house, a bordello and a basement bar into which 'a skinny man with a waxed moustache quickly disappeared ... to a place where he could meet others like himself'.[122] In this 'underworld' of racial others and illicit sexuality, the 'skinny man' seeks both community and concealment, his furtive presence beneath the streets unsettling the foundations of the glamorous world of wealth and privilege which Greta and Lili are about to enter. Later in the narrative, it is during an evening assignation by a lake in a public park that Lili's admirer Henrik expresses his feelings for her and reassures her that he 'already know[s]'.[123] In a moment of alienation in which she imagines Einar witnessing the scene, Lili withdraws from Henrik and observes the following: 'a man loitering near the toilets, lighting a book of matches one by one. A second man walked by and then looked over his shoulder.'[124] The men become visible to Lili at the very moment that Einar's presence is imagined, as if manifesting a fear that Lili's heterosexual desire for Henrik might be interpreted as a symptom of Einar's homosexuality. The glamour of socially sanctioned heterosexual romance is contrasted with the subterfuge of male homosexual desire, and Henrik's chivalrous courtship of Lili is juxtaposed with sexual solicitation. In Germany, homosexual people seem to be more visible and socially recognised. While walking in another public park, Lili is declared '"*Lesbienne*"'[125] by two children and she wonders how 'these pretty little boys had managed to hurl something so cruel, and wrong'.[126] By this stage in the narrative, just before she undergoes surgery, Lili's gender identity has been established as taking precedence over Einar's. However, questions of sexual identity and, more explicitly, fears about being mistaken as homosexual still serve as the dominant criteria by which successful gender presentation is judged. 'Loitering' at the edges of Lili's narrative in Paris, homosexuals make a more public appearance at the opera in Dresden, which Einar visits while waiting for admission to Professor Bolk's Women's Clinic: 'Einar went to the box office of the Semperoper and bought a ticket to *Fidelio*. He knew that homosexuals gathered at the opera, and he feared that the woman behind the glass, which was smudged with breath, might think he was one of them.'[127] Here the existence of a public, albeit coded, homosexual culture and community is acknowledged but still disowned. It is clear that Einar is sensitive to these codes but anxious to distance himself from possible membership of the community which they signify.

The imperative to evade categorisation as homosexual arguably finds its vindication in *The Danish Girl* during Einar's privately conducted Paris education, which takes place in two locations: a brothel and a public library. It is only after Einar is expelled from the former that he seeks enlightenment in the latter. If the conversion of Grete/Greta from a Danish artist in *Man into Woman* to an American expatriate in *The Danish Girl* and her transformation from a supporting character in the auto/biographical source to a leading protagonist in the novel is one of the most substantial creative interpolations in Ebershoff's reworking, then the introduction of pivotal scenes taking place in a brothel is perhaps the most provocative departure. These scenes are provocative not because of their sexual content but because of the role they play in implying that it is sexual identity which secures gender identity, positing a mutually reinforcing relationship which queer theory has done much to disentangle. While Greta labours to meet the demands of the new market for her art in Paris, both Lili and Einar develop daily routines marked by leisure and recreation. Lili becomes a regular at a public swimming pool and Einar becomes a habitual visitor to Madame Jasmin-Carton's establishment, where he pays to occupy rooms whose internal windows enable him to watch women exposing their bodies to male clients. He is quick to insist that his motivations are 'not the same as other men';[128] he attends only to watch and to 'examine women, to see how their bodies attached limb to trunk and produced a female'.[129] While Greta is busy filling a notebook with a 'career's worth'[130] of drawings of Lili, Einar is engaged in a different kind of life class. While Lili has ample opportunity to observe the diversity of female anatomy engaged in unselfconscious behaviour in the single-sex swimming pool, Einar turns to sex workers, who dance 'angrily'[131] in their booths, as models for the female form. As a male heterosexual client Einar can pay for the privilege of intimately scrutinising women's bodies and does so in a context where their bodies are sexualised and commodified. When Einar pays a special fee to watch a man and woman engage in sexual intercourse, this scene proves pivotal in his conception of the meaning and origins of Lili's gender identification. He watches a younger man penetrate an older woman as they 'thrash' on the floor, then ejaculate over her 'puckered face'.[132] Realising that he has been aroused to the point of ejaculation himself, Einar makes the following deduction: 'Only then, when Einar looked down into his own lap, did he discover the salty stain, as if a teacup of seawater had overturned. Then he knew, although he supposed he had always known: he wanted the boy to do that to Lili.'[133] The possible sexual and gender identifications available in this scene are multiple and ambiguous and do not exclude the homoerotic possibility that Einar is aroused by the thought of being the object of a man's sexual desire. However, the 'evidence' of Einar's sexual arousal – in a narrative where he is depicted as rarely taking the initiative in his sexual relationship with Greta – is here offered as 'proof' of his heterosexuality. It seems that Einar's identification of Lili's heterosexuality can only be expressed through the vehicle of male sexual agency: hence, Einar vicariously imagines the man he has been observing penetrating Lili, who becomes the passive object, not agent, of this far from tender sexual encounter. A subsequent encounter serves to further complicate the lessons which Einar learns from his education in the brothel. The room that Einar habitually occupies has two windows and he scrupulously avoids the one on the left: 'But the other window shade Einar never touched. That was because he knew what was in there. He somehow knew that once he had pulled that shade he would never return to the window on the right.'[134] The window on the left opens on to a naked man and when Einar does lift the shade he finds himself unconsciously moved to undress. Einar's 'unbuckled pants' are 'bunched at his ankles'[135] as he falls to his knees, in a posture which suggests urgent desire. However, he is also wearing Lili's 'oyster-grey knickers and a matching camisole',[136] and as he realises that he is being watched by a man in another window he experiences a revelation:

> It was as if it were the most natural thing in the world for a man to be staring at her in her intimate underthings, the straps of the camisole across her shoulders. As if something inside Einar had snapped, like the canvas window blind, and told him, more plainly than ever before, that this was who he was: Einar was a guise.[137]

Einar exposes Lili's body to the gaze of this male stranger, imitating the movements of the female sex workers. Again this scene is full of ambiguity; it is Einar who falls to his knees in desire at the sight of a naked man and who opens his mouth to another man's penis (when the other client enters his room), but his response is given as vindication of Lili's existence as a heterosexual woman. It is the gaze of a fellow client in a brothel which brings Lili into being, despite the fact that this man was seemingly in pursuit of a same-sex encounter. The possibility that the man is attracted to Lili as a transgender woman is not entertained in Einar's mind. Rather this scene serves to confirm Lili's gender via her sexuality; sexuality becomes the arbiter of appropriate gender identity and Lili's femininity is finally affirmed by men's heterosexual desires for her. In other words, in *The Danish Girl*, the conclusions which Einar draws from his 'education' in the brothel and the Bibliothèque are distinctly normative. From his experiences in the brothel he identifies Lili as heterosexual, and from his research in the library he deduces that he is in possession of female sex organs: in other words sexuality is depicted as determining sex (if Lili is attracted to men she must be female), and sex is depicted as determining gender (if Einar has female sex organs they must be the cause of his femininity), with Lili's gender emerging as the 'natural' outcome of her 'true' sex and her heterosexuality as the guarantor of her gender.

Lili Elbe's apparently uncritical subscription to normative gender roles in *Man into Woman* prompted Sandy Stone to express scepticism about this memoir's status as an 'authentic record', as claimed in the title of the first edition of its English translation. In 'The Empire Strikes Back: A Posttranssexual Manifesto', Stone asks: 'Not by whom but *for* whom was Lili Elbe constructed? Under whose gaze did her text fall? And consequently what stories appear and disappear in this kind of seduction?' [emphasis in original][138] It is evident that *Man into Woman* exhibits a complex relationship both to literary genre and to dominant ways of thinking about sex, gender and sexuality: borrowing from the conventions of fiction, memoir and biography, its subject self-consciously reflects on the conditions of her negotiations with both narrative and identity. The question of 'what stories appear and disappear'[139] becomes more pronounced when this unique testimony serves as a source text for historical fiction. Written from the vantage point of the late twentieth century, *The Danish Girl* does not impose contemporary categories of identity on to the past but neither does it significantly historicise Elbe's experience in ways which might offer new perspectives on her narrative. The tripartite structure of *The Danish Girl* locates each section of the narrative in a single European city and a specific year – Copenhagen in 1925, Paris in 1929 and Dresden in 1930 – but effects an omission which is worthy of a final note. In *Man into Woman* Andreas's first operation is undertaken by a 'Dr Hardenfeld' in Berlin prior to his entry into Professor Kreutz's Women's Clinic in Dresden. By contrast, in *The Danish Girl*, Einar's treatment takes place in Dresden only and the Berlin interlude is entirely excised. Weimar Berlin in the early 1930s presents considerable opportunities for a historical novelist exploring the lives of people whose sexed, gendered or sexual identity was perceived to be, or experienced as, at odds with the prevailing norms. In this interwar period, between the founding of the Republic in 1919 and the rise of Hitler in 1933, Berlin was widely renowned for its thriving gender and sexual subcultures. Moreover, it was also the home of Magnus Hirschfeld's pioneering Institute for Sexual Research, whose libraries and archives were destroyed by the Nazis in 1933. Indeed, Hirschfeld is identified as supervising Elbe's treatment in Berlin in some accounts of her life.[140] In this context the exclusion of the Berlin passage – and the opportunities to explore new formations of identity and community which it presents – might be seen as symptomatic of a tension between privatising and historicising impulses in this historical fiction, with personal experience and period detail arguably privileged over the imagining of collective identity and historical change.

Notes

1. Prosser, *Second Skins*, p. 101.
2. Amin, 'Temporality', *TSQ: Transgender Studies Quarterly Special Issue – Postposttranssexual*, p. 219.
3. Republished by Blue Boat Books, UK, in 2004 under the title *Man into Woman: The First Sex Change – A Portrait of Lili Elbe*.
4. Prosser notes that Elbe's biography is cited in memoirs by Stephanie Castle (1992), Jan Morris (1974) and Reneé Richards (1983). See also Meyerowitz, *How Sex Changed: A History of Transsexuality in the United States*.
5. *Man into Woman*, p. 24.
6. Morland, '"The Glans Opens Like a Book": Writing and Reading the Intersexed Body', pp. 335–48.
7. David L. Eng, J. Halberstam and José Esteban Muñoz describe queer studies as a '"subjectless" critique' which 'disallows any positing of a proper subject *of* or object *for* the field by insisting that queer has no fixed political referent'. 'Introduction: What's Queer about Queer Studies Now?', p. 3.
8. Getsy, 'Capacity', *Postposttranssexual*, p. 48.
9. I will refer to 'Andreas' and 'Lili' (*Man into Woman*) and to 'Einar' and 'Lili' (*The Danish Girl*) according to the different narrative positions and perspectives which these characters occupy in each text. I will use 'Elbe' when referring to the historical person who exists outside of the texts.
10. *Man into Woman*, p. 18.
11. *Man into Woman*, p. 60.
12. *Man into Woman*, p. 60.
13. *Man into Woman*, p. 237.
14. *Man into Woman*, p. 267.
15. *Man into Woman*, pp. 237, 255, 267.
16. *Man into Woman*, p. 266.
17. Prosser, *Second Skins*, p. 102.
18. *Man into Woman*, p. 267.
19. *Man into Woman*, p. 267.
20. Prosser, *Second Skins*, p. 113.
21. Amin, 'Temporality', p. 219.
22. Salamon, *Assuming a Body: Transgender and Rhetoric of Materiality*, p. 87.
23. Amin, 'Temporality', p. 220.
24. *Man into Woman*, p. 111.

25. Morland, 'Intersex', *Postposttranssexual*, p. 114.
26. *Man into Woman*, p. 24.
27. Foucault, 'Introduction', *Herculine Barbin*, p. vii.
28. Foucault, 'Introduction', p. viii.
29. Chase, 'Hermaphrodites with Attitude', p. 189.
30. Wilkerson, 'Normate Sex and its Discontents', in McRuer and Mollow (eds), *Sex and Disability*, p. 193.
31. *Man into Woman*, p. 262.
32. Fausto-Sterling, *Sexing the Body: Gender Politics and the Construction of Sexuality*, p. 37.
33. Dreger, *Hermaphrodites and the Medical Invention of Sex*, p. 11.
34. *Man into Woman*, p. 4.
35. *Man into Woman*, p. 5.
36. *Man into Woman*, pp. 8, 34.
37. *Man into Woman*, p. 93.
38. *Man into Woman*, p. 111.
39. *Man into Woman*, p. 159.
40. *Man into Woman*, p. 215.
41. *Man into Woman*, p. 222.
42. *Man into Woman*, p. 219.
43. Mak, *Doubting Sex: Inscriptions, Bodies and Selves in Nineteenth-Century Hermaphrodite Case Histories*, p. 27.
44. *Man into Woman*, p. 220.
45. *Man into Woman*, p. 221.
46. *Man into Woman*, pp. 92, 171.
47. Ebershoff, *The Danish Girl*, p. 56.
48. Ebershoff, *The Danish Girl*, p. 58.
49. Ebershoff, *The Danish Girl*, p. 52.
50. Ebershoff, *The Danish Girl*, p. 85. This metaphor seems to draw on the trope of being 'trapped in the wrong body' which has been the subject of much debate and critique in contemporary transgender studies and activism. See Bettcher, 'Trapped in the Wrong Theory: Rethinking Trans Oppression and Resistance', p. 388.
51. Ebershoff, *The Danish Girl*, p. 86.
52. Ebershoff, *The Danish Girl*, p. 128.
53. Ebershoff, *The Danish Girl*, p. 159.
54. Ebershoff, *The Danish Girl*, p. 159.
55. Ebershoff, *The Danish Girl*, p. 159.
56. Ebershoff, *The Danish Girl*, p. 148.
57. Ebershoff, *The Danish Girl*, p. 160.
58. Ebershoff, *The Danish Girl*, pp. 160, 170.
59. Ebershoff, *The Danish Girl*, p. 85.
60. *Man into Woman*, p. 64.
61. *Man into Woman*, p. 264.
62. *Man into Woman*, p. 135.
63. *Man into Woman*, p. 157.

64. *Man into Woman*, p. 164.
65. *Man into Woman*, p. 158.
66. *Man into Woman*, p. 158.
67. *Man into Woman*, p. 187.
68. *Man into Woman*, p. 222.
69. *Man into Woman*, p. 223.
70. *Man into Woman*, p. 61.
71. Ebershoff, *The Danish Girl*, p. 5.
72. Ebershoff, *The Danish Girl*, p. 3.
73. Ebershoff, *The Danish Girl*, p. 41.
74. Prosser, *Second Skins*, p. 5.
75. Salamon, *Assuming a Body*, pp. 171–2.
76. Halberstam, *Female Masculinity*, p. 165.
77. Ebershoff, *The Danish Girl*, p. 38.
78. Ebershoff, *The Danish Girl*, p. 185.
79. Ebershoff , *The Danish Girl*, p. 40.
80. In comparison to the historic presence of people of Chinese heritage in California, migration to Denmark is thought to have been mostly male and an effect of sea faring and trade.
81. Ebershoff, *The Danish Girl*, p. 7.
82. Ebershoff, *The Danish Girl*, p. 22.
83. Ebershoff, *The Danish Girl*, p. 259.
84. Ebershoff, *The Danish Girl*, pp. 51, 219.
85. Ebershoff, *The Danish Girl*, pp. 14, 61, 76, 259.
86. Ebershoff, *The Danish Girl*, p. 61.
87. Ebershoff, *The Danish Girl*, pp. 8–9.
88. See Ebershoff, *The Danish Girl*, pp. 24–5, 27, 100, 113.
89. Ebershoff, *The Danish Girl*, p. 14.
90. Ebershoff, *The Danish Girl*, p. 76.
91. Ebershoff, *The Danish Girl*, p. 87.
92. Ebershoff, *The Danish Girl*, p. 51.
93. Ebershoff, *The Danish Girl*, p. 4.
94. Ebershoff, *The Danish Girl*, p. 64.
95. Ebershoff, *The Danish Girl*, p. 111.
96. *Man into Woman*, p. 42.
97. Ebershoff , *The Danish Girl*, p. 22.
98. Ebershoff, *The Danish Girl*, p. 61.
99. Matta, 'Ambiguous Bodies and Deviant Sexualities: Hermaphrodites, Homosexuality, and Surgery in the United States, 1850–1904', p. 75.
100. Reis, 'Divergence of Disorder? The Politics of Naming Intersex', p. 540.
101. Dreger, *Hermaphrodites and the Medical Invention of Sex*, p. 8.
102. Fausto-Sterling, *Sexing the Body*, p. 71.
103. Johnson, 'Transgender Subject Access: History and Current Practice', p. 671.
104. Quoted in Dreger, *Hermaphrodites and the Medical Invention of Sex*, p. 136.

105. Prosser, *Second Skins*, p. 139.
106. *Man into Woman*, p. 56.
107. *Man into Woman*, p. 54.
108. *Man into Woman*, p. 73.
109. *Man into Woman*, p. 73.
110. *Man into Woman*, p. 74.
111. Ebershoff, *The Danish Girl*, p. 134.
112. Ebershoff, *The Danish Girl*, p. 134.
113. Ebershoff, *The Danish Girl*, p. 148.
114. Ebershoff, *The Danish Girl*, p. 128.
115. Ebershoff, *The Danish Girl*, p. 127.
116. Ebershoff, *The Danish Girl*, p. 173.
117. Ebershoff, *The Danish Girl*, p. 115.
118. Ebershoff, *The Danish Girl*, p. 134.
119. Ebershoff, *The Danish Girl*, p. 168.
120. Ebershoff, *The Danish Girl*, p. 57.
121. Ebershoff, *The Danish Girl*, p. 50.
122. Ebershoff, *The Danish Girl*, p. 50.
123. Ebershoff, *The Danish Girl*, p. 70.
124. Ebershoff, *The Danish Girl*, p. 70.
125. Ebershoff, *The Danish Girl*, p. 206.
126. Ebershoff, *The Danish Girl*, p. 207.
127. Ebershoff, *The Danish Girl*, p. 216.
128. Ebershoff, *The Danish Girl*, p. 121.
129. Ebershoff, *The Danish Girl*, p. 121.
130. Ebershoff, *The Danish Girl*, p. 122.
131. Ebershoff, *The Danish Girl*, p. 122.
132. Ebershoff, *The Danish Girl*, p. 126.
133. Ebershoff, *The Danish Girl*, p. 126.
134. Ebershoff, *The Danish Girl*, p. 142.
135. Ebershoff, *The Danish Girl*, p. 143.
136. Ebershoff, *The Danish Girl*, p. 143.
137. Ebershoff, *The Danish Girl*, p. 144.
138. Stone, 'The Empire Strikes Back: A Posttranssexual Manifesto', in Stryker and Whittle (eds), *The Transgender Studies Reader*, p. 224.
139. Stone, 'The Empire Strikes Back', p. 224.
140. See Meyerowitz, *How Sex Changed*, p. 20.

Chapter 5

Blue Births and Last Words: Rewriting Race, Nation and Family in Jackie Kay's *Trumpet* (1998)

In her 1998 biography of the white American jazz pianist and bandleader Billy Tipton (1914–89), *Suits Me: The Double Life of Billy Tipton*, Diane Wood Middlebrook offers a regretful authorial aside in the course of her reconstruction of Tipton's life and times: 'Too bad for us that, unlike some of the male impersonators we know about, Billy did not write a memoir or leave a letter marked with the instruction "To be opened after my death."'[1] Tipton was a successful professional entertainer and musical agent, as well as a husband and father to four sons, whose death attracted national attention when the fact of his female-sexed body was made public knowledge by the press. Middlebrook's fantasy of a deathbed disclosure reveals an assumption that there is a secret which needs to be revealed and betrays a conviction that Tipton's gender identity is a mystery requiring resolution. In the absence of such a document the author draws her own conclusions, with the reference to Tipton as a 'male impersonator' anticipating the emphasis on theatrical performance which will characterise her biographical standpoint. By contrast, Jackie Kay's 1998 novel *Trumpet* – inspired by the life of Billy Tipton and published in the same year as Middlebrook's biography – does incorporate the discovery of a letter inscribed 'To be opened after my death', written by the deceased jazz trumpeter Joss Moody and addressed to his son Colman. The contents of the letter are not disclosed until the penultimate chapter – entitled 'Last Word' – which is one of only two chapters in the novel which represent Joss's narrative perspective. However, the reader who shares Middlebrook's curiosity, anticipating dramatic and possibly intimate revelations, is likely to be disappointed. Joss's letter to his son does contain personal reflections on identity, but these reflections pertain not to his sex, gender or sexuality but to his identity as a Scottish man of African heritage. It tells a story – or rather stories – of origins, but these origins extend to his own father and beyond, situating his life within a collective history of migration and mobility, both forced and elective. Natal birth is no more the definitive origin of Joss's sex or gender than it is of his identity as a black man and a Scot. This arguably subversive narrative shift serves two purposes: firstly, it challenges the cultural (and legal) construction of birth as the immutable origin of identity, and secondly, it reminds the reader that gender is only one of a number of identities and identifications which constitute a sense of self. In 'Trans/scriptions: Homing Desires, (Trans)sexual Citizenship and Racialized Bodies', Nael Bhanji suggests that a 'failure to take into account racial and ethnic differences'[2] has served to perpetuate 'unspoken white privilege'[3] within transgender theory. In this context, Kay's novel explores the ways in which sex, gender, sexuality and race are closely intertwined, with Joss's 'last words' drawing attention to the ways in which gender is a racially constructed category. In '"My Father Didn't Have a Dick": Social Death and Jackie Kay's *Trumpet*', Matt Richardson argues that 'the undoing and reworking of black gender categories is a key facet of social death';[4] this chapter examines Kay's resistance to the attempted 'undoing and reworking' of transgender identity in relation to her representation of a Scottish man of African heritage.

The motif of birth – a legally and medically mediated life event which has been complicit in the state management of sexed, gendered, raced and other categories of identity – is highlighted in the first chapter dedicated to Joss's point of view in *Trumpet*. In 'Music', Kay employs free indirect discourse to render Joss's creative unconscious in a non-linear and fragmentary manner. Through the vehicle of transformative performance – an experience depicted as interiorised and subjective rather than externalised and theatrical – Joss descends to a 'place down there' which 'forces him to witness his own death':[5]

> Down there at the bottom he can see himself when he was a tiny baby, blue in the face. The trumpet takes him back to the blue birth. In the music at the bottom the cord starts to swing. It swings round and round and up and down until he slices it, cuts the cord and watches the cord slither into a bucket.[6]

The reference to a 'tiny baby, blue in the face' combined with an encircling umbilical cord is suggestive of an averted infant death, with the motif of posthumous life extending back almost to the point of birth. Indeed, the 'blue birth' takes on multiple meanings in the course of the narrative, which questions ideas of origin, heredity and heritage. In the immediate narrative context of a virtuosic jazz improvisation, the 'blue birth' signifies the musical heritage of the African diaspora – especially as it is mediated through American culture – which is a central feature of Joss's sense of identity as an artist and as a black man. In other narrative contexts the significance of 'birth' as a determining concept is explored in relation to sexed and gendered identity (and its corresponding colour codings), national identity (the blue of the Saltire) and family identity (the distinction between 'birth' and adopted family). This chapter will begin by considering the novel within the contexts of transgender life writing, focusing on its purposeful thwarting of narrative imperatives which privilege 'birth' over agency and identification when it comes to considering sex and gender. It will then turn to the idea of origin in relation to racial and national constructions of identity, looking at how the narrative challenges the unspoken equation of Scottishness with whiteness. Finally, it will turn to the motif of adoption – and especially transcultural adoption – exploring the ways in which the narrative borrows and reworks key motifs from adoption narratives, including those concerning secrecy and tracing. These themes will be brought together in a consideration of the significance of the recurring figure of the 'small black girl'[7] – Josephine Moody – who appears in the dreams and memories of a number of key characters, including Joss, his wife Mille and their son Colman. While such a figure might be seen as evidence of the persistence, albeit ghostly, of identities assigned at birth, I will argue that this figure signifies ideas of continuity which undermine the binary logic of male and female and the temporal logic of 'before' and 'after' which often inform narrative attempts to forcibly expose transgender lives.

'Everybody wants to know the wrong thing': Tipton, *Trumpet* and Transgender Lives

Jackie Kay's novel *Trumpet* explores what Halberstam has termed the 'violent ... and imprecise project'[8] of transgender biography through the figure of Sophie Stones, an ambitious English tabloid press journalist who attempts to enlist Joss's son Colman in her quest to produce a sensationalist account of his father's life. The consistent refusal of Joss's family, friends and colleagues to comply with Stones's script of deception and betrayal provides the narrative structure for the novel, which concludes with the anticipated reconciliation of the grieving and estranged mother and son rather than with the kind of revelations which Stones assumes her editors and readers will relish. This fictional narrative strategy is all the more striking when compared with a biographical account of Billy Tipton's life which was published in the same year.

Commissioned by Kitty Tipton Oakes, one of Billy Tipton's former wives, and written with access to family archives and a licence to exercise editorial autonomy, Diane Wood Middlebrook's 1998 biography *Suits Me: The Double Life of Billy Tipton* is meticulously researched and imaginatively conceived, conjuring a portrait of Depression-era America peopled by wing-walking aviators (Tipton's father, G. W. Tipton), dance marathon 'horses' (Tipton's first partner and civil wife, Non Earl Harrell) and itinerant entertainers and entrepreneurs. Middlebrook's depiction of Tipton's birthplace, Oklahoma City, as a place brought into being by a land rush which saw the city settled within the space of a single day – 22 April 1889 – situates his story within a particular American mythology of self-invention. The testimony of fellow musician and bass player Wayne Benson is not untypical of those given by Tipton's family, friends and colleagues:

> When I read this article I called him [a guitar-playing friend]. I said, 'Jim, do you remember Billy Tipton?' He said, 'Sure – everyone down here knew she was a woman.' I said, 'That's what I've been trying to tell everyone!' But no one thought anything about it, no one cared, the people I knew – no one cared at all! So what!'[9]

The object of Benson's incredulity is not the posthumous revelation of Tipton's sex but the construction of the fiction that this information constitutes shocking news. Tipton is not the only female-sexed person living as a man in his milieu – Buck Thomason, a programmer at the KFXR radio station in Oklahoma City, played an important role in Tipton's career and is a similarly accepted fixture in the local entertainment business circuit. For others, Tipton's gender was never in doubt and even if the disclosure of his sex does prove unexpected it does not compromise their loyalty to his memory. Clarence Clagle, a young piano player taken in by Tipton and Harrell, insists: '"You're not going to get me to say anything bad about either one of them! I wouldn't even think about it, you know, because they were nice people."'[10] Betty Cox, another of Tipton's wives, discloses to the author: '"I cannot in my wildest dreams accept the fact I finally know to be true."'[11] However, despite the recurring affection and loyalty to

Tipton evident in these testimonies the motifs of 'deception, dishonesty, and fraud'[12] which Halberstam foregrounds in her critique of transgender biography remain prominent in Middlebrook's account of his life. From the outset, Middlebrook emphasises what she refers to as the 'scale of the deception and the scarcity of explanations',[13] drawing analogies between Tipton's profession as a performer and his life as a man to depict him as a 'skilled impersonator'[14] with a 'gift for mimicry'[15] and a capacity to conjure the 'illusion of masculinity'.[16] When she describes Tipton as 'both acting the role and acting the actor who played it'[17] Middlebrook mobilises performance as a metaphor for dissimulation, a persistent trope which prompted Talia Mae Bettcher's satirical comment that 'If all the world's a stage on which we all play a part, trans individuals play actors'.[18] For Middlebrook, Tipton's wives are unwitting accomplices who have been shrewdly enlisted to maintain the illusion of his masculinity and it is their assumed point of view which Middlebrook adopts, at one point speculatively inserting her younger self into the narrative:

> What if I had met Billy at age eighteen, Betty's age when they became lovers? In 1957, I was as ignorant about the specifics of sexual intercourse as most of my girlfriends, and I did not know much about male anatomy. Would I have discovered Billy's secret?[19]

Elsewhere she enlists Tipton himself as complicit in her own biographical project, imagining the scene of his death as premeditated to ensure discovery: 'The dramatic way she surrendered her secret at the time of her death suggests that she wanted the disguise to become part of the record too.'[20] Tipton's sex was identified by an attending paramedic and revealed to his unsuspecting youngest son; his biographer turns this scene of unwitting exposure into an act of agency, interpreting his final breath as anticipating her own endeavour: 'That sigh was a secret escaping.'[21] The transgender subject is depicted as legitimating the biographer's attempt (in Halberstam's words) to 'erase the carefully managed details of the life of a passing person'.[22] In response to intrusive questions about her life with Tipton, Kitty Oakes is recorded as having exclaimed: '"Everybody wants to know the wrong thing."'[23] This heartfelt complaint finds echoes in the depiction of Joss's wife Millie in Kay's novel *Trumpet*, whose experience serves to illustrate the 'brutal'[24] effects of asking the wrong questions about transgender lives.

The 'brutal erasure'[25] of transgender lives by state apparatus and media representation is a central concern in Kay's *Trumpet*, which explores the tensions between protocols of identity documentation in death, the imperatives of tabloid journalism and the lived experience of gender identity in familial, domestic and workplace settings. This erasure is often a posthumous exercise, whereby revelations of sexed identity after death are employed to rewrite the life of the transgender subject. In *Trumpet* it is Joss's widow, Millie, through whom the emotional effects of this erasure are registered, translating public discourses of scandal into private and personal expressions of grief. Millie is firmly placed within the domestic sphere of family and marriage, her first-person narratives always given the same heading – 'House and Home' – whereas those attributed to Colman and Stones vary. The narrative structure of the novel reflects the convergence of news reporting and lifestyle journalism by mimicking the format of the broadsheet press Sunday supplements, with chapters alluding to personal finance ('Money' and 'Shares'), arts and culture ('Music' and 'Today's Television'), leisure and recreation ('Travel' and 'Good Hotels') and design and fashion ('Interiors' and 'Style'), as well as 'Features', 'Editorials' and 'Obituaries'. Indeed, in Millie's nostalgic recollection of the past, the Sunday newspapers are an integral feature of a cherished routine, providing recognition of Joss's professional and artistic standing through interviews and reviews as well as the harmless diversion of gossip:

> Sundays with Joss at home, not travelling with the band. Sundays at home with me. We wake and fall back to sleep together several times before we get up. Each time we wake we smile kindly at each other, full of sleepy love . . . I like Sundays. First the lovemaking, then the newspapers.[26]

By contrast, after Joss's death the same newspapers become a menacing agent of intrusion, violating the private space of the couple's marriage. Withdrawing to her family's holiday home on the east coast of Scotland, Millie is unable to escape the 'assault' of the tabloid media:

> Even here now the sound of cameras, like the assault of a machine-gun, is still playing inside my head . . . Their fingers on the triggers, they don't take them off until they finish the film, till I've been shot over and over again . . . With every snap and flash and whirr, I felt myself, the core of myself, being eaten away.[27]

Besieged by the flashlights of the press and fleeing like a fugitive, Millie turns to the imagery of post-war film noir to describe her plight, comparing herself to the dying (male) protagonist of Billy

Wilder's 1944 film *Double Indemnity* and picturing herself as 'an actress in an old black and white movie who has just bumped off her husband and is escaping'.[28] As Millie herself insists, 'I haven't killed anyone. I haven't done anything wrong,'[29] but she feels criminalised by the relentless and punitive attention of the press. The distortion of reality by sensationalist and voyeuristic journalism is a recurring theme in Millie's narrative: 'When Joss was alive, life was never like this. It was real . . . Reality has stopped.'[30] Crucially, the authenticity of her relationship with Joss is not in question. What Millie is grappling with is the double death which she has suffered, not only the loss of her husband but the destruction of his memory in the public sphere: 'For that first three days, I felt my whole life ruined. Not just by Joss's death, but by the reporting of his death.'[31]

While the flashlights which cast Millie's life into sinister shadows are wielded by anonymous hands, the intrusions of exploitative tabloid journalism are embodied in a single figure in Kay's narrative: Sophie Stones, a tenacious but inexperienced investigative journalist whose ambition is fuelled by personal insecurity. If Millie's cinematic reference points suggest a generational coming of age in the post-war years, Stones situates herself and her work within a specific contemporary moment: 'The nineties are obsessed with sex, infidelity, scandal, sleaze, perverts. The nineties love the private life. The private life that turns suddenly and horrifically public. The sly life that hides pure filth and sin.'[32] Stones's references to the reporting of a 'sex scandal' which ended the political career of MP David Mellor in 1992, the accidental death by erotic asphyxiation of MP Stephen Milligan in 1994 and the arrest of British screen actor Hugh Grant for 'lewd conduct in a public place' in Los Angeles in 1994 would seem to support this portrait of the preoccupations of the British tabloid press in the 1990s. However, they also serve an expedient purpose, implicitly supplying justification for her actions by allusion to assumed reader interest and routine industry practice and providing a discourse of sexualised deviance to which Joss's life is subsumed. Stones variously refers to Joss as a transvestite or a lesbian, commenting with approval that 'Transvestite has a nice pervy ring to it'[33] and relishing the possibility of access to Edith Moore, 'The mother of the famous transvestite'.[34] However, there is some crude recognition of the inadequacy (if not the offence) of these terms, with Stones conceding: 'No, this isn't a straightforward tranny. Wasn't there an army officer that lived her life as a man? Good background.'[35] This allusion to James Miranda Barry – rather than figures more prominent in the history of popular press coverage, such as Christine Jorgensen – suggests a paucity of precedents for transgender masculinity. Whether that of a transvestite or a lesbian, Joss's story represents for Stones a narrative of scandalous revelation and implied imposture:

> Lesbian stories are in. Everyone loves a good story about a famous dyke tennis star or actress or singer. And this one is the pick of the bunch. The best yet. Lesbians who adopted a son; one playing mummy, one playing daddy. The big butch frauds. Couldn't be better.[36]

Stones's recruitment of Joss's adopted son Colman as an accomplice to her project lends a dynamic of personal and familial betrayal to a plot in which Stones would otherwise remain an outsider. Exploiting Colman's distress, confusion and grief following the death of his father, Stones triumphantly notes her apparent success in enlisting him to her own narrative point of view: 'This boy gets better every day. He's grasped the plot.'[37] Indeed, Colman's attitude to his father's sex seems to have already been shaped by pathologising and criminalising media representations, with the impact of films like *Psycho* (USA, dir. Alfred Hitchcock, 1960) and *The Silence of the Lambs* (USA, dir. Jonathan Demme, 1991) possibly playing a part in the lurid images that he conjures after seeing his father's corpse: 'I take a quick look. But that look is still in my head now. It has stayed in my head – the image of my father in a woman's body. Like some pervert. Some psycho. I imagine him now smearing lipstick on a mirror before he died.'[38] However, even at his most compromised Colman is aware of the role he is playing, albeit remaining hostage to the anger and hurt which is driving him. Stones and Colman vie for authorship of Joss's life, but Colman is under no illusion about the motivation driving his involvement or its emotional subtext: 'I'll write his fucking biography. I'll tell his whole story. I'll be his Judas. That's what Oscar Wilde said, isn't it. My dad often quoted it and laughed. "Every man needs his disciples but it's Judas that writes the biography."'[39] The prospect of Colman acting as a Judas to his own father in the telling of his life serves to forcefully underline the role of betrayal in the 'violent and imprecise'[40] project of transgender biography.

The dramatic structure of this 1998 novel seems to suggest that the posthumous intervention of the popular press poses a greater threat to Joss's identity as a man than what Dean Spade has called the 'administrative violence' of 'normal life'.[41] In life Joss is able to successfully navigate state-sanctioned relationships, such as marriage and adoption, which are reliant on identity documentation; it is in death that these apparatus become problematic. It is in the formal registration of Joss's death and management of his body – by the doctor, the registrar and the undertaker – that his gender becomes subject to contestation by individuals acting on behalf of the state. Caught between their official duties and responsibilities and their personal doubts and sympathies, these characters represent both the violence and the vulnerability of systems of state-regulated identity. This tension is exemplified in the motif of handwriting which is prominent in these encounters: the personal idiosyncrasies of the hand are at odds with its official function in the service of impersonal power, and the individual character of the written word testifies to the diversity of lived identity in the face of bureaucratic categorisation. The doctor who attends to Joss's body after his death resists the depersonalising effects of the process of completing a death certificate: 'it was not just a body to her. It was a man, a person.'[42] Dr Krishnamurty is the first to formally 'erase'[43] Joss's identity under the pressure of her official function, but the manner in which she does so is suggestive of doubt: 'She crossed "male" out and wrote "female" in her rather bad doctor's handwriting. She looked at the word "female" and thought it wasn't quite clear enough. She crossed that out, tutting to herself, and printed "female" in large childish letters.'[44] The reversion to a 'childish' hand even as she seeks to assert her professional authority suggests a loss of certainty and the multiple crossings-out draw attention more to what has been erased than to what has been affirmed. If Dr Krishnamurty's hand is 'bad' and 'childish', the registrar who formally records Joss's death prides himself on his elegant and well-practised calligraphy. Like Krishnamurty, Mohammad Nassar Sharif recognises the potentially alienating effects of the process: 'The certificates were not simply pieces of paper with names and numbers on them. There were people in there.'[45] For Sharif the art of the fountain pen represents a humanising touch in the face of the more functional and impersonal mass-produced ballpoint pen: 'He knew of coroners and doctors who were overfond of the red pen. Compared to his beautiful black Indian ink, the red biro was a brash, loudmouthed, insensitive cousin who ought not to have received *anything* in the family fortune' [emphasis in original].[46] The violence of the red pen, with its disciplinary overtones of correction, is evoked by the undertaker Albert Holding in his desire to resolve the apparent contradiction presented to him by Joss's corpse:

> Holding pulled open his special drawer to check that his red pen was still there. If there was anything untoward in the death certificate, he would be duty bound to correct it with this very red pen . . . He

almost wished it would happen. If he could have the satisfaction of brutally and violently obliterating 'male' and inserting female in bold, unequivocal red, then at least he would have something to do.[47]

By contrast with the 'duty bound' red pen, there is significantly some leeway in Sharif's deployment of his fountain pen and – by extension – his interpretation of his role: this extends to suggesting names for infants registered by indecisive parents and, conversely, advising parents regretful of their choices that common usage is more important than official record. Millie's request that Joss be 'registered in death as he was in life'[48] is met with a sympathetic and pragmatic response from Sharif: 'He dipped his marble fountain pen in the black Indian ink and wrote the name *Joss Moody* on the death certificate. He wrote the date. He paused before he ticked "female" on the death certificate, then handed the pen to her.'[49] Joss's name is the marker of his lived identity and gender and by retaining it Sharif goes some way to preserving Joss in death as he was in life. The hesitant hand over the category of sex remains ambiguous but the force of erasure is suspended in a gesture which underlines the disparity between the function of names in state-sanctioned documentation and their vernacular meaning in social contexts. The role of people of South Asian heritage in the state-sanctioned adjudication of Joss's sex and gender after his death, and the uses to which 'black Indian ink'[50] is put in official documentation, draws attention both to a history of migration mediated by Empire and to the diversity of British identity, despite its frequent conflation with white Englishness. These themes are explored in Kay's novel through two significant departures from the historical life of Billy Tipton: where Tipton was a white American, Joss is a Scot of African origin.

'Scotland. Africa. Slavery. Freedom': The Black and the Blue in *Trumpet*

Jackie Kay's novel tells the story of three Scottish men of African heritage: John Moore, who is sent to Scotland as a boy for an education and made to work as a servant to his patron; Joss Moody, son to John and his white Scottish wife, Edith; and Colman Moody, the mixed-race son of unknown parents who is adopted by Joss and his white Scottish wife, Millie. Both Edith and Millie are depicted principally as widows, whose lives lose meaning and purpose after the loss of their husbands and whose relationship with their children is strained or remote. In this way the novel seems to emphasise a paternal lineage (in contrast to Kay's 1991 poetry sequence *The Adoption Papers*, which gives voice to a white birth mother, a white adoptive mother and their mixed-race daughter), but this strategy can equally be described as foregrounding questions of racial identity, African heritage and black culture. In this way both texts address what Carole Jones describes as 'a dominant theme in [Kay's] work – the inherent contradiction as some people see it in being black and Scottish'.[51]

While Tipton played the piano and Joss plays the trumpet, both are members of a musical culture inextricably linked to both the history of racial oppression in America and the immense creative legacy of people of African origin in America and beyond. As a musician and performer Tipton came of age at a time when music originating in African American culture was finding a wider audience, both through the advent of new recording and distribution technologies and through the popularisation of black American music by white musicians and performers. Indeed, in her biography *Suits Me*, Middlebrook suggests that Tipton's musical style resembled that of Teddy Wilson (1912–86), an African American piano player who, as a member of the Benny Goodman Trio, was one of the first black musicians to perform and record in a racially integrated band. Indeed, the composition identified by Middlebrook as Tipton's signature tune – Benny Goodman and Lionel Hampton's 'Flying Home', first recorded in 1939 – is commemorated in the title of Ralph Ellison's celebrated 1944 short story about an African American airman returned to the American South by the accident of a crash landing. Principally a performing rather than a recording artist, Tipton was a popular entertainer whose repertoire was dominated by the dance music standards of the day. Some of these standards feature as signature songs in Kay's novel, while lyrics from George and Ira Gershwin's 'They Can't Take That Away from Me' (1937) serve as an epigraph to the novel. The suggestive 'She Had to Go and Lose It at the Astor' (1940) becomes the humorous musical accompaniment to Joss and Millie's romance and the popular World War Two hit 'Boogie Woogie Bugle Boy of Company B' (1941) (both written by Don Raye and Hugh Prince) is played at Joss's funeral. While these compositions, written by white musicians, represent the populist end of jazz music culture and consumption, Joss is depicted more as an artist than an entertainer; the performance which is rendered in a modernist stream of consciousness in the chapter 'Music' evokes the virtuosity, creative risk-taking and ambition of solo improvisation rather than the tested routines of the bandleader. Moreover, Joss is insistent on the crucial role played by music in expressing the collective identity of the African diaspora. As Colman recalls, in his father's words: 'Black people and music. Black people and music; what would the world be without black people and music . . . the stories in the blues. All blues are stories. Our stories, his father said, our history.'[52] In this sense the 'blue birth'[53] to which Joss returns in the self-disintegrating ecstasy of his performance most obviously refers to the musical heritage of the African American tradition, with the blues standing symbolically for a range of genres emerging in the early twentieth century at the time of the Great Migration from the rural South to the urban North. However, despite the prominence of African American culture in Joss's sense of musical identity, jazz is depicted as a vehicle for the expression of a wider diasporic experience and history.

Joss's attitude to questions of origin in relation to racial identity is one which asserts a strong sense of identification with African heritage while at the same time resisting any single or definitive narrative account of how he – as a descendant of a person of African origin – came to 'arrive' on Scottish shores. Like many artists of the African diaspora of his generation, the impact of an Afrocentric aesthetic is evident in his musical output. In the discography listed in the chapter titled 'Obituaries', the release of a 1966 disc entitled 'Fantasy Africa' coincides with the rise of black consciousness movements in America and beyond. The title is suggestive of Joss's awareness of the symbolic significance of Africa as an idea, distinct from the actual continent; as a source of creative inspiration this fantasy may obscure the political and historical realities of Africa, but the recognition that there is no homeland to which a 'return' is possible also suggests a refusal to essentialise the idea of origin:

> Joss had built up such a strong imaginary landscape within himself that he said it would affect his music to go to the real Africa. Every black person has a fantasy Africa, he'd say. Black British people, Black Americans, Black Caribbeans, they all have a fantasy Africa.[54]

If the 'real' Africa is remote in this refusal, the commonality of people of African origin is strongly expressed in this assertion. Indeed, when Joss resists his son's requests for personal histories of origin, his offering of multiple alternative beginnings can be interpreted as an expression of solidarity with other black people and a refusal to be reduced to a single explanatory story:

> Look, Colman, I could tell you a story about my father. I could say he came off a boat one day in the nineteen hundreds, say a winter day. All the way from the 'dark continent' on a cold winter day, a boat

that stopped at Greenock ... Or I could say my father was a black American who left America because of segregation and managed to find his way to Scotland where he met my mother. Or I could say my father was a soldier or a sailor who was sent here by his army or his navy. Or I could say my father was from an island in the Caribbean whose name I don't know because my mother couldn't remember it. Or never bothered to ask. And any one of these stories might be true, Colman.[55]

Indeed, Joss emphasises the contingency of stories of origin, insisting on the exercise of individual and collective agency in creating meaningful narratives of belonging: 'He said you make up your own bloodline, Colman. Make it up and trace it back. Design your own family tree ...'[56] If Joss declines to satisfy the reader's desire for a gendered story of origin in his 'last words', he does give way to Colman's desire to understand his heritage as a black man: 'You wanted the story of my father, remember? I told you his story could be the story of any black man who came from Africa to Scotland. His story, I told you, was the diaspora. Every story runs into the same river and the same river runs into the sea.'[57] Despite the prominence of America in the musical and cultural landscape of Joss's life and identity, it is the relationship between Africa and Scotland which is the central concern of the two chapters depicting Joss's narrative perspective. Indeed, questions of racial identity cannot be divorced from questions of national identity.

What makes the genre of transgender biography so 'violent',[58] especially when premised on posthumous revelation, is the way in which it invites the deployment of hindsight to retrospectively rewrite transgender lives irrespective of the lived experience or subjective agency of the transgender subject. In such narrative contexts, the reader is alerted, often by covert strategies of suggestion and insinuation, to look for 'clues' which will disclose the mystery of transgender identity, whether in terms of repressed psychological cause, hidden motivation or strategies of subterfuge (to use the register of suspicion which characterises this kind of writing/reading). In *Trumpet*, Millie denounces the misreadings which hindsight invites, conscious that even her own son, in his vulnerable state, is susceptible to its distorting gaze: 'When Colman goes through our house, pointing hindsight's big torch everywhere, he will find things in our garden that we never planted ... [ellipsis in original] One of the newspaper articles had the headline *Living a Lie* ... Hindsight is a lie.'[59] In the tradition of transgender biography which Halberstam critiques, the reader is invited to search for moments of doubt, uncertainty or disparity in relation to the expression, construction and reception of gender identity; in this way the reader is made complicit not only in the policing of gender norms but also in marginalising other aspects of identity. While Millie's recollected life is not one lived in fear of 'discovery' there are isolated but significant moments where her relationship with Joss attracts a visibility which might prove problematic. During their courtship in post-war Glasgow Millie recalls that 'Out in the streets people stare at us, particularly Joss. He knows quite a few of the guys in this club. Some strangers know him. He is already building up a reputation for himself, playing a few jazz bars and pubs and clubs.'[60] The meaning of this public gazing – curious at best and at worst hostile – is seemingly defused when it is attributed to Joss's growing local fame. A reading informed by the hermeneutics of suspicion lent by hindsight might detect other motives behind these stares, ones invisible to the naive Millie, who is then cast as an unreliable witness to her own past. However, while the conventions of transgender biography would attribute all signifiers of cognitive dissonance to gender variation, in the context of this period it seems just as, if not more, likely that the couple attract attention on the grounds of racial difference. In this way, reading Millie and Joss exclusively as a transgender couple obscures their experience as an interracial couple in a period when such relationships were less common and often subject to public disapproval. Even more striking is Millie's account of her wedding to Joss, which stands as the only scene in the narrative in which Millie gives open, if indirect, expression to fears about 'exposure'. This fear is given form in a suggestively intertextual fashion: 'At the Registrar's Office I kept thinking of that bit in *Jane Eyre* where the minister asks if anyone knows of any reason why Mr Rochester and Jane should not marry and the man from the Caribbean suddenly stands up and says, Yes.'[61] The location is one where Millie will later attempt to navigate the preservation of her husband's identity in death; it is in this encounter with the state regulation of personal relationships that Millie anticipates the possibility of an objection in the name of the law. In Charlotte Brontë's novel it is Bertha Mason's brother who alerts Jane to Rochester's prior marriage to his sister. His identification here as the 'man from the Caribbean' brings out the racial and colonial subtexts of Brontë's novel, in which Bertha's madness is implicitly attributed to her mixed racial heredity as a Creole woman. However, in the context of Kay's novel it also draws attention to Joss's mixed-race heritage and uncertain origins: the passage could be read as suggesting that if an objection were to be made it might be as much to do with constructions of race as with assumptions about gender.

In her essay '"An Imaginary Black Family": Jazz, Diaspora, and the Construction of Scottish Blackness in Jackie Kay's Trumpet', Carole Jones observes that 'Jazz functions to foreground black culture in Kay's novel',[62] suggesting that Kay 'employ[s] characteristics of African-American culture, particularly jazz, to illustrate the production of a specifically black Scottish identity which is part of the African diaspora'.[63] The prominence of jazz as a theme and metaphor in the novel might seem to give pre-eminence to the role of America in mediating the triangular relationship between African heritage, African American culture and Scottish identity in the narrative, but when Joss 'goes down, swirling and whirling till he's right down at the very pinpoint of himself'[64] it is not America (the provenance of the music he performs) that he finds but 'Scotland. Africa. Slavery. Freedom.'[65] Just as questions of gender give way to questions of race, as the narrative swerves away from the generic conventions of transgender biography, so questions of racial identity prove to be entwined in questions of national affiliation. In his pivotal contribution to the 2004 collection *Blackening Europe: The African American Presence*, Paul Gilroy challenges the 'peculiar synonymity of the terms European and white', identifying two consequences of this seeming impasse:

> historians of Europe's repressed, denied, and disavowed blackness must be willing to say the same things over and over again in the hope that a climate will eventually develop in which we will be able to find a hearing . . . and . . . we must be prepared to step back boldly into the past.[66]

Recent years have seen an expansion in historical and cultural scholarship on the relationship between Scotland and Africa and the history of people of African origin in Scotland, with a particular focus on Scotland's involvement in Caribbean slavery. John Moore's arrival on Scottish shores significantly predates the wave of post-war immigration from the Caribbean, symbolised by the *Empire Windrush*, which is often posited as a formative event in the history of black British (and implicitly English) people. Hence his embedded story in Joss's final chapter, 'Last Word', serves as another challenge to myths of origin in the novel.

In his 2015 book *Scotland and the Caribbean c. 1740–1833: Atlantic Archipelagos*, Michael Morris argues that 'Caribbean slavery profoundly shaped Scotland's economic, social and cultural development'.[67] In doing so, he contests a tendency by which 'the evils of slavery are consistently identified with England' through a process of 'denial, evasion and elision',[68] a displacement compounded in specific ways by national histories of Scottish subjection and English power. As Morris and others have demonstrated, a disproportionate number of Scots participated in and profited from plantation slavery in the Caribbean as a consequence of a number of historical factors, including the phenomenon of migration (whether economic or political, forced or elective) which has been a key factor in Scottish national history from the Highland Clearances onwards. In his 2003 historical novel *Joseph Knight*, James Robertson tells the story of a Scottish fugitive from the aftermath of Culloden who acquires new wealth through plantation slavery in the Caribbean, returning to Scotland with a house slave – the Joseph Knight of the title – whose challenge to the status of chattel slavery in Scottish law in 1777 was to make legal history. However, it was not only enslaved individuals who undertook a transatlantic crossing to Scotland but also the children of white Scottish settlers and women of African origin. The sexual exploitation of female slaves by white men was integral to the system of plantation slavery, which allowed white men to rape with impunity and to profit through the sale of the children which were conceived through coercion. However, as historians including David Alston and Daniel Livesay have demonstrated, not all of these children were denied or disowned; some were claimed by their fathers and 'returned' to Scotland for their education and upbringing. In his 2015 article 'A Forgotten Diaspora: The Children of Enslaved and "Free Coloured" Women and Highland Scots in Guyana before Emancipation', David Alston concludes that 'A number of children born to enslaved and "free coloured" women were raised in the Highlands, sometimes from a very young age' and that '"Coloured" children were enrolled in many schools in the Highlands in the early nineteenth century'.[69] Moreover, in his 2008 article 'Extended Families: Mixed-Race Children and Scottish Experience, 1770–1820', Daniel Livesay examines the 'remigration' of mixed-race children as part of a racialised project of social mobility, with the white Scots who had attained economic advancement as part of the British imperial project seeking to ensure racial advantage: 'many Scots sent their children of colour to Britain in order to "whiten" them along class and cultural lines, rather than subject them to the legal and racial impediments built into West-Indian society.'[70] Alston's and Livesay's studies are concerned with the period before emancipation, seventy years and more before the arrival of John Moore at Greenock at the turn of the twentieth century in Kay's novel. But with this history in mind his passage acquires historical precedent and significance, and ceases to seem exceptional and anomalous. Matt Richardson notes the resemblance between John Moore's narrative and the African American slave narrative, a genre most closely associated with nineteenth-century American slavery and the movement for its abolition. A recurring motif in the slave narrative, exemplified in Frederick Douglass's *Narrative of the Life of Frederick Douglass, An American Slave* (1845) amongst others, is the depiction of literacy as the path to freedom, its acquisition often requiring immense perseverance and ingenuity in the face of legal prohibition and punishment. Indeed, John 'luxuriates in language' but his facility provokes the resentment of the white working-class cook who sees his eloquence as an assault on her status: 'Who was he to go about the kitchen with his sharp curved words, glinting about the place like carving knives.'[71] As a child John is sent to Scotland by his father for an education under the care of a Scottish captain. However, he is instead taken into the home of Robert Duncan-Brae where he is employed as a (presumably unpaid) household servant until he acquires independence through an apprenticeship as a housepainter in Dundee. John and his father are betrayed by the breaking of the promise – 'He could see exactly where one decision violently parted company with another and a new future flared up before him'[72] – but the fact that his father had any hope of his bargain being honoured suggests that he was able to command some social status and authority. The possibility that John's father is white and that John is his mixed-race son potentially places him in the history of the children of colour being sent to Scotland for their education, although his origin is given as African, not Caribbean. John reads 'many books to see if they might remind him of what he wanted to remember' and it is his 'mother's hot breath on his cheek' which he recalls, not his father's.[73] However, the memory of his 'own country' is 'lost', 'drowned at sea in the dead of a dark, dark night'.[74] Some generations after the abolition of slavery, John's identity is lost to the limbo of a kind of middle passage and it is striking that the land on which he alights has a liminal quality as a 'ghost country' peopled by 'shadow people'.[75] However, this formative experience of estrangement and displacement does not preclude John from developing a strong sense of identification with the culture of his adopted home: 'My father had a wonderful singing voice and could sing from memory just about any folk song I wanted. Every time he sang a Scottish folk song, he'd have this far-away look on his face. *Heil Ya Ho, boys, Let her go, boys, Swing her head round, And all together.*'[76] The 'Mingulay Boat Song', named after an island in the Outer Hebrides and based on a traditional Gaelic melody, suggestively speaks of passage across the sea. John's Scottish-born son

Joss is an international traveller rather than a forced migrant, whose professional success affords him freedom of movement. However, he is also an internal migrant, moving to London for the sake of his career but making an annual return to the holiday home of his wife's family on the east coast of Scotland. When Joss's son Colman mistakes a fellow passenger on a train to Scotland for his dead father it is as if he imagines his father in eternal motion, forever crossing borders (between England and Scotland) and riding the rails which became such a potent and complex symbol in African American contexts of escape (the underground railroad), social mobility (through employment on the railroad and as a vehicle of urban migration) and segregation:

> Walking down the train with such dignity, such fine balance, his back straight, his eyes staring ahead, with neither kindness nor cruelty in them. Walking up and down the train as if that is all he does with his day, walk up and down the infinite train in this way, as if that is all he has been doing his whole life.[77]

John's musicality is not his only legacy to his son Joss, who also demonstrates a proud sense of Scottishness which he is eager to share with his Scottish-born but London-raised son, Colman: 'Determined that everyone would know he was Scottish . . . My father kept telling me I was Scottish. Born there. But I didn't feel Scottish. Didn't feel English either.'[78] However, if Colman is sceptical during his father's life, after his death his unexpected adoption of his father's speech and tastes is a gently humorous sign of his growing reconciliation with his father's memory. First he acquires a craving for whisky: 'Now that his father is dead, he will always drink malts. After years of hating the bark and the flame of peppery malt, Colman now finds himself relishing it. Strange that – how your mouth can suddenly switch allegiances.'[79] Then, as a further sign of his mouth's shifting loyalties, he finds himself using his father's vernacular when he returns to Scotland to trace his father's mother, Edith: 'He chaps the door cautiously, then louder. He hasn't used the word "chap" in his puff. He is becoming his father.'[80] If Colman does express any sense of unease or discontent about his 'mixed' identity, it is more to do with his national and cultural identity than his racial identity:

> His father was always telling him: you are Scottish, you were born in Scotland and that makes you Scottish. But he doesn't feel Scottish. He doesn't speak with a Scottish accent. He can do a good one, like

all children of Scottish parents, but it's not him. What is him? This is what he's been asking himself. It's all the train's fault: something about the way the land moves out of the window; about crossing a border.[81]

As Matthew Mead has argued, in an essay on the prominence of the *Empire Windrush* in conventional accounts of black British history, an emphasis on a '*culturally imagined moment of arrival*' [emphasis in original][82] can risk constructing black British people as always from elsewhere, their presence conditional on permission and easily transformed into intrusion. However, John's passage from Africa is placed in a history in which migration is not seen as an exclusively black experience but as a defining Scottish phenomenon. Joss and Millie's courtship is very specifically located in the streets and dance halls of post-war Glasgow and one of their favoured meeting places seems especially significant: 'I've waited for Joss sheltered under the rain, under the Hielan' Man's umbrella, imagining the Highland men years ago, fresh down from the Highlands talking excited Gaelic to each other.'[83] This is the vernacular nickname for a Victorian architectural landmark in Glasgow: the railway bridge which carries the platforms of Glasgow Central station across Argyle Street and whose shelter served as an informal meeting place for Highlanders displaced by the Clearances and newly arrived in the city. If Glasgow stands for the modernity of the city, social mobility and leisure, the fictional port of Torr, the location of the Moody holiday home, seems to represent stability, continuity and community but in ways which are at odds with the conservative politics which this association might suggest. When Millie retreats to Torr after Joss's death in an attempt to escape the intrusions of the metropolitan media, the neighbours tending the family-run businesses of the village (the butcher, the grocer, the Italian café and ice cream parlour) are the only ones to treat her as a grieving wife. As Millie comments of Mrs Dalsasso: 'She is the first person to make me feel like an ordinary widow, to give me respect, not prurience.'[84] It seems that an identity established over generations, through first-hand familiarity and within the continuity of community cannot be compromised by the impersonal mass media and its attempts to sabotage the public perception of Millie's marriage to Joss.

When Joss shares the story of his father with his son in his 'Last Word', having declined to do so during his life, John Moore emerges as an important ancestor for both Joss and Colman in ways which exceed the imperatives of biogenetic connection. He most obviously represents the collective history of the African diaspora to which both Joss and Colman are heir and, more specifically, the long history of people of African heritage in Scotland, significantly predating the post-war waves of migration and settlement. However, he can also be seen to represent a longer and no less complex history of transcultural adoption. As a six-year-old child John is handed over to the care of others by his father, transported from one continent to another ostensibly in the name of improvement through education. While the Duncan-Braes are 'not unkind',[85] John is nevertheless denied a family life and an education, is subject to a form of indentured servitude (working for his 'adoptive' family without pay) and suffers the loss of his 'mother, his country, his mother-country'.[86] John's history can be placed in a racialised history of the transatlantic exchange and commodification of children of African origin; some generations after the end of the slave trade and the abolition of slavery, John is nevertheless deemed destined for servitude. However, John's history is also the story of the making of black Scottish heritage and the creation of family, as he becomes a husband and father whose memory will be cherished long after his death.

'What gets me is why he didn't tell me': Adoption Narratives in Jackie Kay's *Trumpet*

There is a thought-provoking slippage between discourses of race, gender and adoption in Kay's novel. When the child of adoptive parents angrily rebukes his deceased transgender father with the words 'What gets me is why he didn't tell me',[87] his complaint could equally well refer to the secrecy which has accompanied some adoption practices in the West, whether legally required or informally practised. Similarly, when Joss addresses his son in his posthumous letter, the collective identity he invokes is that of people of the African diaspora but his words could also be applied to the experience of adoptees: 'That's the thing with us: we keep changing our names. We've all got that in common. We've all changed names, you, me, my father.'[88] Colman's adoptive history is not concealed from him in this narrative but it perhaps makes him particularly vulnerable to the hurt and anger which familial secrecy can cause and may go some way to explaining the significance of his anger on discovering his father's sex. While Joss does not share an experience of adoption with his son Colman, his own father experiences a form of transcultural adoption which arguably offers Colman a different kind of familial continuity, beyond the more conventional biogenetic kind. Indeed, the posthumous revelation which so unsettles Colman's sense of self also inspires a project of family tracing, a venture which has become associated with contemporary adoption narratives but which is here concerned with a grandmother to whom he is not biogenetically related. The significance of secrets, the changing of names and the tracing of lost family histories are all tropes reminiscent of adoption narratives but which here combine considerations of race, gender and family to challenge the essentialising of 'birth' as the determining origin of all three.

Colman's adoption by Joss and Millie Moody takes place in a specific moment in black British history and the history of adoption practices in the UK. As John McLeod has written, in his 2015 book *Life Lines: Writing Transcultural Adoption*:

> In the UK, new shifts in patterns of migration after the Second World War saw the advent of a new black British population as many travelled from the colonies to the metropolis to find work ... The social and cultural constraints that soon obtained contributed to the appearance of a distinct constituency of adoptees by the 1960s, black or (more often) of mixed race, that welfare officers found hard to place due to racist attitudes both at large and in the welfare services themselves.[89]

Colman is one of a new generation of children entering the adoption services of the post-war British welfare state whose fortunes were shaped by negative attitudes to both interracial relationships and mixed-race children, in addition to the stigmas and social prejudices with which unmarried mothers and illegitimate children had to contend. Children like Colman faced specific barriers to adoption in comparison to their white peers, and the construction of the mixed-race child as 'difficult to place' is evident in Kay's novel in the relief expressed by social workers when Millie and Joss present themselves as potential parents: 'They told me that the agency was extremely pleased with them given my colour. They said the agency called them "a find" as I remember. A find. I am the same kind of colour as my father. We even look alike. Pure fluke.'[90] Whether Colman's 'colour' is perceived as an obstacle to his adoption by white parents or whether the agency perceives some commonality of ethnic identity to be important to the child's welfare is not clear, but the reduction of complexities of racial, cultural and national identity to the category of 'colour' suggests an attitude to 'matching' which possibly privileges assimilation above all else: the skin tone that Colman and

Joss happen to share suggests – misleadingly – a biogenetic continuity which will not challenge normative ideas about family affinity.[91] The 'interracial' nature of Millie and Joss's marriage might have proved an obstacle to their adoption of a white child, but in this context it presents a 'solution' to the 'problem' of Colman's future.

We have seen how 'secrecy' can be a problematic motif in transgender biography, since it imputes deception and dissimulation to the transgender subject and implicitly licenses the biographer to violate privacy and overwrite identity in the name of 'truth'. In Kay's novel, 'secrecy' takes two different guises: it refers to the cherished intimate life of Millie and Joss, and it refers to Colman's perception that a key feature of his father's identity has been concealed from him by his parents. Millie is protective of the 'secret world that is just his and mine. Nobody else's, just his and mine',[92] a world which is immune to intrusion or disruption, including in the form of infidelity: 'For a split second, I feel jealous, imagining what it would be like if Joss were ever unfaithful to me. Then I remember and feel safe. We have our love and we have our secret.'[93] For Millie, the cherished 'secret' of her intimacy with Joss is not a truth concealed but a truth which has no need to be shared: 'It was our secret. That's all it was . . . Our secret was harmless. It did not hurt anybody.'[94] However, the private world of his parents' intimacy begins to take on new meanings for Colman after the revelation of his father's sex: the legitimately private world of the 'secret' is transformed into the purposeful concealment of 'secrecy': 'She said he never would be unfaithful and gave me an odd smile that makes perfect fucking sense now. See that's what I mean. I'm going to have to go back over my whole life with a fine-tooth comb and look for signs like that.'[95] Hindsight transforms Colman into a kind of reluctant detective, revisiting his memories and the artefacts and archives of his childhood with a newly sceptical eye. It is here that a key trope of adoption narratives emerges: tracing. Colman finds parallels between his attempts to uncover his father's secrets and the possibility of tracing his adoptive parents:

> 'Yeah, I thought I could snoop around. See what I can dig up. I want to get on his case. I can see myself as a kind of private dick investigating him, know what I mean? . . . Funny, I always thought one day I might get around to tracing my other father. Ironic, isn't it?'[96]

McLeod has commented on the emergence of 'tracing' as a key motif in contemporary adoption narratives, in the face of past practices and attitudes which held that the severing of all connections – whether past or future – between the birth parents (more often the birth mother) and the adoptee was in the best interests of the child, their adoptive family and society more broadly. McLeod observes that 'in a relatively short space of time tracing has been transformed from a task which those inward of the [adoption] triad must be legally prohibited from pursuing to an activity which adoptees in particular often feel under pressure to perform'.[97] The tracing of birth parents and biogenetic relatives can be understood as a response to the secrecy which forcefully curtailed the agency of birth parents and adoptees. McLeod powerfully captures the harmful impact of secrecy on the adoptee's sense of self and place:

> Secrecy keeps one in the dark about consanguineous lines of connection and limits the knowledge of an adoptee's embedding within biogenetic and adoptive life lines. It amplifies feelings of fraudulence, powerlessness and insubstantiality – all inimical to adoptive being – because keeping secrets usually means telling lies.[98]

However, McLeod also questions the assumption that 'identity must be a matter of biogenetic attachment to people, place, race, culture or nation', suggesting that it is this assumption that constructs the experience of adoption as a puzzle, whether an 'enigma, with secrecy sitting where the reassurances of roots should be found' or 'as a jigsaw puzzle with missing pieces, incomplete and lacking its full dimensions'.[99] Colman does not undertake to trace his birth parents in Kay's narrative but he does trace his father's elderly mother, Edith, and his journey to visit her in her home in a sheltered housing community is characterised by anxieties to do with disclosure, recognition and acceptance familiar to those who have sought encounters with biogenetic parents for the first time in adult life. In some sense, 'secrecy' does continue to prevail in Colman's meeting with his grandmother, where he does not declare (as he had anxiously anticipated) that 'My father was your daughter'[100] but is warmly welcomed by the energetic Edith as a 'friend of Josephine's'.[101] However, Colman emerges from the encounter – whose detail is left to the reader's imagination – with a determination to withdraw his co-operation with Stones's sensational exposé and a readiness to be reconciled both with his father's memory and with his living mother. The photograph with which he leaves – of Josephine Moore as a child – serves not to contradict or cancel out his memory of his father as a man but rather to foster a sense of affection and loyalty to his newly expanded sense of family.

Colman's particular outrage at discovering that information has been withheld from him by his adoptive parents and his sense of humiliation at discovering he has been the unwitting victim of an apparent conspiracy of silence attain special meaning when considered in the context of transcultural adoption narratives. As McLeod writes:

> Transcultural adoptees often carry a distinctive degree of consciousness regarding the racial, national, cultural and social norms of personhood and identification, as their often conspicuous presence within, but not fully of, their daily environments may leave them vulnerable to the designs of others.[102]

However, Colman's ultimate refusal to subscribe to discourses of origin – whether sexed, gendered, racial or other – suggests that he can be read as representing the mode of 'adoptive being' theorised by McLeod as being characterised by a 'capacity to reconfigure the multidirectional material particulars offered by both biogenetic and adoptive attachments'.[103] Colman's complaint against his father – 'What gets me is why he didn't tell me'[104] – is in some way answered by his father's 'Last Word': where Colman is painfully stung by his apparent exclusion from his father's confidence, Joss's words to his son interpolate him within a collective 'we' to which he and Colman (and not his white mother) uniquely belong. The changing of names – whether forced or by choice – is a recurring motif in Kay's novel, as a number of critics have recognised, but acquires added meaning when addressed to a son whose birth name is not shared with his father. Throughout the novel there is a persistent discrepancy between the names recorded and registered in state-sanctioned documentation – from the registrar's office to the school classroom – and the names which have meaning and value in social contexts. This discrepancy points to a tension between the disciplinary regulation of names as a means of managing individuals and populations and the spontaneous generation of new names and denominations by individuals and communities. May Hart recalls the school days she shared with her childhood friend Josephine Moody: 'Everyone was called the name on the register. At least half the people in her class were not known by these names. Some of them weren't even similar. They all had two personalities.'[105] The question of which name you are willing to answer to extends beyond childhood, and for Joss's drummer there is pride and mischief in his legend as 'Big Red': 'Ever since he was a boy he's been graffitied with nicknames. . . . Big Red was his favourite because he believed in communism and had a red hot temper. Nicknames were magic; they let people know what they were in for.'[106] The world of the playground and of the itinerant jazz musician are both places rich in vernacular language and in the Scottish context of Kay's narrative there is the added tension between the national tongue and the Standard English of the central state. However, the 'changing names' to which Joss refers in his letter to his son evokes the specific history of the African diaspora, as mediated by transatlantic slavery and colonialism, in which the imposition of names serves to erase cultural identity and to assert ownership. It is interesting to note that Colman's birth name – William Dunsmore – shares an etymological root with the name given to his African grandfather after his arrival in Scotland: 'more' and 'moor' are suggestive of a much longer history of European discourses of African origin. By contrast, names which are chosen rather than imposed have a special meaning and value. When Colman's adoptive parents elect to give him a new name their decision is in keeping with the emphasis on severing all ties with the past in the adoption practice of the time, but they disagree over whether to give him a name that would mark his Scottish heritage or that would pay homage to his father's profession. When Millie mocks the names of famous jazz and blues musicians (Jelly Roll, Howling Wolf, Bird, Muggsy, Fats, Leadbelly, Pee Wee) Joss responds with anger and violence:

> Joss wanted Miles, I wanted Campbell. Joss wanted Louis. I wanted Alastair. Joss wanted a jazz or blues name . . . Joss slapped me across my face. 'That's enough,' he said. 'White people always laugh at black names.'[107]

In the African American context evoked by the names of these artists, 'adopted' names, rooted in community and shared language, may have more authenticity than inherited names which may carry the legacy of slave ownership.

The Small Black Girl: Recovering Josephine Moody

I wish to conclude by considering the persistence of a recurring figure in the dreams and fantasies of characters in Kay's novel. A 'small black girl'[108] appears in the dreams of Millie, Colman and Joss's childhood friend May Hart. The same figure also makes an appearance in 'Music', the chapter in which Joss's altered consciousness during the throes of musical performance takes on a dream-like quality. The girl appears in contexts to do with loss or death: in Millie's case she acts to reunite her with her deceased husband, while in May's and Colman's dreams she is herself in fatal danger from which her friend and son are compelled to rescue or save her. Joss identifies the girl as his childhood self and in May's and Colman's dreams she is explicitly identified as Josephine Moody. The recurring significance of this figure and the fierce protection which she inspires can be interpreted in different ways. On the one hand, the potent and poignant revival of Joss's 'birth' name and identity might be seen to threaten his chosen gender identification. Josephine appears after Joss's death but it is as if Josephine has herself suffered an earlier death following Joss's gender transition; in seeking to 'save' her it might seem that May and Colman are attempting to reinstate the sexed and gendered identity assigned to Joss at birth. However, her appearance heralds a renewed sense of continuity, rather than contradiction, in May's and Colman's understanding of Joss's gendered identity.

The 'small black girl' first appears in a dream to Millie in the first days of her retreat to Torr. The child brings comfort to the widow in her grief and distress at the intrusion of the media, restoring her to her husband:

> As I unlock the door of our house, I know we've been burgled ... Joss isn't there. The sheets have been ripped off the bed and someone has written something horrible in the mirror. But I can't read it because it is written in mirror writing. His trumpet is missing ... A small black girl climbs in through the window. She takes my hand and we walk down the stairs, down Rose Street till we come to Renfield Street, round the corner till we come to 14 Abercromby Place. She stops. Waves goodbye to me. I go into the stranger's house and there is Joss sitting in front of the dresser mirror in somebody's bedroom playing the trumpet. He is playing Millie's Song.[109]

This child is not explicitly identified as Josephine, a figure whose existence has only briefly been acknowledged by Joss during his marriage to Millie, and may stand for the 'imaginary daughter' which Millie has had to 'let go'[110] along with her dreams of a child conceived with her husband. Interestingly, it is the memory of a celebrated African American pioneer of transcultural adoption, the dancer and jazz age icon Josephine Baker (1906–75), which prompts Joss to make a rare allusion to his childhood: 'I don't know anything about his childhood. I know that his name was Josephine Moore ... It came out one day quite casually when we were watching a programme on Josephine Baker adopting a 'rainbow tribe' of children ... He always spoke about her in the third person.'[111] The association raises the possibility that Baker might have been the inspiration for the birth name given to Joss by John and Edith Moore, but it also seems to anticipate the expansive notion of kinship which Joss will later advocate to his son.

In the chapter entitled 'People: The Old School Friend', which depicts the aftermath of an interview conducted by Stones, the repeated appearance of Josephine Moore in May Hart's dreams is indicative of her (misplaced) feelings of guilt and remorse at the prospect of having unwittingly played a part in Stones's exposé: 'This morning May Hart realized it was talking to that woman that was giving her these nightmares. Josephine Moore has died every night for four nights on the trot. She is always eleven years old.'[112] Motifs of peril, protection and rescue are prominent in a repeated nightmare in which the seventy-year-old May finds herself tending to the eleven-year-old Josephine, who has been the victim of a collision with a lorry on the M8 motorway connecting Glasgow with Edinburgh. Unable to do more than hold her hand, May is herself threatened with sedation when she attempts to prevent an enraged policeman from injecting Josephine against her will. Helpless to protect her vulnerable friend from the disciplinary and medicalising interventions of the state, May appears in the dream as the same age as her friend in a version too 'terrifying'[113] to remember. Revisiting an old school photograph at Stones's request May is overwhelmed with emotion: 'As she stared transfixed at the photograph all the old love came spilling back. There's no love like the love you have as girls ... May Hart would have died for Josie. She loved everything about her.'[114] In this context the dream might suggest not only that Joss's memory is at risk from the intrusion of exploitative journalism but that the memory of the girl that she was – and that May loved – is at risk from the revelation of her gender identity as a man. In this sense, Josephine's 'death' is the price of Joss's gender; one lives at the expense of the other and their mutual existence cannot be reconciled. However, May's response to a photograph of the adult Joss – which Stones misinterprets as speechless shock – reveals a continuity of attachment and a renewal of feeling rather than their disruption: 'Looking at Josie all dressed up as a man, May realized that she'd missed her all her life. Didn't she have style! Look at that suit! Her Bert had never looked like that in a suit. She was moved to tears.'[115]

The compulsion to save or rescue the 'small black girl' from danger is also manifest in Colman's dream after his visit with Edith:

> *Edith Moore is in front of him at the seaside, holding the hand of a small girl, his father. The girl has a mass of curly black hair, like himself. She is deaf. The girl takes a liking to him and starts to play with him ... All the time they are speaking in sign. Suddenly the*

whole place starts to fill with water. He is going to have to save her from drowning.
  ... He has got the little girl's life on his back. He has to save her. Has to save her. Has to.[116]

Prior to his visit with Edith, Colman has begun to have doubts about the outcome of his co-operation with Stones and these doubts find their focus in the fate of a photograph of Josephine as a child: 'This book is starting to eat away at him. Imagine this photograph of his father as a little girl in a book with sinister captions.'[117] The desire to protect the child – whose gender identity is reiterated in the phrases 'small girl' and 'little girl' – might again seem to position the memory of Josephine against that of Joss: the girl must be protected from the intrusive and exploitative gaze which the man has invited. However, both passages anticipate Colman's gradual reconciliation with the memory of his father as a man in their reference to 'a small girl, his father' and 'his father as a little girl'. Indeed, this dream is a prelude to Colman's termination of his contract with Stones and his refusal to be party to the 'sinister captions' which her narrative distortion would lend to his father's life. Josephine's vulnerability is compounded in Colman's dream by the fact that she is deaf, but the dream is less concerned with the absence of hearing than with the language which she and Colman uniquely share. The content of their speech is not disclosed but in a sense it anticipates the communication which Colman will receive from his father after death. Indeed, the photograph of Josephine Moody as a child, and its entry into private and public circulation, serves to signify the uses of memory in this narrative. From Stones's perspective its existence is irrefutable evidence of Joss's true sex and its intended role is to negate and demean Joss's identity as a man. However, in a chapter entitled 'Editorial', which at first sight seems to adopt the forcefully interpellating gaze of the tabloid newspaper, the photograph refuses to yield the evidence demanded of it. Despite the commanding register of the passage and its apparent incitement to a gender policing gaze – 'Look at this photograph. Look at it again. And again'[118] – the force of hindsight cannot induce the photograph to yield any clues to its subject's gender identity:

Look at this photograph. No matter how long you stare at the photograph, the clothes she is wearing will not change. Does he look at all tomboyish with that confident sparkle in her eye, that wild look? No. No, that couldn't be said. She looks just like a little girl. A happy little girl.[119]

In every dream in which Josephine Moody appears – whether to Millie, May or Colman – her existence as a girl does not serve to negate the existence of Joss the man but rather acts as a prelude to a return, renewal or reconciliation with his memory. Indeed, while Joss does not dwell on his childhood in Millie's company, Josephine is no stranger to his inner thoughts and her appearance serves as a prelude to the pivotal moment of 'blue birth' in the chapter entitled 'Music': 'He watches himself in flashback. He's a small girl skipping along an old disused railway line in a red dress, carrying a bunch of railway flowers for her mother.'[120] The railway line which Colman will later have him travelling for eternity is his playground here, albeit a place of possible peril from his mother's perspective. The aesthetic of jazz improvisation doubles as a narrative vehicle for the deconstruction of self, but while the signifiers of identity may fall away, the 'small girl, his father' remains:

> Running changes. Changes running. He is changing all the time. It all falls off – bandages, braces, cufflinks, watches, hair grease, suits, buttons, ties. He is himself again, years ago, skipping along the railway line with a long cord his mother had made into a rope. In a red dress. It is liberating. To be a girl. To be a man.[121]

The critical reception of Jackie Kay's novel reflects many of the concerns which have shaped the depiction of transgender lives in women's writing and feminist literary criticism, as examined in the preceding chapters. In her 2001 essay '"A Woman's a Man, for a' That": Jackie Kay's *Trumpet*', Jeanette King considers the possibility of reading the narrative as a story either of women's strategic gender crossing (to overcome professional obstacles) or of lesbian desire, but opts for an interpretation informed by Judith Butler's theories of performativity. Questions of lesbian identity are also central to Irene Rose's 2003 essay 'Heralding New Possibilities: Female Masculinity in Jackie Kay's Trumpet', in which she reads Joss as 'a validation of the often forgotten, and sometimes extreme, social costs paid by butch lesbians for transgressing both heteronormative and homonormative boundaries'.[122] Moreover, in her forcefully argued essay '"The Truth Is a Thorny Issue": Lesbian Denial in Jackie Kay's *Trumpet*', Ceri Davies argues that Millie 'endeavours to manipulate the truth to deny her possible lesbianism while seeking to affirm Joss's masculinity, and by extension, their heterosexuality'.[123] By contrast, this chapter has approached Kay's *Trumpet* as a fictionalised life story which thwarts the problematic conventions of transgender biography (including the attribution of gender identification to hidden or covert motivations) in two significant ways: on the level of plot, through its depiction of a tabloid journalist's failed attempt to 'violently erase'[124] a transgender life through the medium of sensationalist journalism, and at the level of character and relationship, through an emphasis on continuity rather than contradiction. As Joss's son Colman succinctly puts it: "'Don't bother with this him/her bullshit. That's bollocks, man. Just say him.'"[125]

Notes

1. Middlebrook, *Suits Me: The Double Life of Billy Tipton*, p. 49.
2. Bhanji, 'Trans/scriptions: Homing Desires, (Trans)sexual Citizenship and Racialized Bodies', in Cotten (ed.), *Transgender Migrations: The Bodies, Borders and Politics of Transition*, p. 157.
3. Bhanji, 'Trans/scriptions', p. 158.
4. Richardson, '"My Father Didn't Have a Dick"', p. 361.
5. Kay, *Trumpet*, p. 132.
6. Kay, *Trumpet*, pp. 132–3.
7. Kay, *Trumpet*, p. 33.
8. Halberstam, 'Telling Tales: Brandon Teena, Billy Tipton, and Transgender Biography', in Sánchez and Schlossberg (eds), *Passing: Identity and Interpretation in Sexuality, Race, and Religion*, p. 13.
9. Middlebrook, *Suits Me*, p. 92.
10. Middlebrook, *Suits Me*, p. 87.
11. Middlebrook, *Suits Me*, p. 175.
12. Halberstam, 'Telling Tales', p. 14.
13. Middlebrook, *Suits Me*, p. xiii.
14. Middlebrook, *Suits Me*, p. 9.
15. Middlebrook, *Suits Me*, p. 10.
16. Middlebrook, *Suits Me*, n.p.
17. Middlebrook, *Suits Me*, p. 10.
18. Bettcher, 'Trapped in the Wrong Theory: Rethinking Trans Oppression and Resistance', p. 398.
19. Middlebrook, *Suits Me*, p. 175.
20. Middlebrook, *Suits Me*, p. 9.
21. Middlebrook, *Suits Me*, p. 3.
22. Halberstam, 'Telling Tales', p. 13.
23. Middlebrook, *Suits Me*, p. 10.
24. Halberstam, 'Telling Tales', p. 13.
25. Halberstam, 'Telling Tales', p. 13.
26. Kay, *Trumpet*, pp. 196–7.
27. Kay, *Trumpet*, p. 2.

28. Kay, *Trumpet*, p. 3.
29. Kay, *Trumpet*, p. 1.
30. Kay, *Trumpet*, p. 153.
31. Kay, *Trumpet*, p. 267.
32. Kay, *Trumpet*, p. 169.
33. Kay, *Trumpet*, p. 126.
34. Kay, *Trumpet*, p. 234.
35. Kay, *Trumpet*, p. 128.
36. Kay, *Trumpet*, p. 170.
37. Kay, *Trumpet*, p. 123.
38. Kay, *Trumpet*, p. 63.
39. Kay, *Trumpet*, p. 62.
40. Halberstam, 'Telling Tales', p. 13.
41. See Spade, *Normal Life: Administrative Violence, Critical Trans Politics and the Limits of Law*.
42. Kay, *Trumpet*, p. 43.
43. Halberstam, 'Telling Tales', p. 13.
44. Kay, *Trumpet*, p. 44.
45. Kay, *Trumpet*, p. 73.
46. Kay, *Trumpet*, p. 77.
47. Kay, *Trumpet*, pp. 112–13.
48. Kay, *Trumpet*, p. 79.
49. Kay, *Trumpet*, p. 81.
50. Kay, *Trumpet*, p. 81.
51. Jones, '"An Imaginary Black Family": Jazz, Diaspora, and the Construction of Scottish Blackness in Jackie Kay's *Trumpet*', p. 191.
52. Kay, *Trumpet*, p. 190.
53. Kay, *Trumpet*, p. 132.
54. Kay, *Trumpet*, p. 34.
55. Kay, *Trumpet*, p. 59.
56. Kay, *Trumpet*, p. 58.
57. Kay, *Trumpet*, p. 271.
58. Halberstam, 'Telling Tales', p. 13.
59. Kay, *Trumpet*, p. 95.
60. Kay, *Trumpet*, p. 16.
61. Kay, *Trumpet*, p. 26.
62. Jones, '"An Imaginary Black Family"', p. 194.
63. Jones, '"An Imaginary Black Family"', p. 192.
64. Kay, *Trumpet*, p. 131.
65. Kay, *Trumpet*, p. 136.
66. Gilroy, 'Migrancy, Culture, and a New Map of Europe', in Raphael-Hernandez (ed.), *Blackening Europe*, p. xii.
67. Morris, *Scotland and the Caribbean*, p. 6.
68. Morris, *Scotland and the Caribbean*, pp. 6, 8.
69. Alston, 'A Forgotten Diaspora', p. 62.

70. Livesay, 'Extended Families', p. 2.
71. Kay, *Trumpet*, p. 275.
72. Kay, *Trumpet*, p. 274.
73. Kay, *Trumpet*, p. 273.
74. Kay, *Trumpet*, p. 273.
75. Kay, *Trumpet*, p. 271.
76. Kay, *Trumpet*, p. 275.
77. Kay, *Trumpet*, p. 194.
78. Kay, *Trumpet*, p. 51.
79. Kay, *Trumpet*, p. 212.
80. Kay, *Trumpet*, pp. 223–4.
81. Kay, *Trumpet*, p. 190.
82. Mead, '*Empire Windrush*: The Cultural Memory of an Imaginary Arrival', p. 139.
83. Kay, *Trumpet*, p. 14.
84. Kay, *Trumpet*, p. 24.
85. Kay, *Trumpet*, p. 275.
86. Kay, *Trumpet*, p. 275.
87. Kay, *Trumpet*, p. 54.
88. Kay, *Trumpet*, p. 276.
89. McLeod, *Life Lines*, p. 11.
90. Kay, *Trumpet*, p. 50.
91. McLeod examines in detail the paradoxical ways in which both supporters and opponents of transcultural adoption have deployed similar ideas about 'racial distinctiveness, consanguineous kinship, cultural heredity, the assumption that race carries culture or that culture is a matter of racial ancestry'. *Life Lines*, p. 14.
92. Kay, *Trumpet*, p. 198.
93. Kay, *Trumpet*, p. 29.
94. Kay, *Trumpet*, p. 10.
95. Kay, *Trumpet*, p. 48.
96. Kay, *Trumpet*, p. 121.
97. McLeod, *Life Lines*, p. 135.
98. McLeod, *Life Lines*, p. 43.
99. McLeod, *Life Lines*, p. 18.
100. Kay, *Trumpet*, p. 214.
101. Kay, *Trumpet*, p. 229.
102. McLeod, *Life Lines*, p. 229.
103. McLeod, *Life Lines*, p. 127.
104. Kay, *Trumpet*, p. 54.
105. Kay, *Trumpet*, p. 248.
106. Kay, *Trumpet*, p. 145.
107. Kay, *Trumpet*, p. 5.
108. Kay, *Trumpet*, p. 33.
109. Kay, *Trumpet*, p. 33.

110. Kay, *Trumpet*, p. 39.
111. Kay, *Trumpet*, p. 93.
112. Kay, *Trumpet*, p. 246.
113. Kay, *Trumpet*, p. 246.
114. Kay, *Trumpet*, p. 251.
115. Kay, *Trumpet*, p. 252.
116. Kay, *Trumpet*, p. 260.
117. Kay, *Trumpet*, p. 256.
118. Kay, *Trumpet*, p. 255.
119. Kay, *Trumpet*, pp. 254–5.
120. Kay, *Trumpet*, p. 132.
121. Kay, *Trumpet*, p. 135.
122. Rose, 'Heralding New Possibilities: Female Masculinity in Jackie Kay's *Trumpet*', in Lea and Schoene (eds), *Posting the Male: Masculinities in Post-war Contemporary British Literature*, pp. 149–50.
123. Davies, '"The Truth Is a Thorny Issue"', p. 5.
124. Halberstam, 'Telling Tales', p. 13.
125. Kay, *Trumpet*, p. 142.

Chapter 6

Never an Unhappy Hour: Revisiting Marriage in Film Adaptations of *Albert Nobbs* (2011) and *The Danish Girl* (2016)

The retelling of transgender lives in diverse contexts, for different audiences and with varying effects has been a central concern of this book, with a particular focus on the impact of intertextual relationships, whether between memoir, biography, drama or fiction. This final chapter explores the afterlives of two of the texts analysed in previous chapters through a focus on the depiction of transgender characters in film adaptation, a genre characterised by its complex relationship to source texts and to changing cultural conditions of production and reception. The films examined in this chapter are both period dramas: *Albert Nobbs* (directed by Rodrigo García, screenplay by Glenn Close, John Banville and Gabriella Prekop, 2011) centres on the lives of two late-nineteenth-century working-class men, Albert Nobbs and Hubert Page, while *The Danish Girl* (directed by Tom Hooper, screenplay by Lucinda Coxon, 2016) depicts a historical subject, Lili Elbe (1882–1931), reputed to be the first recipient of successful gender reassignment treatment. They are adaptations of fiction published at the start and at the close of the twentieth century – George Moore's *Albert Nobbs* (1918) and David Ebershoff's *The Danish Girl* (2000) – and the relationship between these films and their ostensible literary sources is made more complex by the presence of further intertexts: Simone Benmussa's 1977 stage adaptation of Moore's novella, *The Singular Life of Albert Nobbs*, and Niels Hoyer's 1931 'memoir', *Man into Woman*. Released in a contemporary context in which issues to do with the representation of transgender people in all forms of media have attracted new scrutiny, these films offer portraits of transgender characters evidently intended to elicit audience sympathy. However, they also exhibit an uneven relationship to gender norms, often enlisting their transgender protagonists as agents of normative gender and sexuality. Indeed, the dramatic focus on heterosexual marriage in these film adaptations is especially striking: in *Albert Nobbs* Hubert Page is depicted as the unassuming saviour of turn-of-the-century masculinity and marriage, whereas in *The Danish Girl* the demise of a heterosexual marriage competes with the premature death of its protagonist as the tragic climax of the drama.

Before turning to the films in question it is important to situate them in the context of cinematic representations of transgender characters and to consider their place in relation to film genre, including period drama and literary adaptation. The history of the representation of transgender characters in film drama has been a contentious one. In his 2006 book *Transgender on Screen*, John Phillips suggests that two genres have predominated in the portrayal of transgender characters in cinematic narrative: 'comedies almost exclusively represent cross-dressers, exploring temporary transformations of gender in a largely playful manner, while thrillers deal with the frightening prospects of a more serious threat to gender identity.'[1] From *Some Like It Hot* (directed by Billy Wilder, 1959) to *Tootsie* (directed by Sydney Pollack, 1982) disparities between the sexed and gendered body have been used to provoke laughter, albeit sometimes to satirical effect, and from *The Silence of the Lambs* (directed by Jonathan Demme, 1991) to *The Skin I Live In* (directed by Pedro Almodóvar, 2011) the possibility of changing sex or gender – whether by will or through coercion – has been depicted as the cause of horror. The lack of distinction drawn in Phillips's book between 'cross-dressers' and people who identify as transgender is perhaps symptomatic of the expedient uses to which transgender motifs have been put. Indeed, Phillips identifies a recurring narrative structure of 'disguise/deception' followed by 'unveiling/revelation'[2] and this trope is especially evident in film dramas which rely on visual spectacles of revelation, such as *The Crying Game* (directed by Stephen Frears, 1992). Indeed, the forcible 'exposure' of a sexed body seemingly at odds with a gendered identity has been the subject of sustained critique by transgender theorists, including Jack Halberstam in his groundbreaking essay 'Telling Tales: Brandon Teena, Billy Tipton, and Transgender Biography'. Kimberly Peirce's 1999 film *Boys Don't Cry*, based on the brutal murder of Brandon Teena in Nebraska, USA, in 1993, is seen by many film commentators as a turning point in the representation of transgender characters on screen. As Melissa Rigney argues: 'For the first time, audiences were introduced to a transgender character that was not demonized as either killer, sexual predator or deranged psychopath.'[3] Motifs of family and marriage, especially in relation to fatherhood, have begun to recur in film and television dramas such as *The Adventures of Priscilla, Queen of the Desert* (directed by Stephan Elliott, 1994), *Transamerica* (directed by Duncan Tucker, 2005) and *Transparent* (Amazon Studios, 2014–) and the figure of the transgender child has emerged as a new focus of interest in films such as *Ma vie en rose* (directed by Alain Bernier, 1999) and *Tomboy* (directed by Céline Sciamma, 2011). With the integration of transgender characters into dramas of relationship and family, questions of casting have become the object of increasing public debate in recent years. Transgender roles on screen have historically served as star vehicles for leading performers and as pathways to film award nominations: Hilary Swank received the Academy Award for Best Actress for *Boys Don't Cry* and Felicity Huffman, Glenn Close and Eddie Redmayne were all nominated for Best Actress or Actor awards for *Transamerica, Albert Nobbs* and *The Danish Girl* respectively. In the marketing and reception of these films the transgender character is seen as providing the stage on which the performer can demonstrate his or her versatility. Indeed, an actor's willingness to 'risk' their gendered screen identity is often applauded as a signifier of professional courage and artistic integrity by critics and audiences alike. In this context, this chapter will pay close attention to the mode of performance given by non-transgender actors in transgender roles, comparing the performances given by Glenn Close and Janet McTeer in *Albert Nobbs* and examining Eddie Redmayne's performance as Lili Elbe in *The Danish Girl*. Where more recent film and television drama has tended to turn its attention to the contemporary moment, both of the films explored in this chapter can be considered period dramas. *Albert Nobbs* (2011) and *The Danish Girl* (2016) can be seen as testifying to the historical existence of transgender people – whether in nineteenth-century Ireland or early-twentieth-century Europe – but their relationship with the past is inevitably mediated by the conventions of historical film genres. In period drama, costume, interior set design and exterior locations are granted a privileged role in establishing the respective historical setting, rather than details of social, economic or political contexts. The aesthetic and spectacular pleasures of period design and dress are especially prominent in *The Danish Girl*, in which an emphasis on conventional femininity and the imperatives of 'passing' are aligned with the conventions of costume drama. Period drama and literary adaptation have historically enjoyed a close relationship, especially on British screens and in the form of the 'classic' adaptation. The capacity of film and television adaptations to bring not only new readers but also enhanced critical status to their source texts is widely recognised. However, where adaptations of texts by canonical authors can often rely on the audience's advance familiarity with the source text, *Albert Nobbs* and *The Danish Girl* are adaptations of narratives by authors whose reputation has been critically overlooked (Moore) or yet to be established (*The Danish Girl* was Ebershoff's debut novel). For many audiences and readers the film may have been encountered before the novel, supplanting the novel as the 'original' against which the source text is later compared. Moreover, despite taking their titles from a literary source, both films have a significant relationship with further source texts, which complicates their status as adaptations. Close consideration of these two films as adaptations serves to highlight questions to do with the relationship between the 'original' and the adaptation, between the historical or literary source text and its appropriation, and the role of intertextuality in mediating the representation of transgender lives.

Simone Benmussa's 1977 stage adaptation *The Singular Life of Albert Nobbs* has played an essential role as a bridge between George Moore's 1918 novella *Albert Nobbs* and Rodrigo García's 2011 film adaptation of the same title. The stage adaptation brought a little-known story by an often-overlooked Irish author to a wider audience, not only through theatrical performance but also through its canonisation in feminist theatre criticism. Moreover, it secured a champion in the form of Glenn Close, the American stage and screen actor whose experience of playing the role of Albert Nobbs in the American Off-Broadway premiere in 1982 was motivation for her longstanding and persistent efforts to bring the story to the cinema screen.[4] The critical reception of the play has undoubtedly shaped the film's re-emergence in the twenty-first century; despite the film's nominal fidelity to Moore's novella, the legacy of Second Wave feminist readings of Albert Nobbs's story (as mediated by Benmussa's stage adaptation) as a narrative of women's cross-dressing is evident in an inserted scene in the film adaptation which depicts Albert as 'resuming', albeit temporarily, his gender identity as a woman. Albert's plight is depicted as commanding pity in the 2011 film, with the discovery of Albert's sex after his death prompting the hotel doctor to declare, with compassionate despair: 'I don't know what makes people live such miserable lives.' However, in dramatic contrast, the charismatic working-class masculinity of Hubert Page – whose narrative as a female-bodied man doubles that of Albert Nobbs in Moore's novella – is not only intact but flourishing at the end of the film, with a planned second marriage promising a continuation of family life and domestic contentment. Indeed, one of the most notable features of the film adaptation is its transformation of Hubert into a character whose presence in the narrative is continuous, rather than limited to the two appearances which bookend the beginning and end of the story in Moore's novella: inserted scenes, locations and characters dramatise Hubert's contented home life as a married man, providing a counterpoint to Albert's solitude. Albert and Hubert emerge as 'two men, so dissimilar'[5] in even more pronounced ways in the 2011 film adaptation and this is underlined further in significant departures from Moore's novella in relation to period and plot. Firstly, the transposition of the action from the 1860s (as established in the novella and retained in the stage adaptation) to turn-of-the-century Dublin mobilises ideas about social, moral and national instability in the *fin de siècle* era; it situates Albert's and Hubert's lives in a historical context of uncertainty and change rather than stability and continuity. Secondly, the introduction of themes to do with masculinity, illegitimacy and migration in the extended narrative of Helen Dawes and Joe Mackins's courtship serves to place Albert's and Hubert's narratives in a wider social, cultural and historical context, one identifiably Irish in its allusion to specific national and moral crises. These changes set the scene for Hubert's emergence as figure of compensatory and even redemptive masculinity, with marriage serving as the principal vehicle through which his gender identity is affirmed in the context of the film narrative.

Hooper's 2016 film replicates the title of Ebershoff's 2000 novel, *The Danish Girl*, and the closing credits acknowledge that it is 'based upon' the book. However, the relationship between adaptation and source text is complicated by the novel's relationship to *Man into Woman*, a generically hybrid narrative which borrows the conventions of memoir, biography and fiction. In a poignant passage towards the end of *Man into Woman* – a narrative of the life of Lili Elbe first published in 1931 – Lili recalls the 'terribly hard contest between my sister and me for recognition as a person'[6] following her return to her family home in rural Jutland. The terms of the 'contest' concern the tension between Lili's identity as a woman and her sister's attachment to the memory of a beloved brother and her grief at his loss. The 2000 novel and the 2016 film adaptation similarly centre on a 'hard contest' but the emotional drama is transferred from the familial bond between siblings to the marital relationship between spouses. The first sentence of Ebershoff's novel anticipates the emphasis which this historical fiction will place on heterosexual marriage in its retelling of Lili Elbe's life: 'His wife knew first.'[7] Its prominence in the narrative is retained and expanded in the film adaptation, with Alicia Vikander's Academy Award winning performance as Elbe's former wife serving as the vehicle through which feelings of abandonment and grief at the loss of a husband compete with sentiments of empathy and loyalty towards a dearly loved life companion. At one point in the drama, an exasperated Gerda, having attended the launch of her first major exhibition alone, rebukes Lili with the words 'It's not all about you'.[8] It might be reasonable to expect a film biopic of a pioneer of gender reassignment treatment to be 'all about' its biographical subject, but in this drama the focus shifts from Elbe's experience to its impact on her former marriage. Indeed, 'the Danish girl' of the title is implicitly identified as Gerda – rather than Lili – in the film when she is introduced in these terms to Hans, Einar's childhood friend and Gerda's future partner. This chapter will explore this shift in emphasis in the film adaptation, with a focus on its relationship to the depiction of Lili's transition. Close comparative analysis of *Man into Woman* (as a historical and auto/biographical source text), Ebershoff's novel (as a literary source text) and *The Danish Girl* (as a film adaptation) will serve to demonstrate how the life of a historical subject is triply mediated in this nominally biographical film. The film reproduces pivotal scenes from the novel which have their origins in *Man into Woman* – Lili's 'birth' at a portrait sitting and her 'debut' at an artists' ball – but places them in a narrative context in which motifs to do with sexuality and femininity are prominent. Indeed, the sexualisation of Lili's transition and the mobilisation of tropes associated with female impersonation serve to suggest that what is at stake in the 'hard contest' between Lili and Gerda is femininity itself. This chapter aims to investigate how an early-twentieth-century narrative of transsexual transition is transformed into an early-twenty-first-century narrative of 'passing', in which normative constructions of gender and sexuality are reiterated through a focus on heterosexual marriage.

'Disguised as ourselves': Class, Costume and Contagion in *Fin de Siècle* Dublin in *Albert Nobbs* (2011)

Albert Nobbs was first published in 1918 in the story-cycle *A Storyteller's Holiday*. Its narrator – a fictionalised George Moore – recalls events which took place in Dublin in the era of his childhood in the 1860s and does so from a narrative present situated in the aftermath of the 1916 Easter Rising and the end of the First World War. In this context, an element of nostalgia infuses the narrative's return to 'the 'sixties'.[9] Indeed, the narrator admits to his interlocutor, Alec: 'I'm telling you these things for the pleasure of looking back and nothing else. I can see the sitting room and myself as plainly as I can see the mountains beyond, in some ways plainer, and the waiter that used to attend on us.'[10] Indeed, if the Dublin hotel in which the narrative is located serves as a microcosm of Anglo-Irish society, the familiarity of the hotel household and predictability of its daily regimes represents the (remembered) stability of a period prior to the Irish Land Act of 1870 and the Long Depression of the 1870s. By contrast, the film adaptation shifts the historical setting of the drama from the 1860s to the 1890s, a very significant period in terms of Irish cultural and literary history, coinciding with the Irish Literary Revival or 'Celtic Twilight'. Stephen Regan has argued that 'the 1890s witnessed the most powerful burst of cultural nationalism in Irish history'[11] and the period saw the founding of the Irish Literary Society (also known as the National Literary Society, 1892), the Gaelic League (1893) and the Irish Literary Theatre (1897), with Moore playing an active role in the founding of the last. More broadly, the *fin de siècle* has been characterised by cultural historians as witnessing a 'process of cultural fragmentation' that 'threw the norms of the Victorian age into crisis: empires were threatened, feminism was on the march, and the first socialist parties in Britain were formed'.[12] While Morrison's Hotel is unlikely to be the principal haunt of the artistic milieu of the Literary Revival and the political events of the era are not explicitly cited, the film borrows from popular cultural associations of the *fin de siècle* period to evoke a sense of troubling social instability. The hotel depicted in the film adaptation is at some remove from the family hotel of the 1860s which the child Moore visited with his parents. Indeed, two significant departures from the novella suggest that Morrison's is no longer the paragon of respectability and bourgeois propriety that it once was. The first is a costume ball, in which the decadent dress and behaviour of a new generation of English upper-class guest suggests an abdication of class responsibility. The second is an outbreak of typhus and the temporary closure of the hotel. Not only do these scenes serve to establish the end of the nineteenth century as a period of moral and social degeneration, they also contribute to a sense of narrative anticipation concerning the 'exposure' of Albert's sex.

The opening scenes of the 2011 film adaptation *Albert Nobbs* evoke the familiar generic conventions of popular British period drama, from *Upstairs, Downstairs* (London Weekend Television, 1971–5) to *Downton Abbey* (Carnival Films, 2010–15), as the hotel staff stand to attention in crisply laundered uniforms to greet an increasingly idiosyncratic cast of guests as they assemble in the dining room. Where Morrison's Hotel is depicted as a labyrinth of stairways and corridors in Moore's novella, its staff rendered as disembodied voices and its guests as depersonalised room numbers, the film adaptation takes full advantage of the conventions of period and costume drama to materialise the internal and external spaces of the hotel and dramatise the bustling household of working and paying residents, individuating them through appearance, behaviour and personality. The impressions and opinions held in reserve by the waiting staff when in the presence of guests are given free expression at the kitchen breakfast table, at which is assembled an intergenerational grouping whose informal familiarity, accommodation of personal eccentricity and teasing banter have all the hallmarks of an extended family. The table is headed by the cook, Polly (Brenda Fricker), a mature woman whose management of the servant household involves both manual and emotional labour; the younger maids, Helen (Mia Wasikowska) and Emmy (Antonia Campbell-Hughes), bicker and flirt, and the failing comprehension of the elderly Patrick (James Greene) is kindly indulged. The head waiter, Albert Nobbs (Glenn Close), is seated at the other end of the table, facing Polly, his position suggesting seniority and deference as the paternal head of the household staff. However, the arrival of Dr Holloran (Brendan Gleeson) at the kitchen table is the first indication of a breach of class boundaries. As a paying guest he belongs in the formal dining room but as a long-term resident he resembles the live-in staff. Moreover, his apparent status as unofficial house doctor complicates his class status since he is at once an educated professional and a worker in service to the hotel, its guests and employees. Holloran is soon after found in another unexpected location, his head emerging from between the legs of Galway-born Mary, one of the more mature maids, as a service bell comically interrupts their mutual pleasure by summoning her to work. A keen drinker, Holloran can rely on Albert to supply his favourite whiskey with his breakfast tea and he familiarly addresses Mrs Baker (Pauline Collins), the proprietor of the hotel, as 'Duchess'. Whilst Mrs Baker is a capable and fair-minded businesswoman in the novella, her behaviour in the film is comically manipulative and morally compromising; she is flirtatious with men of all classes and connives with her upper-class male guests to enable their illicit sexual behaviour. When she inadvertently discovers Albert's considerable savings following his death, she uses them to redecorate the hotel, fulfilling an ambition which had been the pretext for a flirtatious encounter with the travelling housepainter Hubert Page (Janet McTeer) earlier in the film, when she invited him to appraise her property and join her in imagining 'more salubrious rooms'. However, while Holloran's behaviour – combined with his full beard and collar-length hair amidst the clean-shaven chins of the other hotel staff and guests – suggests a raffish character, he emerges as a figure of moral as well as medical authority, his emancipated compassion compelling him to forbid Mrs Baker to expel a serving maid who has fallen pregnant outside of marriage. Holloran's indifference to social convention is revealed as principled rather than exploitative; his relationship with Mary, for example, is depicted as consensual, faithful and a source of pleasure to them both. Holloran is the only new character of any significance introduced into the film adaptation and his medical expertise places him in a crucial position to intervene at moments of crisis in the narrative, a position which anticipates his role as arbiter of Albert's gender identity after his death. Holloran's judgements – whether philosophical or medical – play a pivotal role in scenes in which a *fin de siècle* sensibility is communicated.

The introduction of a costume ball into the film narrative provides an opportunity to dramatise the contrast between the families of Anglo-Irish gentry who frequent Morrison's Hotel in Moore's novella and the new generation of English aristocratic guests who are cultivated by Mrs Baker in the film adaptation. During the opening scenes in the dining room, the viewer is introduced to the hotel's returning or long-resident guests, including a Mr and Mrs Moore, whom the viewer familiar with the source text will identify as the parents of the 'little red-haired boy'[13] who was the child George Moore. While Mr Moore (Rhys Burke) is depicted as slightly contemptuous of Mrs Baker's pretensions to quality, Mrs Moore (Lauren Kinsella) is openly appreciative of the attentions of Albert, who is shown more than once rather pedantically switching vases of flowers to ensure that Mrs Moore to able to enjoy her favourite bloom – the white rose – both in her room and at her table. It is Mrs Moore who lingers as the guests rush to leave the hotel following the outbreak of typhus, expressing mute concern for an ailing Albert who struggles to rise from his seat to salute her. The rituals of long service and the sentiments of loyalty that characterise this relationship typify class dynamics defined by deference. If Mr Moore is not an especially gracious guest, Viscount Yarrell (Jonathan Rhys Meyer) is satirically profuse in his apologies when he and his companions enter into the dining room in an explosion of unrestrained laughter and uninhibited movement. His party consists of two young couples, unchaperoned by older relatives and seemingly without the responsibility of family. Later that night Albert stands aside as the four guests return to their rooms, the Viscount's male companion crawling along the floor in a state of high-spirited inebriation. The next morning, as Albert observes his duties in the Viscount's rooms, the Viscount drains the dregs of a champagne bottle, his dressing gown gaping open to reveal his naked chest; the camera cuts away to his male companion, whom he addresses as 'Bunny', lying naked on a bed in the same suite, the stem of an empty bottle in the foreground comically concealing his exposed genitals from the camera's gaze. By contrast to the Moores and other time-honoured guests, the Viscount's party represents a breakdown in social hierarchy and class responsibility which is further underlined in the depiction of the hotel's annual costume ball. This event takes place in the guest dining room, formerly the scene of muted and formal social interaction but now transformed into a more dynamic social space, where guests move freely, talking, drinking, promenading and dancing. The costumes are elaborate, representing a diverse range of national, historic and theatrical dress, including a medieval jester in a three-cornered hat, a Highland ghillie, a Cavalier, a harlequin and an American cowboy in Stetson and buckskin jacket. Mr and Mrs Moore arrive dressed as a conquering Roman soldier, in armoured breastplate and laurels, and a Celtic goddess, in a long feathered cloak – costumes which gesture respectively to a history of colonialism and the current revival of interest in Irish mythology. Most significantly, the Viscount and his party attend the ball cross-dressed. The two women wear top hats and tails, the flattering tailoring of their evening dress and the jaunty angle of their hats evoking the popular male impersonators of the stage in the period. By contrast, the men wear Regency style gowns, indecorously straining at the neck or falling from their shoulders, with their heads and hair undressed, in contrast to the elaborate headgear of most of the other guests. Whether sprawling in their companions' laps or dancing parodically with each other there is a subtext of social aggression in their behaviour. If the cross-dressing Viscount and his party bring a touch of decadence to the gathering, it is characterised by nihilism rather than glamour and lends an air of incipient chaos. While the women's cross-dressing borrows from recognised theatrical convention, the men's cross-dressing seems to have an undercurrent of misogyny. The ball is the scene of further licence in relation to class when Joe Mackins (Aaron Johnson) enters the room in his working clothes, picking at the buffet and enlisting one of the servants to serve him some punch, until he is spotted by Mrs Baker and unceremoniously expelled. Joe is an imposter twice over: not only is he an uninvited guest at the ball but his very presence in the hotel is the consequence of mistaken identity, when he fails to correct Polly's presumption that he is the man come to fix the boiler and presents himself as an apprentice to the trade. Holloran's role in crossing and confounding class boundaries is further confirmed in these scenes. He is the only guest not to sport a costume but is given the privilege of leading Mrs Baker – sporting a Venetian columbina – in the first dance of the evening. As the evening progresses, and after much consumption of alcohol, Holloran approaches the ever impassive Albert to enquire why he is not wearing a costume; now sporting a stethoscope – a belated concession to the theme of masquerade – Holloran declares: 'We are both disguised as ourselves.' His comment could allude to the prevalence of performance in the management of social roles in everyday life and by sharing his thoughts with the waiter Holloran confirms a sense of fellow feeling. However, in the narrative context of the film his comments acquire a foreshadowing function because they are addressed to Albert in particular. Motifs of masquerade, costume and disguise proliferate in narratives which depict transgender as a form of cross-dressing. In this context it would seem as if the audience is positioned to view Albert's gender identity with the sceptical or satirical eye that dramas of dissimulation invite. Dramatic irony is deployed in this scene, which anticipates the pivotal role Holloran will play in the 'exposure' of Albert's 'disguise' and the 'revelation' of his sex. If the costume ball presents a certain risk for Albert, because of the way it invites scrutiny of the role played by dress in determining social identity, the outbreak of a contagious disease in the hotel represents an even greater danger given the licence it gives to figures of medical authority to inspect the body.

In the 2011 film adaptation an outbreak of typhus in Morrison's Hotel provides a dramatic hinge which throws the social world it has conjured into crisis, placing key characters in jeopardy and propelling the action towards its denouement. An unidentified young kitchen maid is the first to fall ill, collapsing on the scullery floor, and Holloran is quick to identify the gravity of the situation, commanding those nearby to scrub their hands with carbolic soap to prevent further infection. However, for Mrs Baker the crisis is principally economic and she entreats her rapidly departing guests not to leave, begging a health official not to damage her business by identifying it as the site of contagion. In her essay 'Typhus in Nineteenth-Century Ireland', E. Margaret Crawford describes the sentiments of fear, shame and denial that an outbreak of the disease could provoke in a community.[14] Indeed, the nailing of the public health notice to the door and the drawing of the shutters, as the hotel is closed for business, evoke the rituals of public mourning. Crawford describes the popular association between typhus and hunger, adding the stigma of poverty to the disease. However, as she notes, the 'culprits responsible for typhus were not cesspools, stagnant air nor even hunger but body lice that found hospitality in the clothing of the poor',[15] thriving particularly in 'the cramped conditions in gaols, barracks and ships'.[16] The date given on the public health notice, 1898, was the year of a significant local epidemic of typhus in Ireland (although not the year of the Public Health Act named on the notice, which was in 1878). However, the depiction of the outbreak is more than an act of historical fidelity; the symbolic meanings of contagion serve a number of significant purposes. The outbreak can be seen as a signifier of the transgression of class boundaries; the proximity of the poor and the wealthy, the crossing of class distinction (including in intimate personal contexts) and the presence of interlopers in the building are all factors which conspire to make contagion more likely. The borders of this social space have been breached and the hotel's status as an upper-class enclave is compromised. A hotel is not a gaol, barrack or ship but it does rely on a kind of bonded labour in the context of institutional living; those who can escape the hotel (the guests) do so, and those who remain are revealed as a kind of prisoner. Albert is the only named character in the hotel staff to be depicted as falling ill but surviving (the elderly Patrick's death from the disease is noted after the fact); that he suffers alone in his room seems a noble act of self-sacrifice, protecting the other members of the household from contagion. However, his illness takes on the form of another crisis in this narrative context, since the viewer is now well aware of Albert's fear of exposure; in these circumstances, his withdrawal can be seen as an attempt to evade the attentions of a doctor even at the risk of his own health.

The *fin de siècle* setting provides an ideal opportunity to present Albert and Hubert as figures of social and gender transgression, whether as subversive individuals defying the moral and social conventions of the era or as pathologised subjects symptomatic of degenerate trends: the narrative motifs of costume and contagion could set the scene for the exposure of travesty or diagnosis of pathology. However, the film adaptation retains the novella's depiction of Albert as a character whose greatest ambition is inclusion within social norms, principally through the vehicle of marriage. Moreover, in its significant expansion of Hubert's role within the narrative and its focus on his status as a husband, the film offers Hubert as a solution to some of the crises of late-nineteenth-century Ireland, specifically in relation to masculinity, illegitimacy and migration. The contrasting character of the 'two men, so dissimilar' depicted in Moore's novella is significantly extended in the film adaptation and underlined by the performances given by Glenn Close and Janet McTeer in these roles.[17] The characterisation of Albert in the film at first seems to position him as a comic character, with scenes of his apparently miserly hoarding accompanied by a signature musical score in which the striking of piano keys and the plucking of harp and violin strings suggest that he is not to be taken seriously. The soliloquies which Glenn Close performs in character as Albert Nobbs are clearly a relic of the stage adaptation and seem at odds with the more naturalistic ensemble acting of the rest of the film. Close's performance as the timid, tightly buttoned Albert moves between comic and tragic registers, inviting our amusement at his naiveté and our pity at his suffering. By contrast, Janet McTeer's embodied performance as Hubert is expansive, humorous and charismatic. Where Close's Albert is reserved and withdrawn, his face consistently assuming the impassivity which the other servants adopt only when on duty, McTeer's Hubert is expressive and expansive, his face mobile with wry smiles and teasing insinuations as he swings around the hotel with assurance. However, the treatment of motifs of revelation in relation to Albert and Hubert in the film adaptation suggests that they represent not only two contrasting characters, but two contrasting modes of representing transgender characters in contemporary culture.

'You'll find nothing there': Revealing Masculinity in *Albert Nobbs* (2011)

In George Moore's 1918 novella Albert's and Hubert's identity as men with female-sexed bodies is quickly established. Indeed, one of the most interesting features of Moore's treatment of the topic is the fact that his narrative is not invested in dramatic dynamics of suspense and revelation. Albert's and Hubert's sexed identity is established principally through first-person narrative disclosure, but prompted by a fleeting moment of physical exposure pertaining to Albert only. However, the exact nature and meaning of what has been seen remains ambiguous. From this point onwards the narrator of Moore's novella uses female pronouns to refer to Albert and Hubert, a practice which creates some narrative dissonance given that their gender identity as men is accepted without question by the other characters in the novella. In the 2011 film adaptation both Albert and Hubert are subject to moments of spectacular revelation. Such moments can have violent effects where transgender identity is concerned, mobilising the dynamics of film language to privilege what is seen over what is experienced by providing visual 'proof' that contradicts the transgender subject's identity. As Danielle M. Seid has argued:

> Structuring an audience's knowledge of a character's transgender status as a reveal can contribute to the perception that living a transgender life involves concealing 'the truth' of sexed bodies. The moment of the reveal provokes a struggle over the meaning of the trans body, a struggle in which the trans person often 'loses' to dominant discourses about trans lives, the conclusion being: that's *really* a man. [emphasis in original][18]

However, the revelation of Albert's and Hubert's sexed identity is treated in very different ways in the film: where Albert is implicitly depicted as a cross-dressing woman, the disclosure of Hubert's female body does not compromise his identity as a man.

Albert's body is subject to two forms of exposure in both the novella and the film adaptation. The first is inadvertent and accidental, when Hubert sees him undressed in the bedroom that they share, and the second is posthumous, when Albert's corpse is examined by a doctor; in both cases he is 'authored by others', who draw conclusions about his identity from the apparent evidence of his sex. In Moore's novella, Hubert glimpses Albert's exposed body when the latter undresses in the night in order to contend with a flea lodged in his shirt tail. However, the pivotal nature of this moment is somewhat qualified when the narrator observes: 'If Albert had had the presence of mind to drop her shirt over her shoulders and to answer: You're dreaming, my man, Page may have turned over and fallen asleep and in the morning forgotten all about it, or thought he had been dreaming.'[19] From this the reader might conclude that whatever visual evidence Hubert has witnessed was not so surprising or conclusive as to be impossible to forget. The reference to the dropping of the shirt suggests that Hubert has glimpsed Albert's upper body, but the novella makes no reference to practices such as binding by which the existence of breasts might have been concealed. At Albert's death in Moore's novella, an unidentified doctor supplies no explanation for his report that 'Albert was a woman'[20] and none is required of him. In the adaptation, by contrast, the mystery of what Hubert and the doctor have seen is dispelled. Albert falls from the bed he shares with Hubert as he wrestles to release himself from his clothes, lifting his shirt to reveal a torso which is both bound and corseted; in his haste to relieve his discomfort, the camera briefly discloses Albert's breasts and nipples escaping from the top of his disordered undergarments. A rapid cut to a reaction shot traces this sight line to Hubert's point of view, as he starts up from his slumber to exclaim in his deep Dublin vernacular: 'Jesus!' In her 2010 book *Assuming a Body: Transgender and Rhetoric of Materiality*, Gayle Salamon observes that 'Culture often insists that sex equals genitals. But in the workings of culture, sex attribution has almost nothing to do with genital configuration.'[21] Here it is the presence of the breasts (a secondary sex characteristic) rather than the absence of the penis which determines Hubert's deduction. Similarly, on the discovery of Albert's dead body Holloran is called to Albert's room in his dressing gown and slippers, where he presses his ear to Albert's chest to determine that his heart has stopped beating. A look of slight consternation prompts him to gently press his hands against Albert's chest and then to unbutton Albert's necktie, jacket and shirt, revealing binding, which he partially unravels, and a corset. Again, the concealment of breasts is presented as sufficient evidence of sexed identity, requiring no further investigation and transforming Albert into 'a woman'.

By contrast, Hubert is subject to no such exposure in Moore's novella. Following his disclosure he does invite an unbelieving Albert to 'feel for yourself if you won't believe me. Put your hand under my shirt; you'll find nothing there.'[22] This invitation lends further ambiguity to what it is that the shirt conceals, the 'nothing' presumably referring to the genitals (more obviously concealed by garments of the lower body) rather than the breasts. This discretion is entirely undone in the film adaptation where Hubert's upper body is exposed in the public space of the laundry room, which he has been employed to paint. However, this exposure is self-managed and hence it can be interpreted as an expression of his individual agency rather than a symptom of its loss. Moreover, the manner in which this evidence is revealed has the effect of confirming, rather than contradicting, his masculinity as a man; Janet McTeer's performance as Hubert, here and elsewhere, is crucial in ensuring this effect. In Moore's novella Albert and Hubert tell their narrative over the course of a single night in the privacy of Albert's room in the servants' quarters of the hotel, Hubert's disclosure following Albert's in quick and uncanny succession. By contrast, in the film adaptation Albert's narrative is considerably deferred, in both time and place, and Hubert's narrative is not only postponed until daylight but its telling is dispersed across the working spaces of the hotel, both interior and exterior. In the film adaptation, Hubert quickly regains his composure after being roused from his sleep by Albert's agitation. Reclining on Albert's side of the bed, fully dressed but with his braces loose by his waist and rolling a cigarette between his fingers, Hubert silently considers Albert with a cocked head, raised eyebrow and lopsided smile. McTeer's performance embodies Hubert's innate authority and easy command of space; his demeanour is in striking contrast to that of Albert, who cowers on the floor, shrinking into the wall and pleading with Hubert on his knees. Hubert's charm and good humour are more in evidence in the morning, and he teasingly rebuffs Albert as he anxiously pursues him around the hotel with offerings of tea. Hubert relents when Albert makes another approach, this time armed with a plate of dinner, and assures him that his 'secret is safe with me', as he wipes his hands with a rag in the laundry room sink. The traffic of staff through the room indicates that it is not the most secure space for private confidences. However, Hubert silences Albert's repeated pleas by bearing down towards him to close the door, one hand unbuttoning his waistcoat and a cigarette hanging from the side of his mouth. Turning to face Albert, Hubert plants his feet squarely and seizes the dense fabric of his waistcoat and shirt in his clenched fists; he pauses for a beat before pointedly opening his arms to reveal a naked chest and a pair of large breasts, free of any binding or corsetry. As Albert recoils in shock, Hubert swiftly buttons his shirt and reaches for the handle of the laundry room door, allowing Albert to make his exit. Silence, dominance of space and decisive action are all characteristics of physical masculine authority, but in this context Hubert's actions can equally be read as an expression of solidarity between two female-bodied men. The secrecy, shame and fear which characterised Albert's unwitting exposure of his body are entirely absent; on the contrary, there is a quality of bravado in Hubert's risk-taking which suggests that his gender identity is far from precarious.

If the revelation of Hubert's sexed body does not seem to contradict his masculinity the insertion of two further scenes further confirms it. The inclusion of Hubert's wife, renamed Cathleen in the film adaptation, and the depiction of her home life with Hubert, is one of the most significant interpolations in the film adaptation. Albert's two visits to Hubert's home prove pivotal in the film narrative but for different reasons as far as Albert's and Hubert's gender identity is concerned. The first visit confirms Albert in his ambition to secure a wife, but the second – which incorporates the most dramatic departure from the source text – suggests an unexpressed femininity when Albert and Hubert venture outside in Cathleen's dresses. By contrast, these encounters both serve to confirm Hubert's masculinity, firstly in his marriage to Cathleen and secondly in his grief as a husband following her death. When Albert takes the opportunity to enquire whether Hubert is still married as they go about their work in the hotel, Hubert's answer is whispered into Albert's ear with self-conscious drama and humour: 'Yes . . . And her name's Cathleen!' This revelation prompts Albert to leave the city, travelling by horse-drawn trap to the coast, where Hubert and Cathleen's home bears a painted sign reading 'Sewing – Plain or Fancy'. Albert visits Hubert on the pretext of returning a mislaid button but it is clear to all that his curiosity about Hubert's wife is the real motivation behind the visit. Cathleen (Bronagh Gallagher) receives her awkward guest with quizzical amusement, but soon seizes on the return of the button as a merry pretext to extend her hospitality to Albert and invite him to dinner. The relationship between Cathleen and Hubert is one marked by humorous banter and affectionate intimacy; they join together in a benevolent conspiracy to make Albert welcome and draw him out of himself. The figure of Helen Dawes – to date Joe Mackins's love interest alone in the film narrative – is revealed to be a standing joke between Cathleen and Hubert, one which provides an occasion for teasing and flirting. Hubert winks at Albert as he recalls what 'a fine girl' she is, pulling a face at Cathleen as she turns to him in mock indignation, noting wryly that Hubert 'took quite a shine to her'. The topic of emigration to America is introduced into the film narrative with comic effect here, with Hubert imagining Cathleen's departure as an opportunity to 'try me luck' with Helen, with her 'sweet little face' and 'lovely blonde curls'. As Cathleen perches on Hubert's lap he extends his arm around her waist and Cathleen swears to thwart Hubert's ambitions by staying put in Dublin; at this she strikes a match to light the cigarette poised in Hubert's mouth (the signature motif of McTeer's performance), shakes her head in indulgent exasperation and leans in to him comfortably with her arms around his neck and her hand stroking the shoulder of his stained woollen sweater. There is a sense that this performance of faux sexual jealousy has been played out again and again, the prospect of a love rival and the threat of abandonment conjured and dismissed for the sheer pleasure of confirming their mutual attachment and contentment. The scene takes place as both Hubert and Cathleen instruct Albert in the art of rolling tobacco in preparation for his future career; however, the scene doubles as an induction in the art of contented married life. It is clear that Hubert's private self is identical to his public self and that his masculinity is central to his relationship with Cathleen.

Cathleen's death is unexplained in Moore's novella but in the film adaptation she is the principal dramatic casualty of the outbreak of typhus. On his recovery from illness, Albert's first enquiry is after the health of Helen, but when he visits Hubert the mourning drapes adorning the front door and bay window of his home indicate a grief which will prove pivotal in both Hubert's and Albert's expression of their gender identity. When Albert offers to take Cathleen's place in the home it becomes all the more clear that Hubert's marriage is much more than a matter of convenience, as its depiction in Moore's novella might suggest; a grief-stricken Hubert, incredulous at Albert's proposal, declares with emotion: 'She was my world – we loved each other.' When Hubert invites Albert to admire Cathleen's self-made dresses her uninhabited gowns laid out on the marital bed strongly evoke her absence. However, Albert's wistful comment – 'I can't remember what it's like' – prompts one of the most unexpected and arguably least plausible interpolations in the adaptation. A cut to the front door of Hubert's home opening into the hall reveals first Albert and then Hubert emerging from the shadows in the dresses which had been admired from a distance in the previous scene. Their short hair concealed in the poke bonnets of their grandmother's era, they proceed to walk out of the door – where a passing gentleman doffs his hat to them – and are next pictured strolling on the beach, Albert responding rapturously to the sensation of the sea breeze as it lifts his bonnet and shawl; he breaks into a run, his head thrown back in pleasure, until he stumbles in his skirts and falls in the sand. Throughout this silent scene Hubert's gaze is trained on Albert, monitoring his response watchfully; it is clear that this adventure is for Albert's benefit entirely. Albert's gown is close fitting and flattering and his carefully controlled gait and erect deportment seem to suit his outfit. By contrast Hubert's gown is short in the sleeves and the length and cuts tightly across his chest; he makes no concessions to his dress in his demeanour, his very visible wrists and ankles swinging and his stride wide. As he comes to Albert's rescue he jogs steadily through the sand, flicking back the lock of hair that habitually falls into his eyes as he comes to an unhurried halt. Hubert betrays no nostalgia for feminine attire whatsoever and his lack of self-consciousness about his ill-fitting gown and old-fashioned hat is entirely consistent with the easy self-confidence. For him, masculine dress is no disguise; if he is 'disguised as himself' in his suit of hollands, he is no more disguised than any other man in the film.

The origins of Glenn Close's interpretation of her character – both as performer in, and executive producer of, the film adaptation – could be traced to the legacy of Benmussa's stage play and its reputation as a drama of women's gender crossing. As we have seen, motifs of imprisonment, alienation and loss recur in the critical reception of the play as a classic of feminist theatre and these themes are evident in Close's depiction of Albert as a woman trapped in masculine disguise, alienated from her femininity and suffering loneliness and isolation. However, while the film goes much further than the novella or the stage adaptation in making a claim to Albert's 'lost' femininity, at the same time it depicts Hubert's lived masculinity as extending beyond the narrative. In other words, while one narrative (Albert's) seems to reinforce the idea of a causal relationship between sex and gender which can only bring grief and alienation if disrupted, another parallel narrative (Hubert's) depicts a gender identity not dictated by sex, and one, moreover, which is characterised by social integration, continuity and futurity. Indeed, Hubert's masculinity has a compensatory quality, substituting for the shortcomings of the other men in the narrative; the turn-of-the-century setting provides narratives of national crisis to which Hubert's masculinity brings welcome relief in this film adaptation.

Three Men, So Dissimilar: Illegitimacy, Masculinity and Marriage in *Albert Nobbs* (2011)

In Moore's 1918 novella, Helen Dawes is a vivid but minor character as the reluctant but shrewd object of Albert's courtship, who colludes with her young man, Joe, to take advantage of Albert's naive liberality. However, Helen and Joe's romance is significantly expanded in the 2011 film adaptation where it culminates with Helen's pregnancy and Joe's departure for America. In doing so it brings together two crises in Irish history: the treatment of unmarried mothers and their children by the Church and state, and the mass emigration of Irish people to America and elsewhere in the decades following the Great Famine. Here the former is the cause of the latter, with Helen tied to her mother country more firmly than ever by the responsibility of a child and the stigma of illegitimacy, and Joe seeking escape from a brutalised history through flight to America. In some ways, the expansion of Helen and Joe's subplot threatens to supplant Albert's story as the eponymous protagonist of the film, their ill-fated courtship mobilising narratives of Irish national history with which audiences may be more familiar. However, this subplot nevertheless exhibits a close and complex relationship with motifs which have their origin in the source text. Moreover, the film narrative closes with the widowed Hubert about to embark on a second marriage, his proposal to Helen providing a 'solution' to crises of illegitimacy, masculinity and migration.

In Moore's novella, Albert's social vulnerability is the effect of a combination of circumstances, including illegitimacy as the child of unmarried parents and exposure to the unwelcome sexual advances of men. The themes of illegitimacy and male violence play a significant role in both the novella and its film adaptation, and in the latter they are brought together in Joe's abandonment of the pregnant Helen. In Moore's novella, Albert Nobbs expresses compassion for those women who, like his own mother, find themselves pregnant outside of marriage: 'what a great misfortune it is for a poor girl to find herself in the family way; no greater misfortune can befall anyone in this world.'[23] Indeed, Albert imagines such a woman as an ideal candidate for his future wife; by providing a home for a vulnerable mother and child, Albert would be able to save them both not only from the stigma of illegitimacy but also from the poverty and possible destitution which might follow from the social and moral penalties imposed on such women in late-nineteenth-century Ireland. However, Albert would also secure the unpaid labour of his wife, not only in the home but also in his intended business venture as a shop keeper. Indeed, his future wife's sexual history arguably places her under even greater obligation; as she would have forfeited her currency in the legitimate marriage market, her capacity to exercise choice would be curtailed and her position in the marriage shaped by obligation. Indeed, Albert speculates that a woman with sexual experience and a child may be more likely to accept marriage as 'a community of interests' rather than a 'sexual adventure',[24] perhaps especially where 'sexual adventure' had ended in pregnancy and abandonment. In Moore's novella Albert sets out to court Helen, despite the fact that she is not an unmarried mother, after a protracted process of selection in which a number of candidates are considered and rejected. By contrast, in the film adaptation Helen falls pregnant with Joe's child, thereby fulfilling Albert's criteria for an ideal wife; she even names her infant after Albert as if anticipating that he might step into the vacated paternal role. When Hubert returns to the hotel to learn of Albert's death and to take up a lucrative commission funded by Albert's stolen savings, he encounters the abandoned Helen with her infant in the yard among the laundry, the location of her wooing by Joe earlier in the film. Helen bitterly and tearfully explains that her continuing employment at Morrison's Hotel is subject to terms which she cannot negotiate:

HUBERT: So Mrs Baker's letting you stay is she?
HELEN: Oh she told you that did she? Out of the kindness of her Christian heart. The truth is, Mr Page . . . the truth is,

she won't tell the priest about my Albert as long as I work here for nothing. But they are going to take him away from me. I know they will. And they will throw me out on to the street. It's just a matter of time.

In order to avoid separation from her child, Helen exchanges one punishment for another, a form of indentured labour wherein her wages and liberty are forfeited. Helen expresses the working woman's legitimate horror of being compelled to labour without pay by a state-sanctioned institution – the Church – in the name of public morality, and in doing so echoes the sentiments of a character from the novella, Kitty MacCan, who is excised in the film adaptation: 'you're not one of them, she said, that think that we should wash clothes in a nunnery for nothing?'[25]

Joe has no story to tell in Moore's novella, where his exploitation of Albert's generosity seems more mischievous than malicious despite its cruel effects. By contrast, in the film narrative, significant efforts are made to secure sympathy for Joe, as if in advance vindication of his subsequent behaviour towards both Albert and Helen. Indeed, Joe is furnished with a back story by which to explain his abandonment of Helen and his experience of male violence is central to this story. In the novella Albert recalls his childhood fear of being 'caught hold of and held and pulled about'[26] by men, a phrase that is elsewhere used by Helen to allude to the accepted sexual negotiations of heterosexual courtship. In the film adaptation, the sinister subtext is made reality when Albert recounts his experience of being 'caught' and 'pulled about' by five men, concluding with emotion and emphasis that 'they hurt me'. In the novella, Hubert was previously a wife and mother whose husband, a housepainter, 'changed towards her altogether after the birth of her second child, leaving her without money for food and selling up the home twice'.[27] Hubert's plight and its solution are economic; he assumes his husband's work clothes and profession in order to make a living. By contrast, in the film adaptation, Hubert's husband is depicted as a violent and abusive man and Hubert's life as a man a consequence of a crisis brought on by his assaults. Hubert discloses his story in response to Albert's evident curiosity: 'It's not much to tell. I was married. To a housepainter as it happens. A drunk and a bully. One night he came home scuttered, gave me the usual hiding, only this time rounded it off with an almighty kick. And that was the end of that.' Domestic violence is presented here as routine – 'the usual hiding' – but the assault which precipitates Hubert's flight has an implicitly sexualised overtone. As Hubert recalls the 'almighty kick' his hand forms a fist over his lower abdomen, suggesting that the target was his belly or even genitals; the 'end' to which he refers – 'And that was the end of that' – encompasses the marital relationship and his endurance of his husband's abuse but might also hint at the possibility of a pregnancy terminated in a miscarriage brought on by the force of the blow. The motif of domestic violence within the home – and the hotel as an unwitting refuge for its victims – is further reinforced in the film adaptation by the family life of Joe Mackins, the newly appointed yardman and Helen's suitor. Joe's father, like Hubert's husband, is a 'boozer' and Joe recounts the dread with which he and his siblings anticipated their father's return as children: 'None of us ever slept. We'd be lying there, shivering with the fright, waiting for him to come home, knowing that if he did, there'd be no place to hide. He'd get up in the morning with no memory of him beating the stuffing out of us the night before.' The memory of Joe's status as an impoverished and neglected child, and the poignancy of his efforts to overcome this history, is reinforced in a scene where we witness Joe copying letters from a child's reader; hastily concealing the evidence of his illiteracy from Helen as she enters his room, he later offers his inability to read as further proof of his unreadiness to be a father. Joe is placed in the position of potential heir to his father's violence, a potentiality of which he himself is very conscious; his courtship of Helen is characterised by sudden appearances and seizures, prompting Helen to cry out 'you're hurting me' when he grasps her in their first encounter in the maze of billowing laundry pegged out to dry in the hotel yard. His feints and embraces are presented as play but have an undercurrent of menace; indeed, when Helen reveals her pregnancy to him he reacts with anger, pounding a kitchen chair against the flagged floor in frustration. Joe's palpable struggle to control his emotions is evident in the confrontations which follow the disclosure of Helen's pregnancy, in which Joe's anger is traced directly to his fear of following in his father's footsteps:

> JOE: I can't do it Helen. I hate meself for it but I can't do it. It's the same old story and you know it. I mean how many times have you seen it happen? It shouldn't have happened.
> HELEN: But it did happen.
> JOE: Yeah but it happened too soon. It will change us. It'll change me. I don't want to be that person. I don't want to be me fecking Da.

Joe's abandonment of Helen, when he leaves Ireland for America without her, is presented as a desperate attempt to escape the legacy of his father's violence. He confides in Helen that the only thing that 'kept me from killing him' was 'the thought of getting on a boat and hopping it to America'. Here and elsewhere Joe struggles to resist the violence which his father's abuse has bred in him and a more radical flight – to America – presents itself as the only solution.

Joe is doubled with both Albert and Hubert in the film and in this way they emerge as '*three* men, so dissimilar'. Hubert's discovery of Albert's sex is cross cut in the film with Joe's struggle with the hotel boiler; as Albert begs Hubert to keep his secret in order to avoid the workhouse, Joe triumphs over the hotel plumbing by a combination of sheer luck and brute force, ensuring that his imposture will not be exposed. Moreover, the scene in which Joe discloses the traumatic memory of a difficult childhood to Helen follows immediately after Albert's disclosure of his childhood to Hubert. This doubling of their stories suggests structural parallels between their narratives while at the same time confirming them as rivals for Helen's attention. Joe is depicted as secretly scrutinising Albert in the kitchen yard as he looks yearningly after a departing Hubert; in a later scene, Joe's offer to help Albert with the luggage with which the older man is struggling is rudely rejected. These scenes portray Joe as an intrusive and suspicious figure, an interloper whose keen eye for fellow imposters might jeopardise Albert's position. This sense of danger is vindicated at the climax of the narrative, when Albert intervenes in an angry confrontation between Helen and Joe: thrown against the wall by Joe, Albert suffers a blow to his head which proves fatal. Where Joe is implicitly posited as a rival and potential danger to Albert, he is doubled with Hubert as an object of sexual or romantic interest on the part of the female staff at Morrison's. When Joe washes barechested at the scullery sink after his labours with the hotel boiler he is surreptitiously observed by two young female servants positioned in doorways at either end of the passage; while one lingers and looks away guiltily after she hands him a towel to dry himself, the other stares open-mouthed until her presence is observed and she sinks back behind the door. Hubert also attracts attention, but of a different kind; he comments humorously on the profusion of offers of tea while working in the laundry room. Where Joe is the object of undisguised sexual interest, Hubert inspires overtures of a more domestic nature, suggesting that he may be the more desirable partner. Moreover, a version of the marriage which Albert imagined is set to take place beyond the end of the film, but involves neither Albert nor Joe but Hubert. In the closing scene of the film, Hubert's response to Helen's confession of her plight as an unmarried mother promises a new future for both of them; taking the infant in his arms, he assures her: 'Well now, we can't let that happen can we?' Hence, it is Hubert – not Joe – who is poised to marry Helen, and it is Hubert – not Albert – who is seemingly accepted with gratitude. Hubert takes both Albert's and Joe's place, fulfilling Albert's dream (in the novella) of marrying an unmarried mother and substituting for Joe's inadequacies as a man inducted into brutalising patriarchal masculinities. In a film narrative where patriarchal masculinity is depicted as either abusive or absent, Hubert emerges as the 'ideal husband' – a man whose masculinity is characterised by economic and emotional responsibility, rather than by violence and abandonment.

The 2011 film adaptation of Moore's *Albert Nobbs* centres on two contrasting performances which arguably typify the tensions between twentieth-century and contemporary interpretations of characters with transgender potential. Where Close's performance as Albert can be situated in traditions of reading female-bodied men as cross-dressing women (exemplified in the canonisation of Benmussa's play as a classic of feminist theatre), McTeer's performance as Hubert implies no contradiction between his sex and his gender. However, the prominent role of marriage in the legitimisation of Hubert's masculinity in the film might suggest that this recognition of gender is nevertheless conditional on conforming to social norms. The vexed nature of the relationship between seemingly progressive representations of transgender identity in film narrative and the role of heteronormative constructions of gender is equally apparent in the 2016 film adaptation of David Ebershoff's novel *The Danish Girl*, with a pronounced focus on femininity.

'What you draw, I become': Cultivating Femininity in *The Danish Girl* (2016) and its Source Texts

David Ebershoff's 2000 novel and its 2016 film adaptation place special emphasis on a conceit that has its origin in the 1931 account of Lili Elbe's life, *Man into Woman*: namely, that Lili has been brought into being through the agency of an artist's authorship. Grete comments on this uncanny sensation in *Man into Woman*: '"It often happens," she continued excitedly, "that when she poses for me as a model a strange feeling comes over me that it is *she* whom I am creating and forming rather than the girl whom I am representing on my canvas"' [emphasis in original].[28] However, Grete also admits to '"prickings of conscience because I was, to a certain extent, the cause of creating Lili, of enticing her out of you, and thus becoming responsible for a disharmony in you'".[29] The myth of a woman brought to life through the agency, will and desire of a Pygmalion figure is given a seemingly modern twist because the artist in this case is a woman. However, while Grete's exercise of nominally masculine prerogatives as an artist challenges gendered power dynamics, Lili's femininity is nevertheless 'authored by others'. Indeed, the pivotal role of women in Lili's social, as opposed to medical, transition – she is named by Anna Larsen, Anna Fonsmark and Ulla respectively in the 'memoir', novel and film adaptation – seems to reinforce the assumption that femininity can only be authenticated and validated by female-bodied people. Ebershoff's novel opens with a scene which is depicted as playing a crucial – even causal role – in the transition of the Danish artist Einar Wegener into Lili Elbe, when Einar agrees to take the place of a female sitter for a portrait which his wife is completing. This scene has its origins in *Man into Woman* but acquires a heightened significance and new meanings in Ebershoff's novel. In *Man into Woman,* it is Grete's absent sitter, an actor named Anna Larsen, who suggests that Andreas take her place. Andreas initially declines but his wife is persistent and he soon succumbs to a venture which they approach as a 'great joke'.[30] While his legs alone are required to serve as a substitute for the intended model, Grete places a 'carnival wig' on Einar's head and 'attack[s]' him with 'rouge and powder'.[31] However, despite the complete absence of serious effort to emulate the appearance of their female friend both Grete and Andreas – and later Anna herself – are taken aback by the effect. Grete is 'delighted' and declares of her husband that he looks '"as if you had never worn anything but women's clothes in your life"'.[32] On her return Anna initially fails to recognise Andreas but 'utter[s] a cry of delight' on realising his identity, announcing that '"you were certainly a girl in a former existence, or else Nature has made a mistake with you this time"'.[33] Anna speaks 'quite slowly, quite deliberately' with the appearance of being 'strangely stirred'[34] and when Andreas recounts this scene on the eve of his first surgery he notes that her words were 'never forgotten'.[35] Indeed, it is Anna who 'christens' Lili and the three friends '[keep] up the rejoicings far into the night'.[36] When an artists' ball is held a few weeks later Lili attends in a pierrette's costume and is assiduously courted by men. Indeed, when Lili attempts to 'disclose her secret' to an officer who is paying 'obtrusive'[37] attentions her efforts are met with disbelief. It is notable that these scenes take place in domestic and social spaces shaped by the artistic milieu of which Andreas and Lili are a part; stigma and shame are notable by their absence and motifs of play and festivity attend Lili's emergence. While Andreas's personal anguish will supplant these light-hearted beginnings as the narrative progresses, questions of acceptance and assimilation within a wider community do not arise. Moreover, Lili's gender identity as a woman is never depicted as being vulnerable to exposure and nor does she express any anxieties about 'passing' as a woman. On the contrary, prior to his transition it is Andreas who is mistaken more than once for a girl or woman 'impersonating'[38] or 'masquerading'[39] as a man.

Both of these scenes are reproduced in Ebershoff's novel but in ways which introduce meanings which depart significantly from *Man into Woman*. *The Danish Girl* opens with the scene in which Einar substitutes for his wife's absent model and this experience is attributed a critical role in Lili's genesis. In Ebershoff's novel the actor Anna Larsen is transformed into an opera singer, Anna Fonsmark, whose professional identity provides an opportunity to introduce motifs of theatrical cross-dressing: 'She was used to men dressing in women's clothes. And women in men's, the *Hosenrolle*. It was the oldest deceit in the world. And on the opera stage it meant nothing at all – nothing but confusion. A confusion that was always resolved in the final act.'[40] However, Fonsmark's experience of travesty roles on the theatrical stage serves as an ironic anticipatory counterpoint to the narrative which is to follow, in which 'confusion' will prevail and resolution will prove hard to attain. Moreover, the analogy with theatrical conventions might seem to place Lili within a cultural tradition of dissimulation in which her gender identity is equated with deceit and subject to narrative structures of exposure and reversal. By contrast with *Man into Woman*, Einar's experience in this scene is markedly sexualised in Ebershoff's novel and associated with motifs of secrecy and sensations of shame. Einar is 'both frightened and excited'[41] at the suggestion that he pose for Anna's portrait. The invitation is issued by his wife and her very words evoke a response suggestive of arousal, closely followed by guilt: 'When she said the word "dress" his stomach filled with heat, followed by a clot of shame rising in his chest.'[42] The gendered clothing which Einar assumes – stockings and shoes – are described in fetishistic terms and when Greta invites him to complete the costume with a dress he feels the 'flesh beneath his skin ripening'.[43] The apparent awakening of dormant desires in Einar is evoked in sexualised and phallic imagery: 'Something began to run through Einar's head, and it made him think of a fox chasing a fieldmouse: the thin red nose of the fox digging for the mouse through the folds of a pulse field.'[44] In Ebershoff's novel, Greta's promise to keep 'our secret'[45] is shattered by Anna's unexpected return; in this scene the laughter is shared by the two women alone and its function is humiliating rather than inclusive:

> While the two women laughed some more, Einar's eyes began to roll back into his head, filling with tears. He was stung by their laughter, along with the perfume of the white lilies, whose rusty pistils were leaving dusty prints in the lap of the dress, against the garish lump in his groin, on the stockings, all over his wet hands.[46]

In this context, the remark which closes this opening chapter seems to seal the shame of Einar's exposure, when he is imperiously renamed by Anna: '"Why don't we call you Lili?"'[47] Secrecy, risk and danger extend into Ebershoff's depiction of the artists' ball in *The Danish Girl*, which Lili approaches with great trepidation: 'Lili felt as if she were carrying the greatest secret in the world – she was about to fool all of Copenhagen. At the same time, another part of her knew that this was the most difficult game she would ever play.'[48] Where the attentions of heterosexual men are the object of comic exasperation in *Man into Woman*, in *The Danish Girl* they play a vital role in bringing Lili to life: 'There was a circle of men in tuxedos with their hands in their pockets, their eyes roaming. Lili was stirring.'[49] It is at the artists' ball that Lili meets the man who will later propose marriage, Henrik Sandahl, but it is in their first encounter that Ebershoff introduces a narrative device which serves to signify moments of traumatic crisis. In *Man into Woman*, Einar experiences mysterious bouts of bleeding which he comes to attribute to the presence of female reproductive organs in his body. In Ebershoff's novel, the introduction of the motif of the 'divided being' is announced by a dramatic nosebleed, when a tension emerges between Lili's desire for Henrik and Einar's loyalty to Greta.[50] In the film adaptation, this bleeding serves to signify an inner struggle which makes itself manifest in the body through symptoms suggestive of internal injury or violent assault. Indeed, an anxious Greta asks if Henrik has harmed Lili and her suitor flees from the scene as if in guilt.

A portrait sitting in which a male-bodied sitter takes the place of a female performer offers rich opportunities for a quality period drama, a genre which places considerable emphasis on the pleasures of costume and set design and on the rewards of performance by talented character actors. In the film adaptation of *The Danish Girl*, Gerda's subject – an actor in *Man into Woman* and an opera singer in Ebershoff's novel – is transformed into a ballet dancer. A favoured subject of post-Impressionist painters, most notably Edgar Degas, classical ballet is also an art form in which gendered roles are very strictly defined and demarcated. Ulla (Amber Heard), the dancer in question, is introduced to the drama in an earlier scene in which Einar visits the Royal Danish Theatre, home of the Royal Danish Ballet and Opera, while his wife paints the portrait of a wealthy male patron. Casting a furtive glance behind him, Einar enters the theatre foyer in a dark overcoat and wide-brimmed hat and carrying a weighty briefcase. He seems an anomalous presence in the backstage spaces of the theatre, where he is revealed on the balcony of a high-ceilinged and ornately decorated space which houses the costume department. Rows of illuminated white tutus are suspended above the rehearsal space below, and Einar runs his hand appreciatively along a rail of stage costumes. A dancer undergoing a costume fitting at a barre beneath the clouds of tulle catches sight of Einar, whose artificially illuminated face has taken on an entranced quality, and hails him, assuring the seamstress who attends her that he is not an unwelcome intruder. This scene serves not only to establish the flamboyant character of Ulla – who warns that Gerda will 'need all her colours' for her portrait – but also to establish the costume department as a significant space in this version of Elbe's transition. Indeed, it will play a central role in two further interpolated scenes which bookend the 'birth' and 'debut' of Lili in this film.

In the film adaptation, Einar offers little resistance to Gerda's request that he substitute for the late-running Ulla, seeming eager to appease his wife's mood following her return from the Danish Royal Academy where her work has been dismissed and rejected by the patrician director. In the portrait propped on Gerda's easel Ulla is depicted in a pose which has become familiar in representations of classical dancers on canvas: a full tulle skirt fans outwards from her waist, with a single exposed leg extending across the foreground of the painting at an oblique angle, evoking the erotic subtext often underlying depictions of female dancers' bodies. This pose is mimicked with self-conscious humour by Einar, whose stockinged lower legs are substituting for Ulla, but when Gerda insists that he hold a full ballet dress against his body to provide perspective his mood undergoes a significant shift. Einar's attention turns inwards as he presses the bodice of the gown to his body, his arms crossing over his chest in a protective and self-caressing gesture and his fingertips tracing the edges of the costume. His lips parted, his breath quickening, his cheeks flushed and his pupils dilated, Einar's response to the proximity to women's clothing is distinctly sexualised and he starts from his reverie with embarrassment when Ulla unexpectedly bursts into the studio. It is Ulla – like Anna Larsen (the actor in *Man into*

Woman) and Anna Fonsmark (the opera singer in Ebershoff's novel) before her – who names Lili, and on this occasion her name is a homage to the flowers which she presents to the blushing Einar, whose position on an elevated platform only reinforces the sense of a theatrical debut. Important motifs are established in this scene: firstly, the sexualisation of Elbe's transition (seeming to suggest sexual motives and in doing so to evoke misplaced associations with transvestism); secondly, an emphasis on conventional femininity as the principal medium through which to achieve an identity as a woman (despite the alternative model of modern womanhood provided by Gerda and others); thirdly, the evocation of tropes of female impersonation (establishing the imperatives of 'passing' as a woman as a key concern for this drama). Indeed, when Einar is pictured from behind, the tips of his fingers clutching his own shoulders in a posture which mimics the embrace of another, the shot seems to be lifted straight from the lexicon of drag performance.

The interlude between Lili's birth in the studio and her debut at the ball is significantly extended in the film adaptation which introduces a lengthy sequence in which Einar and Gerda make elaborate preparations for the latter; the costume department of the Royal Danish Theatre plays an important role in this sequence, in which the full repertoire of female impersonation – make-up, hairpieces, costume and deportment – is deployed. Moreover, in these scenes the sexualised meanings which have been implicitly attributed to Einar's experience of cross-dressing are integrated into the intimate dynamics of a heterosexual marriage. It is in the course of these scenes that body-language motifs emerge which will serve as the signature of Eddie Redmayne's performance as Lili: the modestly crossed legs, ankles and arms; the hands elevated to the chest, neck and face, often in gestures of self-touching; the cradling of the face in the hand, elbow often propped on a knee; the ducked head and lowered gaze, looking up through blinking eyes and fluttering lashes. In the film adaptation, the beginnings of Einar's transition are signified by an interest in women's clothing whose motivation and meaning are initially ambiguous. When he admires Gerda's new silk nightdress as she undresses for bed the compliment can easily be understood as an expression of desire for his wife. However, when he asks her not to remove it and caresses her thigh through the material, it is not clear whether it is the fabric or her body which arouses him. Gerda's teasing comment that she might 'let [him] borrow it' only enhances the eroticism of the encounter in this scene, but after the couple return from a party hosted by their friend Ulla, Gerda discovers the gown beneath Einar's shirt as she begins to undress him. A discovery which might prompt shock, distress or shame is instead incorporated into the couple's love-making. If this adoption of feminine attire is furtive and secretive, Einar's public debut as Lili is made possible by a shared venture in which she is brought to life under Gerda's tutelage. When Einar declines to attend the artists' ball with his wife, she playfully suggests that he go as someone else. There follows a sequence of events which take place within the privacy of the home, the liminal space of the passageway and the fantasy space of a theatrical costume department. Mostly without dialogue and incorporating scenes in which comic mime enhances a register of irreverent play, these scenes depict Einar's transformation into Lili as provisional and temporary and contain it within the dynamics of a heterosexual marriage. In Ebershoff's novel, Einar makes an analogy between his practice as an artist and his new skill in painting his face: 'He'd begun to think of his make-up box as a palette. Brush-strokes to the brow. Light dabs to the lids. Lines on the lips. Blended streaks on the cheek. It was just like painting – like his brush turning a blank canvas into the winter Kattegat.'[51] This analogy is replicated in the film adaptation, except that it is Gerda who applies paint directly from her palette to Einar's lips and eyes. Moved to paint his portrait, Gerda lassoes her subject with a scarf and commands him to sit, Einar adopting exaggerated poses – legs crossed, head thrown back, hands aloft or coyly cupping his chin – which will later become Lili's signature. In these scenes the reversal of gender roles and blurring of gender boundaries pose no challenge to their relationship and the couple collapse in embraces on the chaise longue where Einar is seated. In subsequent scenes this apparently private play is gradually extended further into the public sphere, introducing the frisson of risk and thrill of conspiracy. Gerda again leads the way in instructing Einar how to walk as a woman and the lesson takes place in the cobbled passageway which opens from the courtyard of their home into the bright light of the harbour. One hand on one hip, the other aloft and hips swaying, this stylised mode of feminine motion forms a striking contrast with preceding scenes depicting Gerda walking towards the Academy: moving briskly and with purpose, her body is thrown askew by the weight of a large leather portfolio of artwork slung over one shoulder and the rolled canvases enveloped in her other arm. Indeed, the couple break apart from their impromptu rehearsal when they are interrupted by a fishwife in a paper hat carrying a wicker basket on her arm. The contrast between the exaggerated, even parodic, mode of feminine deportment which Einar adopts and the reality of working women's lives is further underlined by their neighbour's squarely planted posture and grounded step. The motif of impersonation continues in the fish market on the quayside where Einar imitates the hand gestures of a middle-class woman pointing to her desired purchase. At this stage in their preparations Einar and Gerda return together to the costume department of the Royal Danish Theatre, bypassing the courteous doorkeeper to giddily raid the stocks of wigs, costumes and shoes. Abandoning all attempt at subterfuge, the couple leave the theatre in defiantly ill-fitting wigs and hats, and the comedy continues when this scene of high-energy bustle is reversed in a low-level shot of Einar's calves and ankles in stockings and heels stumbling across the wooden floors of their apartment in a visual conceit which has become a staple of cross-dressing film comedies from *Some Like It Hot* onwards.

However, the pleasures of private travesty, which are foregrounded in these scenes, are supplanted by the fear of public exposure in the depiction of the artists' ball which serves as Lili's debut in the 'memoir', novel and film alike. In the film adaptation the bohemian milieu of the costume ball, as depicted in *Man into Woman*, is transferred into a separate party hosted by Ulla at the Royal Danish Theatre, in the same space which had witnessed her first encounter with Einar in the film. Male and female dancers in stage make-up and costume mingle freely with guests, talking, laughing and dancing to the sound of jazz music. While Gerda's ankle-revealing skirts are acknowledged as risqué in other quarters, in this context the film sets Gerda and Einar slightly apart from their peers, with Ulla pointing out that they are the only married couple in attendance. Indeed, Ulla is figured as an outspoken bohemian in the film, with her provocative speech and Ballets Russes style dress, whose narrative function is to construct her married friends as relatively conventional. In contrast to this apparently permissive atmosphere, the artists' ball itself is highly formal, seeming to reflect the cultural tastes and class position of wealthy patrons, rather than artists themselves. The motif of impersonation continues in this scene when an anxious Lili, her head ducked and shoulders stooping, mimics the posture of other young women seated against the walls of the assembly rooms, waiting to be invited to dance. Moreover, when Henrik (Ben Whishaw) draws Lili away from the crowd for a more private conversation he takes her to the life-drawing studio, as if to underline the life class in femininity she has taken under Gerda's direction. It is here that Lili's nose begins to bleed after Henrik has kissed her. In the film adaptation, the visual spectacle of blood seeping over Lili's face and hands and staining her carefully assembled clothes serves all the more powerfully to suggest that this bleeding has a symbolic function. Her face and neck swollen and distended, Lili gasps for breath and is rushed away by a protective Gerda to the evident shock and seeming distaste of the other guests. This public bleeding sets in motion a symbolic dynamic of exposure and shame which seems to imply a secret whose disclosure will attract social stigma and even violence.

The 'hard contest' between Einar and Gerda over the future of their marriage begins in the aftermath of the ball, with Gerda insisting 'We were playing a game' and Einar replying 'I know. But then – something changed.' At this cusp in the narrative the costume department of the Royal Danish Theatre plays a pivotal role once more when Einar returns alone. He turns on the lights as he enters the unoccupied space, the tulle skirts illuminated by his touch. Einar's hand once again trails along the costumes suspended from the rail but this time with greater urgency and, standing in front of a full-length mirror, he begins to remove his clothes, stripping to his underwear. In movements reminiscent of the earlier scene in the studio, Einar presses his arms close to the sides of his chest, crossing his wrists in front of him and caressing his upper body with his fingers. Drawing his underwear down, he conceals his genitals between his closely pressed thighs and poses with his hand on his hips and knees bent, as if to create the curves and angles of the stereotypical silhouette of a woman's body. The scene closes with Einar holding a dress to his naked body and caressing himself through its fabric, the beginnings of a smile emerging on his lips and his head ducking to touch the hand which rests on his upper chest. This sequence cuts between Einar at the mirror and Gerda at her canvas, the tentative pleasure evident in Einar's face at the close of this otherwise portentous scene in sharp contrast with Gerda's tearful fury as she sketches a nude portrait of Lili as if against her will. Tropes of sexualisation and female impersonation in relation to Einar's transition are further accentuated by scenes in which Lili's femininity is counterpointed with the gendered and sexual roles of other women in the narrative. As an artist Gerda is depicted as struggling against the gendered power dynamics of the art establishment; when her portraiture is rejected by the director of the Royal Academy, Rasmussen (Adrian Schiller) is framed by a large female nude in the classical tradition, as if to suggest that the only acceptable role for women in art is as a sexualised object. However, in her own practice Gerda challenges these power dynamics. Einar's first visit to the costume gallery at the theatre at the start of the film is necessitated by the sensitivities of a wealthy male patron who refuses to pose in the sight of another man. Standing at her easel in an artist's smock with a cigarette holder clamped between her lips, Gerda studies her subject with an appraising eye, commanding his movements with authoritative gestures. Her acknowledgement that 'It's hard for a man to be looked at by a woman ... to submit to a woman's gaze' does little to alleviate her sitter's discomfort, especially when she adds that there may be 'some pleasure to be had from it. Once you – yield.' Her sitter starts anew when Gerda issues a command to 'sit', a cut to the couple's pet terrier – to whom the instruction was issued – mocking her subject's instinctive submission to her authority. Gerda's willingness to play with the sexualised dynamic of the relationship between artist and model is characteristic of the bold and assertive persona she exercises in the studio and at the easel. However, while Gerda lays claim to the prerogatives of the male artist, Lili seems to comply with the perceived passivity of the female model, the sexualised poses she adopts for the mirror confirming that it is a woman's role 'to be looked at'. Moreover, the motif of female impersonation extends beyond the pleasures of masquerade. Einar undertakes a very different kind of life class when the couple move to Paris, after Gerda's work is taken up by a French art dealer. In Ebershoff's novel Einar undergoes an illicit education in a Parisian brothel, where his encounters with the female workers and male clients combine, rather paradoxically, to confirm both his sense of his heterosexuality and that of his gender identity as a woman. In the film adaptation, Einar mimics a female sex worker who caresses herself for the satisfaction of clients who have paid to watch from viewing booths. As the woman traces her fingers over her own face, lips and neck, in an alienated performance of auto-eroticism designed to arouse heterosexual men, Einar mimics her from behind the glass of his viewing station, stopping only when she reaches between her legs. What is striking is how closely the woman's movements resemble the body language which has become the signature of Redmayne's performance as Lili. The femininity exhibited by Redmayne's Lili bears little resemblance to the varieties of modern femininity represented in the film more broadly: it is only in a brothel that Lili finds a mirror for herself. It seems that Lili finds her own femininity in forms which mimic sexual exploitation but in a narrative context in which the possibility of Lili as an object of sexual desire or as a desiring subject with sexual agency is barely considered.

'His wife knew first': Marriage in *The Danish Girl* (2016) and its Source Texts

In the 2016 film adaptation, an animated Lili quizzes her childhood friend Hans (Matthias Schoenaerts) about his personal life, in a scene which Gerda had intended as a reunion between her husband and his boyhood companion. On discovering that Hans is unmarried Lili expresses regret, declaring the benefits of marriage with emotion: 'It creates someone else. More than just the two of you.' The 'someone else' brought into being by a marriage might more conventionally take the form of a child but in this marriage it has taken the form of Lili, a being who is in some ways a testament to their mutual love and attachment but whose existence will bring their union to an end. In many ways, *Man into Woman*, Ebershoff's novel and its 2016 film adaptation centre on the portrait of a very modern marriage. Grete/Greta/Gerda and Andreas/Einar are professional artists equally committed to their vocation and members of a cosmopolitan network of fellow artists and friends living urban and itinerant lives at a remove from the bonds of family, class and nation. Companionship is an integral element of these relationships and this extends to a broader network of friends, including other couples. In *Man into Woman* and Ebershoff's novel Grete/Greta and Lili both find new partners, following her transition and the annulment of their marriage by king's decree, and these new partners are integrated into their ongoing relationship. Comparative analysis of the depiction of marriage across the retellings of Elbe's story will demonstrate how this relationship is progressively privatised and the imperatives of heterosexual marriage privileged. In *The Danish Girl* (2016) Gerda's loyalty to her former husband outlives their marriage. She repeatedly rebuffs the offers of support which are tokens of Hans's growing love for her and continues to live with Lili long after the end of their intimate relationship, sharing a marital bed discreetly divided by a muslin curtain. Moreover, Lili remains without a romantic or sexual partner to the end. The sanctity of heterosexual marriage is at the heart of this drama with commitment to the institution (represented by Gerda's persistent devotion) constituting its greatest moral and the end of a marriage (effected by Lili's transition) representing its greatest tragedy.

In *Man into Woman* marriage is a relationship which is embedded into networks of friendship which cross Europe. The narrative opens with Grete and Einar discussing Lili's fate with compassion and candour with another married couple – the husband Italian and the wife French – in a restaurant in Paris. When both Grete and Lili find new partners following her transition these developments do not provoke jealousy or grief but only strengthen the bonds of friendship first forged in marriage. Ridolfo Feruzzi is an Italian officer whom the couple first meet in Florence and whose future significance in Grete's life is intuited by Andreas and recollected by Lili following her transition:

> All of a sudden it dawned upon her what a profound and strange secret was bound up with the vow which, on a far-off evening in Rome, when Andreas, Grete, and Feruzzi were sitting together, Andreas himself had taken: that Grete and the wonderful Feruzzi should be united because they belonged truly to each other, and that Andreas should disappear.[52]

Lili writes to Feruzzi, effectively giving him leave to pay his attentions to Grete: '"I will only tell you that Andreas has kept his word. He is dead. I know that Grete has not yet told you anything about it. Write her and do not neglect her."'[53] For Lili her transition liberates not only herself but also Grete: '"you may become free of a person who is long since dead, from Andreas . . . both of us, you and I, can begin a new life."'[54] This new stage in their lives does not mark an irrevocable break with the past but rather the cementing of new loyalties, with friendship valued above all else: 'Feruzzi wrote to say that he was at the service of both of them, wherever they were and wherever he was, and that if they called he would come, and that his heart belonged to them both.'[55] Feruzzi's friendship predates Lili's transition and as such is a signifier of continuity rather than rupture. Similarly, Lili's first encounter with her new companion, Claude Lejeune, 'her truest friend',[56] takes place before her transition. Lejeune, Grete and Lili form a '"triple alliance"' and, like Feruzzi, this new partner is depicted as augmenting existing relationships built on companionship and loyalty, rather than as a rival or intruder: 'Claude was then Grete's and Lili's most delightful cavalier; he was their brother and protector, and the friendship between them became ever more intimate and permanent, a friendship which stood every test.'[57]

In David Ebershoff's novel *The Danish Girl* both Greta and Lili find new partners but with different effects. Following their first and seemingly ill-fated encounter at the artists' ball, Henrik plays relatively little part as a character in the narrative until his proposal of marriage to Lili towards the end. This proposal serves to affirm Lili's normative aspirations and to confirm marriage as the guarantor of gender identity: 'Lili had always wanted this. She knew one day she would marry; sometimes, when she thought about it, she felt she could play no greater role in this world than as a man's wife, Henrik's wife.'[58] While Henrik is not integrated into Greta and Lili's lives in *The Danish Girl* in the way that Claude is in *Man into Woman*, Greta's new partner in the novel is a character who has a longstanding place in Einar's life: his childhood friend, Hans. One of the most extended departures from *Man into Woman* in *The Danish Girl* is the introduction of passages retrospectively depicting Einar's childhood in rural Jutland. His close attachment to his protective friend Hans, and his attraction to the bodies of other boys when they play tennis in the nude, could be read as an expression of same-sex desire. However, the conversion of Hans from Einar's childhood love into Greta's future husband effectively heterosexualises both his and Einar's identity. Indeed, here and elsewhere heterosexual desire is seen as the basis of gendered identity; when Hans kisses Einar as a child this kiss is seen as prefiguring Lili's future role as the female object of heterosexual men's desire. Familial kinship supplants friendship networks in Ebershoff's novel, with Greta's twin brother playing a leading role in Lili's transition; he is figured as Lili's champion and protector, much like Claude before him, his loyalty arguably motivated more by a sense of family prerogative than elective loyalty.

In the 2016 film adaptation, reproductive heterosexual marriage is foregrounded from the start, with the introduction of a subplot to do with frustrated maternal ambitions qualifying the depiction of a contented marriage. When Ulla demands to know when the couple will bring her a godchild, there is a sense that this is a longstanding source of speculation on the part of their intrusive friend. Indeed, when Einar consents to posing in Ulla's place he is attempting not only to pacify Gerda's frustration at her rejection by the Academy but also to appease her disappointment at not becoming pregnant. However, Gerda questions Einar's expressed regret when she tells him that she has her period, as if suspecting that he does not share her desire for a child. When Gerda sketches the sleeping Einar, following the discovery that he has been wearing her nightgown beneath his clothes, her wakefulness is attributed to her 'wondering if we made a baby tonight'. Two significant departures from *Man into Woman* and Ebershoff's novel signify a striking emphasis on heterosexual marriage in the film: firstly, the privileging of Gerda's fidelity to Lili over her own sexual agency, and secondly, the erasure of Lili's future partner. Following on from Ebershoff's novel, in the 2016 film Hans is depicted as Gerda's future partner. It is evident that Einar's childhood attachment to Hans has been much discussed between the couple and has become the subject of Gerda's teasing. However, Einar's disclosure that there was an 'other' before Henrik, when Gerda questions him about his fidelity, casts the relationship in a different light, and when Gerda traces Hans in Paris she questions him about the kiss which Einar had recounted with feeling. Hans's initial failure to recall the incident suggests that the memory holds less significance for him and when he does remember the kiss it is with laughter rather than nostalgia or regret; Gerda's visible relief when Hans explains that he could not resist because Einar 'was so pretty' in his grandmother's apron suggests that both Hans's and Einar's heterosexuality has been assured. However, Hans's evident concern, loyalty and desire for Gerda are repeatedly refused in the name of her affective commitment to Lili. This devotion to Lili ensures that the dramatic focus of the film narrative remains centred on the interpersonal tensions between husband and wife, as Gerda's grief competes with Lili's need to realise her own identity. In the opening scenes of the film Einar makes an unequivocal declaration of marital devotion: 'Gerda Wegener. My life. My wife.' By focusing on Gerda's experience of Lili's transition as an act of betrayal, and on her agonised struggle to reconcile her love for her husband with his apparent abandonment of her, the film crucially qualifies its focus on Elbe's story and perspective.

In contrast to both *Man into Woman* and Ebershoff's novel, Lili does not find a romantic partner in the film adaptation. Moreover, while the character of Henrik is retained he is transformed into a homosexual man and his companionship serves as a substitute for intimacy. In *Man into Woman*, Claude Lejeune plays an important role in affirming Lili's gender identity at a time when her existence is depicted as competing with Einar's: '"However you dress up and whatever you want to make me believe, you are a genuine girl."'[59] In Ebershoff's *The Danish Girl*, Henrik offers similar assurances of 'recognition', even when Lili tries to tell him her story of transition: '"I know that already," he said. "I already told you that I know. I know who you are."'[60] By contrast, in the film adaptation of *The Danish Girl*, while the character of Henrik is retained it is his misrecognition of Lili's identity which plays a pivotal role in the narrative. The film replicates the formative encounter between Henrik and Lili at the ball at which she makes her debut. Both versions of Henrik tell the fable of the oak tree whose acorns grant wishes, anticipating Lili's transition in a way which seems to suggest that they will play an enabling role. In the 2016 film adaptation, the implication that Henrik 'knows' something about Lili which she barely understands herself is reinforced by a coded language of address, insinuating a hidden affinity: 'I'm a romantic. I prefer the shadows. And I don't mean to presume, but I've been watching you, and I think you might be the same.' However, when Henrik kisses Lili again in the privacy of his apartment and addresses her as 'Einar' she recoils in shock and flees into the street, where she scrutinises her passing reflection in the windows of the neighbouring houses, as if trying to reconcile her sense of self with Henrik's presumption. It is only after her transition that Lili meets Henrik again by chance, recounting her story of transition to his amazement and later reassuring Gerda of her fidelity by disclosing his homosexuality. Henrik's *mis*recognition of Lili as a male homosexual serves a central narrative function in *The Danish Girl*: namely, an insistence on Lili's heterosexuality which is closely related to the imperative to divest her transition of any association with sexual deviance. However, the translation of Henrik from a future husband into a homosexual best friend – Gerda sees them at the quayside walking arm in arm, Henrik's arm folded under Lili's in the conventional feminine role – also deprives Lili of a romantic and sexual partner. Her heterosexuality is defined by men's attraction to her and by her fashioning of her body for their gaze rather than by any expression of sexual agency or desire. A nominally sympathetic portrait of Lili Elbe which carefully avoids the sensationalising or pathologising tendencies of earlier film representations of transgender characters, *The Danish Girl* nevertheless remains mortgaged to normative constructions of gender and sexuality. Drawing on visual tropes of female impersonation at the level of representation and depriving Elbe of sexual agency at the level of plot, the film adaptation arguably invites the audience to interpret her gender identity as conditional on her capacity to pass and to equate her sexual identity with the passivity of the objectified woman. In the closing scenes, a silk scarf which had served as a symbolic token of contested femininity – passed back and forth between Lili and Gerda at pivotal points in the narrative – is relinquished to the wind when Gerda and Hans visit the landscapes of Einar's paintings. Its ascension into the sky posits Lili's death as a form of liberation: she is a martyr rather than a pioneer, her demise allowing the long-thwarted heterosexual romance between Gerda and Hans finally to take centre stage.

    The prominence of marriage in these period adaptations of twentieth-century narratives in many ways exemplifies the ambivalent relationship between representations of transgender identity in mainstream culture and the politics of normativity in contemporary contexts. Campaigns for equal marriage have been a central feature of LGBT civil rights activism in the West in recent years and have attracted considerable attention in the media. Equal marriage legislation also has significance for transgender people in contexts where legal recognition of gender transition is not available; the legalisation of same-sex marriage means that individuals undergoing transition are not required to annul marriages which they wish to maintain. However, this focus on marriage rights has been critiqued by some activists and theorists who align this campaign with the trend which Lisa Duggan has termed homonormativity: that is, a tendency in LGBT activism to seek assimilation within normative institutions and to pursue goals which are symptomatic of the neoliberal focus on the individual. In the first instance, critics observe that as a state-sanctioned institution empowered to award or withhold specific privileges, marriage enshrines inequality. As Dean Spade has observed:

> Even relatively popular feminist critiques of the institution of marriage could not trump the new call for 'marriage equality' – meaning access for same-sex couples to the fundamentally unequal institution designed to privilege certain family formations for the purpose of state control.[61]

Moreover, it has been suggested that marriage equality is a priority only for those who suffer no other structural disadvantages. Jasbir Puar describes 'gay marriage' as 'not simply a demand for equality with heterosexual norms, but more importantly a demand for reinstatement of white privileges and rights – rights of property and inheritance in particular'.[62] Furthermore, critics see this trend as an assimilationist strategy, reflecting broader political, economic and ideological contexts. Puar describes this phenomenon as 'queer incorporation into the domains of consumer markets and social recognition in the post-civil rights, late twentieth century'[63] and Susan Stryker attributes it to the 'assimilative strategies of transnational capital'.[64] In the 2011 film adaptation of *Albert Nobbs*, Hubert's entry into the institution of heterosexual marriage – not once but twice – could be seen as subverting its historic grounding in conventional ideas about sex and gender. Indeed, Hubert is arguably a 'better man' than his male-bodied peers, whose abuse and abandonment of women is a recurring theme in the film drama.[65] However, in the context of contemporary debates, Hubert's marriages can be seen as legitimising his masculinity, his assimilation within normative institutions assuring the audience that he poses no threat to gender norms.[66] By contrast, the protagonist of the 2016 film adaptation of *The Danish Girl* is deprived of the romantic partners she enjoys in both *Man into Woman* and Ebershoff's novel. Moreover, the preservation of heterosexual marriage is placed at the heart of this drama, in which a wife's loss of her husband is pitted against the imperatives of self-determination. If the film is 'progressive' in its depiction of a modern marriage, in which a wife learns to champion her husband's transition, it is relatively conservative in its depiction of marital loyalty as a woman's greatest calling. Progressive politics are arguably defined in neoliberal terms in both films, whether as the assimilation of potentially transgressive individuals into normative institutions in *Albert Nobbs* or through the exercise of permissive tolerance within privatised interpersonal relations in *The Danish Girl*.

Produced and released in an era in which there is much greater awareness of issues to do with transgender rights and representation, these literary adaptations are careful to evade the more demeaning and pathologising stereotypes which have characterised representations of transgender people on screen in the past, but nevertheless demonstrate a complex, and sometimes contradictory, negotiation with normative discourses. These films raise questions to do with the terms by which visibility and recognition are granted to transgender identities and histories within contemporary culture. The persistence of normative discourses and their legitimating function in the field of representation suggests that the questions of 'becoming'[67] which have been explored in this book remain just as pertinent in the twenty-first century. By examining the ways in which transgender lives – whether historical or fictional – have been 'authored by others' in twentieth-century writing and its afterlives, this book has sought to provide new perspectives on histories of representation. In a period in which cultural interventions by transgender artists, activists and theorists have changed the terms by which the experiences, identities and histories of transgender people are understood, it is all the more vital to consider both the enabling and the contentious legacies of the representations of the last century.

Notes

1. Phillips, *Transgender on Screen*, p. 5. Phillips's book examines motifs of cross-dressing alongside depictions of transgender identification from a principally psychoanalytic perspective.
2. Phillips, *Transgender on Screen*, p. 18.
3. Rigney, 'Brandon Goes to Hollywood: *Boys Don't Cry* and the Transgender Body in Film', p. 4.
4. Glenn Close describes the stage production as 'one of the most fulfilling experiences of my career' and testifies to being 'haunt[ed]' by the character of Albert Nobbs, prompting her to acquire the rights to the

novella in 1998. Close, 'On Albert Nobbs', in Montague and Frazier (eds), *George Moore: Dublin, Paris, Hollywood*, pp. 197, 198.
5. Moore, *Albert Nobbs*, p. 8.
6. *Man into Woman: The First Sex Change – A Portrait of Lili Elbe*, p. 222.
7. Ebershoff, *The Danish Girl*, p. 3.
8. The film adaptation reinstates Gerda Gottlieb's first name, whereas *Man into Woman* adopts a pseudonym, Grete, which is anglicised in Ebershoff's novel as Greta.
9. Moore, *Albert Nobbs*, p. 1.
10. Moore, *Albert Nobbs*, p. 3.
11. Regan, 'W. B. Yeats and Irish Cultural Politics in the 1890s', in Ledger and McCracken (eds), *Cultural Politics at the Fin de Siècle*, p. 68.
12. Ledger and McCracken, 'Introduction', in Ledger and McCracken (eds), *Cultural Politics*, p. 1.
13. Moore, *Albert Nobbs*, p. 88.
14. Crawford, 'Typhus in Nineteenth-Century Ireland', in Jones and Malcolm (eds), *Medicine, Disease and the State in Ireland, 1650–1940*.
15. Crawford, 'Typhus in Nineteenth-Century Ireland', p. 122.
16. Crawford, 'Typhus in Nineteenth-Century Ireland', p. 123.
17. This difference is further reinforced in the film adaptation by the fact that Albert is English and Hubert Irish, whereas in the novella both are Londoners.
18. Seid, 'Reveal', *TSQ: Transgender Studies Quarterly Special Issue – Postposttranssexual*, p. 177.
19. Moore, *Albert Nobbs*, pp. 12–13.
20. Moore, *Albert Nobbs*, p. 90.
21. Salamon, *Assuming a Body*, p. 179.
22. Moore, *Albert Nobbs*, p. 32.
23. Moore, *Albert Nobbs*, p. 18.
24. Moore, *Albert Nobbs*, p. 64.
25. Moore, *Albert Nobbs*, p. 76. The film adaptation falls back on highly conventional representations of women working as prostitutes; when Albert visits the premises he hopes to purchase he is accosted en route by a heavily painted woman with an exposed bosom, who is consorting with a sailor. Whereas an unexpected affinity springs up between Kitty and Albert in the novella, in this street scene the narrative function of the prostitute is simply to signal the degraded social status of the neighbourhood.
26. Moore, *Albert Nobbs*, p. 17.
27. Moore, *Albert Nobbs*, p. 33.
28. *Man into Woman*, p. 93.
29. *Man into Woman*, p. 92.
30. *Man into Woman*, p. 67.
31. *Man into Woman*, p. 67.
32. *Man into Woman*, p. 67.
33. *Man into Woman*, p. 66.
34. *Man into Woman*, p. 67.
35. *Man into Woman*, p. 66.

36. *Man into Woman*, p. 67.
37. *Man into Woman*, p. 67.
38. *Man into Woman*, pp. 99, 106.
39. *Man into Woman*, p. 108.
40. Ebershoff, *The Danish Girl*, p. 6.
41. Ebershoff, *The Danish Girl*, p. 6.
42. Ebershoff, *The Danish Girl*, p. 10.
43. Ebershoff, *The Danish Girl*, p. 11.
44. Ebershoff, *The Danish Girl*, p. 8.
45. Ebershoff, *The Danish Girl*, p. 6.
46. Ebershoff, *The Danish Girl*, p. 12.
47. Ebershoff, *The Danish Girl*, p. 13.
48. Ebershoff, *The Danish Girl*, p. 51.
49. Ebershoff, *The Danish Girl*, p. 52.
50. See Ebershoff, *The Danish Girl*, p. 58.
51. Ebershoff, *The Danish Girl*, p. 86.
52. *Man into Woman*, pp. 209–10.
53. *Man into Woman*, p. 210.
54. *Man into Woman*, p. 211.
55. *Man into Woman*, p. 211.
56. *Man into Woman*, p. 80.
57. *Man into Woman*, p. 85.
58. Ebershoff, *The Danish Girl*, p. 278.
59. *Man into Woman*, p. 84.
60. Ebershoff, *The Danish Girl*, p. 279.
61. Spade, *Normal Life: Administrative Violence, Critical Trans Politics and the Limits of Law*, p. 35.
62. Puar, *Terrorist Assemblages: Homonationalism in Queer Times*, pp. 29–30.
63. Puar, *Terrorist Assemblages*, p. xii.
64. Stryker, 'Transgender History, Homonormativity, and Disciplinarity', p. 145.
65. In her analysis of motifs of cross-dressing in popular films of the 1980s and 1990s, Elizabeth Abele observes a tendency to 'blend the theatrical convention of forced transvestism with the postfeminist desire to reform a heterosexual man'. 'Becoming a Better Man as a Woman: The Transgendered Fantasy in 1980s and 1990s Popular Films', p. 6.
66. Elizabeth Grubgeld describes García's film as a 'fairy tale for the era of marriage equality', deducing that Hubert is a 'lesbian who prefers to be the cross-dressing spouse of her feminine wife'. '"The Little Red-Haired Boy, George Moore": Moore, Benmussa, García and the Masculine Voices of Albert Nobbs', in Brunet, Gaspari and Pierse (eds), *George Moore's Paris and his Ongoing French Connections*, pp. 261, 264.
67. See Butler, *Undoing Gender*, p. 57.

Bibliography

'A Mystery Still', *All the Year Round*, Volume XVII (18 May 1867), pp. 492–5; Dickens Journals Online, <http://www.djo.org.uk/all-the-year-round.html> (last accessed 15 January 2018).

Abele, Elizabeth, 'Becoming a Better Man as a Woman: The Transgendered Fantasy in 1980s and 1990s Popular Films', *Scope: An Online Journal of Film and Television Studies*, 21 (October 2011), pp. 1–20.

The Adventures of Priscilla, Queen of the Desert, film, directed by Stephan Elliott. Australia: Polygram Filmed Entertainment, 1994.

Aizura, Aren Z., 'Transnational Transgender Rights and Immigration Law', in Anne Enke (ed.), *Transfeminist Perspectives in and beyond Transgender and Gender Studies* (Philadelphia: Temple University Press, 2012), pp. 133–52.

Albert Nobbs, film, directed by Rodrigo García. UK, Ireland, France: Mockingbird Films, Trillium Pictures, Parallel Film Productions, Morrison Films, Westend Films, 2011.

Alston, David, 'A Forgotten Diaspora: The Children of Enslaved and "Free Coloured" Women and Highland Scots in Guyana before Emancipation', *Northern Scotland*, 6 (2015), pp. 49–69.

Amin, Kadji, 'Temporality', *TSQ: Transgender Studies Quarterly Special Issue – Postposttranssexual: Key Concepts for a Twenty-First-Century Transgender Studies*, 1:1–2 (2014), pp. 219–22.

Ammen, Sharon, 'Transforming George Moore: Simone Benmussa's Adaptive Art in *The Singular Life of Albert Nobbs*', *Text and Performance Quarterly*, 11 (1991), pp. 306–12.

Amnesty International, *The State Decides Who I Am: Lack of Legal Gender Recognition for Transgender People in Europe*, <https://www.amnesty.org/en/documents/EUR01/001/2014/en/> (last accessed 15 January 2018).

Barry, Sebastian, *Whistling Psyche* (London: Faber and Faber, 2004).

Bell, Vikki, *Interrogating Incest: Feminism, Foucault and the Law* (London: Routledge, 1993).

Benmussa, Simone, 'Introduction', *The Singular Life of Albert Nobbs* (1977), trans. Barbara Wright (1979) (London: Alma Classics, 2012), pp. v–xii.

Benmussa, Simone, *The Singular Life of Albert Nobbs* (1977), trans. Barbara Wright (1979) (London: Alma Classics, 2012).

Bettcher, Talia Mae, 'Evil Deceivers and Make-Believers: On Transphobic Violence and the Politics of Illusion', *Hypatia*, 22:3 (Summer 2007), pp. 43–65.
Bettcher, Talia Mae, 'Trapped in the Wrong Theory: Rethinking Trans Oppression and Resistance', *Signs: Journal of Women in Culture and Society*, 39:2 (2014), pp. 383–406.
Bettcher, Talia and Ann Garry, 'Introduction', *Hypatia Special Issue – Transgender Studies and Feminism: Theory, Politics, and Gendered Realities*, 24:3 (2009), pp. 1–10.
Bhanji, Nael, 'Trans/scriptions: Homing Desires, (Trans)sexual Citizenship and Racialized Bodies', in Trystan T. Cotten (ed), *Transgender Migrations: The Bodies, Borders and Politics of Transition* (New York and London: Routledge, 2012), pp. 157–75.
Boys Don't Cry, film, directed by Kimberly Peirce. USA: Fox Searchlight, 1999.
Bristow, Joseph and Trev Broughton, 'Introduction', in Joseph Bristow and Trev Broughton (eds), *The Infernal Desire Machines of Angela Carter: Fiction, Femininity, Feminism* (London and New York: Longman, 1997), pp. 1–23.
Britzolakis, Christine, 'Angela Carter's Fetishism', in Joseph Bristow and Trev Broughton (eds), *The Infernal Desire Machines of Angela Carter: Fiction, Femininity, Feminism* (London and New York: Longman, 1997), pp. 43–58.
Brontë, Charlotte, *Jane Eyre* (1848) (London: Penguin, 2006).
Butler, Judith, 'Gender Performance: *The TransAdvocate* interviews Judith Butler', with Cristan Williams, *The TransAdvocate*, 1 May 2014, <http://www.transadvocate.com/gender-performance-the-transadvocate-interviews-judith-butler_n_13652.htm> (last accessed 15 January 2018).
Butler, Judith, *Gender Trouble: Feminism and the Subversion of Identity* (1990) (New York: Routledge, 1999).
Butler, Judith, 'Performative Acts and Gender Constitution: An Essay in Phenomenology and Feminist Theory', in Katie Conboy, Nadia Medina and Sarah Stanbury (eds), *Writing on the Body: Female Embodiment and Feminist Theory* (New York: Columbia University Press, 1997), pp. 401–7.
Butler, Judith, *Undoing Gender* (New York: Routledge, 2004).
Carroll, Rachel, '"Violent Operations": Revisiting the Transgendered Body in Angela Carter's *The Passion of New Eve*', *Women: A Cultural Review*, 22:2–3 (September 2011), pp. 241–55.
Carter, Angela, *The Passion of New Eve* (London: Virago, 1977).
Carter, Angela, 'The Wound in the Face' (1975), in Jenny Uglow (ed.), *Shaking a Leg: Collected Journalism and Writings* (London: Chatto and Windus, 1997), pp. 109–12.
Case, Sue-Ellen, 'Gender as Play: Simone Benmussa's *The Singular Life of Albert Nobbs*', *Women & Performance: A Journal of Feminist Theory*, 1:2 (1983–4), pp. 21–4.

Chase, Cheryl, 'Hermaphrodites with Attitude: Mapping the Emergence of Intersex Political Activism', *GLQ: Journal of Lesbian and Gay Studies*, 4:2 (1998), pp. 189–211.
Close, Glenn, 'Foreword', in George Moore, *Albert Nobbs* (1918) (London: Penguin, 2011), pp. vii–x.
Close, Glenn, 'On Albert Nobbs', in Conor Montague and Adrian Frazier (eds), *George Moore: Dublin, Paris, Hollywood* (Newbridge, Co. Kildare: Irish Academic Press, 2012), pp. 197–201.
Crawford, E. Margaret, 'Typhus in Nineteenth-Century Ireland', in Greta Jones and Elizabeth Malcolm (eds), *Medicine, Disease and the State in Ireland, 1650–1940* (Cork: Cork University Press, 1999), pp. 121–37.
Cromwell, Jason, 'Passing Women and Female-bodied Men: (Re)claiming FTM History', in Kate More and Stephen Whittle (eds), *Reclaiming Genders: Transsexual Grammars at the Fin de Siècle* (London and New York: Bloomsbury, 2016), pp. 34–61.
The Crying Game, film, directed by Stephen Frears. UK, Japan, USA: Palace Pictures, Channel Four Films, 1992.
Daly, Mary, *Gyn/Ecology: The Metaethics of Radical Feminism* (London: The Women's Press, 1979).
The Danish Girl, film, directed by Tom Hooper. UK, USA, Germany, Denmark, Belgium: Working Title Films, Pretty Pictures, 2016.
Davies, Ceri, '"The Truth Is a Thorny Issue": Lesbian Denial in Jackie Kay's *Trumpet*', *Journal of International Women's Studies*, 7:3 (2006), pp. 5–16.
Day, Aidan, *Angela Carter: The Rational Glass* (Manchester: Manchester University Press, 1998).
Diamond, Elin, 'Refusing the Romanticism of Identity: Narrative Interventions in Churchill, Benmussa, Duras', *Theatre Journal*, 37:3 (1985), pp. 273–86.
Doan, Laura and Jane Garrity, 'Introduction', in Laura Doan and Jane Garrity (eds), *Sapphic Modernities: Sexuality, Women and National Cultures* (Basingstoke: Palgrave Macmillan, 2007), pp. 1–13.
Dolan, Jill, 'Gender Impersonation Onstage: Destroying or Maintaining the Mirror of Gender Roles?', *Women & Performance: A Journal of Feminist Theory*, 2:2 (1985), pp. 5–11.
Double Indemnity, film, directed by Billy Wilder. USA: Paramount Pictures, 1944.
Douglass, Frederick, *Narrative of the Life of Frederick Douglass, An American Slave* (1845) (London: Penguin, 1982).
Dreger, Alice Domurat, *Hermaphrodites and the Medical Invention of Sex* (Cambridge, MA, and London: Harvard University Press, 1998).
Duggan, Lisa, *The Twilight of Democracy? Neoliberalism, Cultural Politics, and the Attack on Democracy* (New York: Beacon Press, 2003).
Duncker, Patricia, *James Miranda Barry* (1999) (London: Picador, 2000).
Ebershoff, David, *The Danish Girl* (London: Phoenix, 2000).
Edelman, Lee, *No Future: Queer Theory and the Death Drive* (Durham, NC, and London: Duke University Press, 2004).

Elam, Harry J., 'Visual Representation in *The Singular Life of Albert Nobbs*', *Text and Performance Quarterly*, 11 (1991), pp. 313–18.

Elliot, Patricia, *Debates in Transgender, Queer, and Feminist Theory: Contested Sites* (London and New York: Routledge, 2010).

Eng, David L., J. Halberstam and José Esteban Muñoz, 'Introduction: What's Queer about Queer Studies Now?', *Social Text*, 84–5, 23:3–4 (2005), pp. 1–17.

Fausto-Sterling, Anne, *Sexing the Body: Gender Politics and the Construction of Sexuality* (New York: Basic, 2000).

Feinberg, Leslie, *Transgender Liberation: A Movement Whose Time Has Come* (New York: World View Forum, 1992).

Foucault, Michel, 'Introduction', *Herculine Barbin*, trans. Richard McDougall (New York: Vintage, 1980), pp. vii–xvii.

Foucault, Michel, *The Will to Knowledge: The History of Sexuality, Volume One* (1976), trans. Robert Hurley (London: Penguin, 1978).

Frazier, Adrian, *George Moore 1852–1933* (New Haven and London: Yale University Press, 2000).

Funke, Jana, 'Obscurity and Gender Resistance in Patricia Duncker's *James Miranda Barry*', *European Journal of English Studies*, 16:3 (2012), pp. 215–26.

Gamble, Sarah, *Angela Carter: Writing from the Front Line* (Edinburgh: Edinburgh University Press, 1997).

Gannon, Shane, 'Exclusion as Language and the Language of Exclusion: Tracing Regimes of Gender through Linguistic Representations of the "Eunuch"', *Journal of the History of Sexuality*, 20:1 (2011), pp. 1–27.

Garber, Marjorie, *Vested Interests: Cross-Dressing and Cultural Anxiety* (Harmondsworth: Penguin, 1992).

Gersdorf, Catrin, 'The Gender of Nature's Nation: A Queer Perspective', *Amerikastudien/American Studies*, 46 (2001), pp. 41–54.

Getsy, David J., 'Capacity', *TSQ: Transgender Studies Quarterly Special Issue – Postposttranssexual: Key Concepts for a Twenty-First-Century Transgender Studies*, 1:1–2 (2014), pp. 47–9.

Gilroy, Paul, 'Migrancy, Culture, and a New Map of Europe', in Heike Raphael-Hernandez (ed.), *Blackening Europe: The African American Presence* (New York and London: Routledge, 2004), pp. xi–xxii.

Greer, Germaine, *The Female Eunuch* (1970) (London: Harper Perennial, 2006).

Grubgeld, Elizabeth, *George Moore and the Autogenous Self: A Study of the Autobiography and the Fiction* (Syracuse: Syracuse University Press, 1994).

Grubgeld, Elizabeth, '"The Little Red-Haired Boy, George Moore": Moore, Benmussa, García and the Masculine Voices of Albert Nobbs', in Michel Brunet, Fabienne Gaspari and Mary Pierse (eds), *George Moore's Paris and his Ongoing French Connections* (Oxford: Peter Lang, 2015), pp. 251–66.

Halberstam, J., *Female Masculinity* (Durham, NC, and London: Duke University Press, 1998).

Halberstam, J., 'Telling Tales: Brandon Teena, Billy Tipton, and Transgender Biography' (2000), in María Carla Sánchez and Linda Schlossberg (eds), *Passing: Identity and Interpretation in Sexuality, Race, and Religion* (New York and London: New York University Press, 2001), pp. 13–37.

Hall, Radclyffe, *The Well of Loneliness* (1928) (London: Virago, 2008).

Hanson, Clare, '"The red dawn breaking over Clapham": Carter and the Limits of Artifice', in Joseph Bristow and Trev Broughton (eds), *The Infernal Desire Machines of Angela Carter: Fiction, Femininity, Feminism* (London and New York: Longman, 1997), pp. 59–72.

Hausman, Bernice, *Changing Sex: Transsexualism, Technology, and the Idea of Gender* (Durham, NC: Duke University Press, 1995).

Heilmann, Ann, '"Neither man nor woman"? Female Transvestism, Object Relations and Mourning in George Moore's "Albert Nobbs"', *Women: A Cultural Review*, 14:3 (2003), pp. 248–62.

Heilmann, Ann and Mark Llewellyn, 'Introduction', in Ann Heilmann and Mark Llewellyn (eds), *George Moore: Influence and Collaboration* (Newark: University of Delaware, 2014), pp. 1–24.

Heyes, Cressida J., 'Feminist Solidarity after Queer Theory: The Case of Transgender', *Signs: Journal of Women in Culture and Society*, 28:4 (2003), pp. 1,093–120.

Higgins, Lynn A. and Brenda R. Silver, 'Introduction: Rereading Rape', in Lynn A. Higgins and Brenda R. Silver (eds), *Rape and Representation* (New York: Columbia University Press, 1991), pp. 1–14.

Hindmarch-Watson, Katie, 'Lois Schwich, Female Errand Boy: Narratives of Female Cross-Dressing in Late Victorian London', *GLQ: A Journal of Lesbian and Gay Studies*, 14:1 (2008), pp. 69–98.

Hollows, Joanne, *Feminism, Femininity and Popular Culture* (Manchester: Manchester University Press, 2000).

Holmes, Rachel, *The Secret Life of Dr James Barry: Victorian England's Most Eminent Surgeon* (Stroud: Tempus, 2002).

Jeffreys, Sheila, *Gender Hurts: A Feminist Analysis of the Politics of Transgenderism* (London and New York: Routledge, 2014).

Jeffreys, Sheila, *Unpacking Queer Politics: A Lesbian Feminist Perspective* (Cambridge and Malden, MA: Polity, 2003).

Johnson, Heather L., 'Unexpected Geometries: Transgressive Symbolism and the Transsexual Subject in Angela Carter's *The Passion of New Eve*', in Joseph Bristow and Trev Broughton (eds), *The Infernal Desire Machines of Angela Carter* (London and New York: Longman, 1997), pp. 166–83.

Johnson, Matt, 'Transgender Subject Access: History and Current Practice', *Cataloging & Classification Quarterly*, 48 (2010), pp. 661–83.

Jones, Carole, '"An Imaginary Black Family": Jazz, Diaspora, and the Construction of Scottish Blackness in Jackie Kay's *Trumpet*', *Symbiosis: A Journal of Anglo-American Literary Relations*, 8:2 (2004), pp. 191–202.

Jonquet, Thierry, *Tarantula* (1995), trans. Donald Nicholson-Smith (London: Serpent's Tail, 2002).

Karaian, Lara, 'Strategic Essentialism on Trial: Legal Interventions and Social Change', in Krista Scott-Dixon (ed.), *Trans/forming Feminisms: Trans/feminist Voices Speak Out* (Toronto: Sumach Press, 2006), pp. 182–91.
Kay, Jackie, *The Adoption Papers* (Newcastle: Bloodaxe, 1991).
Kay, Jackie, *Trumpet* (London: Picador, 1998).
King, Jeanette, '"A Woman's a Man, for a' That": Jackie Kay's *Trumpet*', *Scottish Studies Review*, 2:1 (2001), pp. 101–8.
Ledger, Sally and Scott McCracken, 'Introduction', in Sally Ledger and Scott McCracken (eds), *Cultural Politics at the Fin de Siècle* (Cambridge: Cambridge University Press, 1995), pp. 1–10.
Livesay, Daniel, 'Extended Families: Mixed-Race Children and Scottish Experience, 1770–1820', *International Journal of Scottish Literature*, 4 (2008), pp. 1–17.
Love, Heather, 'Queer', *TSQ: Transgender Studies Quarterly Special Issue – Postposttranssexual: Key Concepts for a Twenty-First-Century Transgender Studies*, 1:1–2 (2014), pp. 172–6.
Ma vie en rose, film, directed by Alain Bernier. Belgium, France, UK: Canal+, 1999.
McLeod, John, *Life Lines: Writing Transcultural Adoption* (London: Bloomsbury, 2015).
Mak, Geertje, *Doubting Sex: Inscriptions, Bodies and Selves in Nineteenth-Century Hermaphrodite Case Histories* (Manchester and New York: Manchester University Press, 2012).
Makinen, Merja, 'Sexual and Textual Aggression in *The Sadeian Woman* and *The Passion of New Eve*', in Joseph Bristow and Trev Broughton (eds), *The Infernal Desire Machines of Angela Carter* (London and New York: Longman, 1997), pp. 149–65.
Man into Woman: The First Sex Change – A Portrait of Lili Elbe (1931), ed. Niels Hoyer, trans. H. J. Stenning (1933) (London: Blue Boat Books, 2004).
Mardorassian, Carine M., 'Toward a New Feminist Theory of Rape', *Signs*, 27:3 (Spring 2002), pp. 743–75.
Matta, Christina, 'Ambiguous Bodies and Deviant Sexualities: Hermaphrodites, Homosexuality, and Surgery in the United States, 1850–1904', *Perspectives in Biology and Medicine*, 48:1 (Winter 2005), pp. 74–83.
Mead, Matthew, '*Empire Windrush*: The Cultural Memory of an Imaginary Arrival', *Journal of Postcolonial Writing*, 45:2 (2009), pp. 137–49.
Meyerowitz, Joanne, *How Sex Changed: A History of Transsexuality in the United States* (Cambridge, MA, and London: Harvard University Press, 2002).
Middlebrook, Diane Wood, *Suits Me: The Double Life of Billy Tipton* (Boston and New York: Houghton Mifflin, 1998).
Moore, George, *Albert Nobbs* (1918) (London: Penguin, 2011).
Morgan, Robin, *Sisterhood Is Powerful: An Anthology of Writings from the Women's Liberation Movement* (London: Random House, 1970).

Morland, Iain, '"The Glans Opens Like a Book": Writing and Reading the Intersexed Body', *Continuum: Journal of Media & Culture Studies*, 19:3 (2005), pp. 335–48.

Morland, Iain, 'Intersex', *TSQ: Transgender Studies Quarterly Special Issue – Postposttranssexual: Key Concepts for a Twenty-First-Century Transgender Studies*, 1:1–2 (2014), pp. 111–15.

Morris, Michael, *Scotland and the Caribbean c. 1740–1833: Atlantic Archipelagos* (New York and London: Routledge, 2015).

Murib, Zein, 'LGBT', *TSQ: Transgender Studies Quarterly Special Issue – Postposttranssexual: Key Concepts for a Twenty-First-Century Transgender Studies*, 1:1–2 (2014), pp. 118–20.

Namaste, Vivian, 'Undoing Theory: The "Transgender Question" and the Epistemic Violence of Anglo-American Feminist Theory', *Hypatia Special Issue – Transgender Studies and Feminism: Theory, Politics, and Gendered Realities*, 24:3 (2009), pp. 11–32.

Oram, Alison and Matt Cook, *Prejudice & Pride: Celebrating LGBTQ Heritage* (Swindon: Park Lane Press/National Trust Enterprises, 2017).

Palmer, Paulina, 'Gender as Performance in the Fiction of Angela Carter and Margaret Atwood', in Joseph Bristow and Trev Broughton (eds), *The Infernal Desire Machines of Angela Carter: Fiction, Femininity, Feminism* (London and New York: Longman, 1997), pp. 24–42.

Peach, Linden, *Angela Carter* (Basingstoke and London: Macmillan, 1998).

Phillips, John, *Transgender on Screen* (Basingstoke: Palgrave Macmillan, 2006).

Pierse, Mary, 'Introduction', in Mary Pierse (ed.), *George Moore: Artistic Visions and Literary Worlds* (Newcastle: Cambridge Scholars Press, 2006), pp. xi–xv.

Pride of Place: A Guide to Understanding and Protecting Lesbian, Gay, Bisexual, Transgender and Queer (LGBTQ) Heritage, Historic England (23 September 2016), <https://historicengland.org.uk/images-books/publications/pride-of-place-guide-to-understanding-protecting-lgbtq-heritage/> (last accessed 15 January 2018).

Prosser, Jay, *Second Skins: The Body Narratives of Transsexuality* (New York: Columbia University Press, 1998).

Psycho, film, directed by Alfred Hitchcock. USA: Shamley Productions, 1960.

Puar, Jasbir K., *Terrorist Assemblages: Homonationalism in Queer Times* (Durham, NC, and London: Duke University Press, 2007).

Rae, Isobel, *The Strange Story of Dr James Barry, Army Surgeon, Inspector-General of Hospitals, Discovered on Death to Be a Woman* (London: Longman, 1958).

Rawson, K. J., 'Archive', *TSQ: Transgender Studies Quarterly Special Issue – Postposttranssexual: Key Concepts for a Twenty-First-Century Transgender Studies*, 1:1–2 (2014), pp. 24–6.

Raymond, Janice G., *The Transsexual Empire: The Making of the She-Male* (London: The Women's Press, 1979).

Regan, Stephen, 'W. B. Yeats and Irish Cultural Politics in the 1890s', in Sally Ledger and Scott McCracken (eds), *Cultural Politics at the Fin de Siècle* (Cambridge: Cambridge University Press, 1995), pp. 66–84.

Reis, Elizabeth, 'Divergence of Disorder? The Politics of Naming Intersex', *Perspectives in Biology and Medicine*, 50:4 (Autumn 2007), pp. 535–43.

Richardson, Matt, '"My Father Didn't Have a Dick": Social Death and Jackie Kay's Trumpet', *GLQ: Journal of Lesbian and Gay Studies*, 18:2–3 (2012), pp. 361–79.

Rigney, Melissa, 'Brandon Goes to Hollywood: *Boys Don't Cry* and the Transgender Body in Film', *Film Criticism*, 28:2 (2003), pp. 4–23.

Riley, Denise, *'Am I That Name?' Feminism and the Category of 'Women' in History* (London: Palgrave Macmillan, 1988).

Ringrose, Kathryn, 'Eunuchs in Historical Perspective', *History Compass*, 5:2 (2007), pp. 495–596.

Robertson, James, *Joseph Knight* (London: Fourth Estate, 2003).

Roen, Katrina, '"Either/Or" and "Both/Neither": Discursive Tensions in Transgender Politics', *Signs: Journal of Women in Culture and Society*, 27:2 (2001), pp. 501–22.

Rose, Irene, 'Heralding New Possibilities: Female Masculinity in Jackie Kay's *Trumpet*', in Daniel Lea and Berthold Schoene (eds), *Posting the Male: Masculinities in Post-war Contemporary British Literature* (Amsterdam: Rodopi, 2003), pp. 141–58.

Rose, June, *The Perfect Gentleman: The Remarkable Life of Dr. James Miranda Barry, the Woman Who Served as an Officer in the British Army from 1813 to 1859* (London: Hutchinson, 1977).

Rubenstein, Roberta, 'Intersexions: Gender Metamorphosis in Angela Carter's *The Passion of New Eve* and Lois Gould's *A Sea-Change*', *Tulsa Studies in Women's Literature*, 12:1 (1993), pp. 103–18.

Rubin, Henry, *Self-Made Men: Identity and Embodiment among Trans-sexual Men* (Nashville: Vanderbilt University Press, 2003).

Salamon, Gayle, *Assuming a Body: Transgender and Rhetoric of Materiality* (New York: Columbia University Press, 2010).

Seid, Danielle M., 'Reveal', *TSQ: Transgender Studies Quarterly Special Issue – Postposttranssexual: Key Concepts for a Twenty-First-Century Transgender Studies*, 1:1–2 (2014), pp. 176–7.

Seitler, Dana, 'Queer Physiognomies: Or, How Many Ways Can We Do the History of Sexuality?', *Criticism*, 46:1 (2004), pp. 71–102.

The Silence of the Lambs, film, directed by Jonathan Demme. USA: Strongheart/Demme Productions, Orion Pictures, 1991.

Singer, T. Benjamin, 'Umbrella', *TSQ: Transgender Studies Quarterly Special Issue – Postposttranssexual: Key Concepts for a Twenty-First-Century Transgender Studies*, 1:1–2 (2014), pp. 259–61.

The Skin I Live In, film, directed by Pedro Almodóvar. Spain: Blue Glaze Entertainment, Canal+ España, Deseo, El, FilmNation Entertainment, Instituto de Crediot Oficial, Instituo de la Cinematografía y de las Artes Audivisuales, Televisión Española, 2011.

Some Like It Hot, film, directed by Billy Wilder. USA: Ashton Productions, Mirisch Corporation, 1959.
Spade, Dean, *Normal Life: Administrative Violence, Critical Trans Politics and the Limits of Law* (Durham, NC, and London: Duke University Press, 2015).
Sreedhar, Susanne and Michael Hand, 'The Ethics of Exclusion: Gender and Politics at the Michigan Womyn's Music Festival', in Krista Scott-Dixon (ed.), *Trans/forming Feminisms: Trans/feminist Voices Speak Out* (Toronto: Sumach Press, 2006), pp. 161–9.
Stone, Sandy, 'The Empire Strikes Back: A Posttranssexual Manifesto', in Susan Stryker and Stephen Whittle (eds), *The Transgender Studies Reader* (New York and London: Routledge, 2006), pp. 221–35.
Stryker, Susan, 'Biopolitics', *TSQ: Transgender Studies Quarterly Special Issue – Postposttranssexual: Key Concepts for a Twenty-First-Century Transgender Studies*, 1:1–2 (2014), pp. 38–42.
Stryker, Susan, 'My Words to Victor Frankenstein above the Village of Chamounix: Performing Transgender Rage', *GLQ: Journal of Lesbian and Gay Studies*, 1:3 (1994), pp. 237–54.
Stryker, Susan, *Transgender History* (Berkeley: Seal Press, 2008).
Stryker, Susan, 'Transgender History, Homonormativity, and Disciplinarity', *Radical History Review*, 10 (Winter 2008), pp. 145–57.
Stryker, Susan, 'Transgender Studies: Queer Theory's Evil Twin', *GLQ: Journal of Lesbian and Gay Studies*, 10:2 (2004), pp. 212–15.
Stryker, Susan, '*We Who Are Sexy*: Christine Jorgensen's Transsexual Whiteness in the Postcolonial Philippines', *Social Semiotics*, 19:1 (March 2009), pp. 79–91.
Tomboy, film, directed by Céline Sciamma. France: Hold Up Films, 2011.
Tootsie, film, directed by Sydney Pollack. USA: Columbia Pictures Corporation, Mirage Enterprises, Punch Productions, Delphi Films, 1982.
Trans People and Stonewall: Campaigning Together for Lesbian, Gay, Bisexual and Trans Equality (London: Stonewall, 2015), <http://www.stonewall.org.uk/sites/default/files/trans_people_and_stonewall.pdf> (last accessed 15 January 2018).
Transamerica, film, directed by Duncan Tucker. USA: Belladonna Productions, 2005.
Transparent, television. USA: Amazon Studios, 2014–.
Trevenna, Joanne, 'Gender as Performance: Questioning the "Butlerification" of Angela Carter's Fiction', *Journal of Gender Studies*, 11:3 (2002), pp. 267–76.
Twain, Mark, *Following the Equator: A Journey around the World* (1897), Project Gutenberg, <http://www.gutenberg.org/files/2895/2895-h/2895-h.htm> (last accessed 15 January 2018).
Valentine, David, *Imagining Transgender: An Ethnography of a Category* (Durham, NC, and London: Duke University Press, 2007).
Vidal, Gore, *Myra Breckinridge* (London: HarperCollins, 1970).

Wallace, Diana, *The Woman's Historical Novel: British Women Writers, 1900–2000* (Basingstoke: Palgrave, 2005).

Warner, Michael, 'Introduction: Fear of a Queer Planet', *Social Text*, 29 (1991), pp. 3–17.

Westall, Claire, '"His almost gendered voice": Gendering and Transgendering Bodily Signification and the Voice in Angela Carter's *The Passion of New Eve*', in Rina Kim and Claire Westall (eds), *Cross-Gendered Literary Voices: Appropriating, Resisting, Embracing* (London: Palgrave Macmillan, 2012), pp. 131–47.

Wheelwright, Julie, *Amazons and Military Maids: Women Who Dressed as Men in Pursuit of Life, Liberty and Happiness* (London: Pandora, 1989).

Wilkerson, Abby L., 'Normate Sex and its Discontents', in Robert McRuer and Anna Mollow (eds), *Sex and Disability* (Durham, NC, and London: Duke University Press, 2012), pp. 183–207.

Woolf, Virginia, *Orlando* (1928) (London: Vintage, 2004).

Wyatt, Jean, 'The Violence of Gendering: Castration Images in Angela Carter's *The Magic Toyshop*, *The Passion of New Eve*, and "Peter and the Wolf"', in Alison Easton (ed.), *Angela Carter: Contemporary Critical Essays* (Basingstoke: Macmillan, 2000), pp. 58–83.

Yogyakarta Principles: The Application of International Human Rights Law in Relation to Sexual Orientation and Gender Identity, <http://yogyakartaprinciples.org/wp-content/uploads/2017/11/A5_yogyakartaWEB-2.pdf> (last accessed 20 February 2018).

Index

Abele, Elizabeth, 232n
adaptation
   screen, 2, 30–1, 191–230
   stage, 2, 26–7, 30, 38, 40,
     51–60, 191, 194,
     208–9
adoption, 160, 168, 177–82,
   183–4
The Adventures of Priscilla,
   Queen of the Desert,
   193
Aizura, Aren Z., 26
Albert Nobbs (film), 2, 30–1,
   191–2, 193, 194–5,
   196–214, 229–30
All the Year Round, 89
Alston, David, 173
Amin, Kadji, 125, 130
Ammen, Sharon, 58
Amnesty International, 32n
autobiography *see* life writing

Baker, Josephine, 183
Barry, James Miranda, 2, 5, 25,
   28, 29, 87–120, 164
Barry, Sebastian, 122n
Bell, Vikki, 77–8

Benmussa, Simone, *The*
   Singular Life of Albert
   Nobbs, 2, 16, 26–7, 30,
   38, 40, 51–60, 191, 194,
   208–9, 214, 230–1n
Bettcher, Talia Mae, 4, 14,
   18, 162
Bhanji, Nael, 159
biographical fiction *see* life
   writing
biography *see* life writing
Boys Don't Cry, 192, 193
Bristow, Joseph, 64, 65
Britzolakis, Christine, 76–7
Brontë, Charlotte, *Jane Eyre*,
   112, 171
Brontë, Emily, 74
Broughton, Trev, 64, 65
Butler, Judith, 11, 13, 15–16,
   17–20, 27–8, 29–30, 31,
   64–5, 81

Carter, Angela, *The Passion*
   of New Eve, 2, 5, 16, 26,
   27–8, 29–30, 37–8, 64–81
Case, Sue-Ellen, 57–8
Cassils, 1

castrato, 94
Chase, Cheryl, 132
class, 26–7, 38–9, 40–51, 101–4, 109–10, 127, 140–5, 196–202
Close, Glenn, 30, 52, 191, 193, 194, 202–3, 208–9, 214, 230–1n
colonialism, 2, 6, 25–6, 28, 68–9, 88, 107–15, 141–2, 172–4, 182
Cook, Matt, 166n
Crawford, E. Margaret, 201–2
Cromwell, Jason, 29
The Crying Game, 192

Daly, Mary, 70
The Danish Girl (film), 2, 30–1, 191–2, 193–4, 195–6, 214–28, 229–30
Davies, Ceri, 186
Day, Aidan, 76
Diamond, Elin, 58
Doan, Laura, 7–8
Dolan, Jill, 58
Double Indemnity, 163–4
Douglass, Frederick, 174
Dreger, Alice Domurat, 132, 134, 146
Duggan, Lisa, 21–2, 229
Duncker, Patricia, *James Miranda Barry*, 2, 5, 16, 27, 28, 29, 37–8, 87–120

Ebershoff, David, *The Danish Girl*, 2, 26, 28–9, 30–1, 125–54, 191, 195–6, 214–28, 229–30
Edelman, Lee, 80
Elam, Harry J., 58–9
Elbe, Lili, 2, 5, 25, 28–9, 30–1, 125–54, 191, 195–6, 214–28
Elliot, Patricia, 81
Ellison, Ralph, 168
Empire, British, 28, 88, 107–15, 167
Eng, David L., 34n
eunuch, 68–9

Fausto-Sterling, Anne, 132, 133, 146
Feinberg, Leslie, 2–3
femininity, 27–8, 28–9, 64–81, 127, 137–46, 196, 208–9, 214–23
feminism, 6, 10–16
 lesbian feminism, 7–9, 11–12, 15, 33n, 58, 71–2
 Second Wave, 6, 12–13, 15, 27–8, 38, 57–9, 64–81, 91, 194
 transfeminism, 11, 13–15
Flaubert, Gustave, 74
Foucault, Michel, 8, 80, 131–2
Frazier, Adrian, 38, 52–4
Funke, Jana, 88

Gamble, Sarah, 65
Garber, Marjorie, 91, 105

Garrity, Jane, 7–8
Garry, Ann, 14
gender crossing, 6, 7, 11–12, 15–16, 27, 28, 37–8, 57–9, 65, 67, 88, 90–3, 96–7, 100–1, 102–3, 106–7, 119, 186, 208–9
gender reassignment, 2, 4, 12–13, 27–8, 28–9, 66–7, 69–71, 72, 78–9, 82n, 125, 131, 132–3
Gersdorf, Catrin, 65
Getsy, David J., 9, 39, 89, 126
Gilroy, Paul, 172
Greer, Germaine, 68–71
Grubgeld, Elizabeth, 54–6, 232n

Halberstam, J., 4–6, 8, 25, 34n, 70, 87, 118, 142, 160, 161–2, 170–1, 192
Hall, Radclyffe, 33n
Hand, Michael, 84n
Hanson, Clare, 85n
Hausman, Bernice, 33n
Heilmann, Ann, 52–3
heterosexuality, 40–51, 79–80, 106–7, 127, 146–53, 195–6, 224, 226–30
Heyes, Cressida J., 14, 70, 81
Higgins, Lynn A., 78
Hindmarch-Watson, Katie, 7
Hirschfeld, Magnus, 153
Historic England, 119

historical fiction, 2, 28, 29–30, 87–120, 125–54, 214–28
historiography
 feminist, 7, 58, 91–2
 queer, 7–8
 transgender, 6–10, 89–92, 119–20, 147
Hollows, Joanne, 67
Holmes, Rachel, 90, 91, 93, 96, 101, 102, 108, 113–15, 116–18
homonormativity, 22–4, 228–30
homosexuality, 29, 34n, 137, 146–53, 228

illegitimacy, 43–4, 94–5, 178, 209–14
intersex, 6, 25, 29, 108, 115–20, 125–7, 130–7, 146–7

Jeffreys, Sheila, 72
Johnson, Heather L., 77
Johnson, Matt, 146
Jones, Carole, 168, 172
Jonquet, Thierry, 82n
Jorgensen, Christine, 107, 164

Karaian, Lara, 84n
Kay, Jackie
 The Adoption Papers, 168
 Trumpet, 2, 5, 26, 29–30, 158–87
King, Jeanette, 186
Krafft-Ebing, Richard von, 136, 146

Ledger, Sally, 231n
lesbian, 164–5, 186
LGBT alliance, 20–5, 31,
  119–20, 228–30
life writing, 4–6, 25, 28–9,
  29–30
  autobiography, 2, 28–9, 32n,
    52–4, 117–18, 125–6,
    127–31, 154n, 196
  biographical fiction, 2,
    26, 28–9, 29–30, 30–1,
    87–120, 125–54, 158–87,
    195–6, 214–28
  biography, 2, 87–8, 90–2,
    160–2, 165, 170–1
Livesay, Daniel, 173
Llewellyn, Mark, 52–3
Love, Heather, 16

Ma vie en rose, 193
McCracken, Scott, 231n
McLeod, John, 178–81
McTeer, Janet, 30, 193, 203,
  205–8, 214
Mak, Geertje, 118–19
Makinen, Merja, 76–8
*Man into Woman: The First
  Sex Change – A Portrait of
  Lili Elbe*, 2, 29–30,
  125–54, 191, 195–6,
  214–28
Mardorassian, Carine M., 78
marriage, 26–7, 30–1, 40–51,
  191–230
masculinity, 11, 26–7, 203–14
Matta, Christina, 146

Mead, Matthew, 176
Middlebrook, Diane Wood,
  158, 161–2, 168
migration, 25–6, 115, 127,
  137–8, 140–6, 159,
  167–70, 172–7, 195,
  202, 207, 209,
  212–13
Moore, George, *Albert Nobbs*,
  2, 5, 16, 26–7, 30, 37–60,
  191–214
Morgan, Robin, 71
Morland, Iain, 25, 126, 131
Morris, Michael, 172–3
Muñoz, José Esteban, 34n
Murib, Zein, 21

Namaste, Vivian, 14–15
National Trust, 119

Oram, Alison, 166n

Palmer, Paulina, 85n
Peach, Linden, 76
performance
  screen, 30–1, 193, 202–3,
    205–9, 214, 219–21
  stage, 52, 194
performativity, 11, 13, 16–20,
  28, 64–5
Phillips, John, 192
Pierse, Mary, 53
Poe, Edgar Allen, 74
pregnancy, 67, 72, 79–80, 102,
  209–11, 226
Prince, Virginia, 2, 32n

Prosser, Jay, 3–4, 4–5, 6, 17–20, 25, 65, 70, 76, 125, 129–30, 141, 147
prostitution *see* sex work
Psycho, 165
Puar, Jasbir K., 229

queer theory, 6–8, 11, 13, 16–20, 28, 31, 64–5, 151, 154n

race, 6, 25–6, 28, 29–30, 82n, 88, 107–15, 127, 139, 140–3, 159, 160, 167–77, 182
Rae, Isobel, 88, 90–3, 95–6, 101–2, 108, 113, 116
rape, 13, 65, 71, 73, 77–80, 98–9, 173
Rawson, K. J., 9, 89
Raymond, Janice G., 12–14, 28, 65, 70–2, 75–7, 81
Redmayne, Eddie, 193, 219, 223
Regan, Stephen, 197
Reis, Elizabeth, 146
Richardson, Matt, 159, 174
Rigney, Melissa, 192–3
Riley, Denise, 81
Ringrose, Kathryn, 69
Robertson, James, 173
Roen, Katrina, 33n
Rose, Irene, 186
Rose, June, 88, 90–3, 96, 101, 108, 110, 113, 116

Rubenstein, Roberta, 76–7
Rubin, Henry, 84n

Salamon, Gayle, 130, 141, 205
Seid, Danielle M., 5, 204
Seitler, Dana, 8
sex work, 43, 48–50, 98, 100, 148, 151–3, 223, 231n
The Silence of the Lambs, 165, 192
Silver, Brenda R., 78
Singer, T. Benjamin, 3
The Skin I Live In, 82n, 192
Some Like It Hot, 192, 221
Spade, Dean, 22–5, 165, 229
Sreedhar, Susanne, 84n
Stone, Sandy, 3, 6, 65–7, 72, 153
Stonewall, 35n
Stryker, Susan, 8–9, 10, 16–17, 22, 24, 107, 229

Tipton, Billy, 5, 29–30, 158, 161–2, 167, 168
Tomboy, 193
Tootsie, 192
Transamerica, 193
transgender
 definitions, 2–4, 8–9
 on screen, 5, 30–1, 66, 73–5, 191–230
 rights, 2, 20–5, 31, 32n, 35n, 228–30
Transparent, 193
Trevenna, Joanne, 64–5
Twain, Mark, 89–90, 95

Ulrichs, Karl Heinrich, 147

Valentine, David, 22–4
Vidal, Gore, 82n

Wallace, Diana, 92
Warner, Michael, 80
Westall, Claire, 77
Wheelwright, Julie, 11, 88, 91

whiteness *see* race
Wilde, Oscar, 52, 147, 165
Wilkerson, Abby L., 132
Wilson, Teddy, 168
Woolf, Virginia, 12, 27, 37–8
Wyatt, Jean, 76

Yogyakarta Principles, 32n